Cultivating Judgment

A Sourcebook for Teaching Critical Thinking Across the Curriculum

by
John Nelson

NEW FORUMS
Stillwater, Oklahoma
U.S.A.

NEW FORUMS PRESS INC.

Published in the United States of America
by New Forums Press, Inc.1018 S. Lewis St.
Stillwater, OK 74074
www.newforums.com

Library of Congress Cataloging-in-Publication Data

Nelson, John, 1946-
  Cultivating judgment : a sourcebook for teaching critical thinking
across the curriculum / by John Nelson.
    p. cm.
  Includes bibliographical references.
  ISBN 1-58107-112-4 (alk. paper)
   1. Critical thinking—Study and teaching—Activity programs.
  2. Creative thinking—Study and teaching—Activity programs.
  I. Title.
  LB1590.5.N45 2005
  370.15'2—dc22

                                              2005023342

This book may be ordered in bulk quantities at discount from New
Forums Press, Inc., P.O. Box 876, Stillwater, OK 74076 [Federal I.D. No.
73 1123239]. Printed in the United States of America.

International Standard Book Number: 1-58107-112-4

TABLE OF CONTENTS

PREFACE

The purpose of this sourcebook is to provide fellow college teachers, across the curriculum, with some specific, classroom-tested activities and assignments to stimulate and cultivate critical thinking by students. The work on this project has been a genuinely collegial endeavor—one reward of belonging to the community of teachers is the generosity of colleagues in sharing their most effective assignments and teaching methods. Some of the activities herein I have developed on my own; others have been passed along by generations of teachers, garnered from my research on critical thinking, or shaped and refined through discussions with other faculty, professional staff, and administrators. This sourcebook is a way to continue a dialogue, to pass on to other teachers the work of their colleagues. Credit for the ideas here goes to many collaborators: the teachers who have tested these activities in classrooms, the scholars who have reflected on the best ways to teach thinking skills, and the students who, through their responses to activities—or, in some cases, lack of response—have helped me to learn what works and what doesn't work when teaching critical thinking.

Whatever our disciplines, whatever subjects may engage our intellects or tease our imaginations, we are all striving to help our students become better thinkers. My own interest in critical thinking has evolved and deepened during the past three decades as a teacher of literature and composition at North Shore Community College in Massachusetts. For most of my career I have worked closely with colleagues on curriculum development as part of a learning community at North Shore (formerly called the Motivation to Education Program, now called the TRIO Linked Learning Program) that offers linked courses to low-income and first-generation college students. As curriculum coordinator for this program, I teamed with colleagues to develop and refine an integrated curriculum centered on critical thinking skills. Our work on this curriculum led me to conduct more in-depth research into the teaching of critical thinking, and from this research emerged the idea of this sourcebook—a practical guide that might be helpful to teachers across the curriculum.

I've begun the sourcebook with some remarks about the nature and value of critical thinking. The rest of it consists of fifty activity modules, loosely organized into five sections: (1) Problems and Puzzles (2) Analyses and Critiques (3) Opinions, Decisions, Values (4) Projects, Experiments, Adventures, and (5) Student as Teacher, Teacher as Student. In each module I describe a specific pedagogic activity or assignment, explain its purposes and benefits, and make suggestions about how to carry out the activity or address difficulties that may arise in carrying it out. Some activities are discipline-specific, some could be used in virtually any discipline, and some could be modified to apply to various disciplines. Certain activities require less time than a standard class period; a few could be the foundation for an entire course. I've also discussed related activities, cited relevant resources and appended material to illustrate how to structure some activities.

I hope that each reader will find at least a few activities that prove useful as teaching tools or generate ideas about how to teach critical thinking. Since I teach literature and composition, I have included many activities from these fields, but I have also—boldly or foolishly—ventured far beyond my range of expertise to suggest activities in other disciplines. Forgive my presumption. At the same time, I have certainly neglected some disciplines, not from lack of interest but because my presumptuousness is insufficient to overcome the awareness that my understanding of these disciplines is hopelessly superficial and elementary. Rather than offer insights on how to teach physics or fire science, my better judgment urges me to keep my mouth shut. The selection of activities reflects my preference for assignments that require active learning and collaboration among students. I especially like role-playing assignments, partly because I share Albert Einstein's view that "playfulness" is an "essential feature in productive thought," an idea echoed in John Dewey's belief that teaching must balance seriousness with play. I am also a true believer in the value of interdisciplinary education. Thinking skills vary from one discipline to the next, and I agree with those who assert that critical thinking is best taught within the realm of a discipline, not as an independent subject, but the evolution of critical thought is all about making new cognitive connections and viewing the world from a variety of angles.

I have included a bibliography on critical thinking, and many of these sources suggest classroom activities or present ideas that could be adapted to college courses. Alverno College in Wisconsin has developed an entire curriculum focused on critical thinking, and the two sources from Alverno (edited by professors Lucy Cromwell and Jane Halonen) provide a wealth of assignments designed for college courses. Holyoke Community College in Massachusetts has also developed an excellent learning communities program that stimulates critical thinking through a variety of innovative interdisciplinary courses, such as "Our Changing Universe: Matter, Energy, and the Environment." I have borrowed extensively from the *Innovation Abstracts* series, published by the National Institute for Staff and Organization Development (NISOD), an invaluable forum for the sharing of innovative practices by colleagues across the country. There are also a number of websites devoted to the teaching of critical thinking, such as Longview College's Critical Thinking Across the Curriculum Project, and I have appended a brief, annotated list of selected websites.

My collaborators on this project are too numerous to mention individually, but I would like to acknowledge a few colleagues from North Shore Community College whose assistance and support made this project possible: Dr. Maureen O'Neill, Chair of the Liberal Studies Division, who offered encouragement and some excellent advice about the presentation of material; Dr. Laura Ventimiglia, Assistant Dean of Academic Affairs, who enthusiastically arranged for institutional support in producing the original version of this sourcebook; and administrative assistant Marianne Neve, who was instrumental in designing the sourcebook and bringing the project to completion. I am also grateful to North Shore Community College for granting me a sabbatical leave to conduct research on this project.

Above all, I thank my wife Mary for her loving support and her faith in me.

THINKING ABOUT CRITICAL THINKING

"To spend too much time in studies is sloth," Francis Bacon wrote in his essay "Of Studies;" "to use them too much for ornament is affection; to make judgment wholly by their rules is the humor of a scholar . . . Read not to contradict and confute, nor to believe and take for granted, nor to find talk and discourse, but to weigh and consider."

Critical thinking has been defined variously as the process of making informed decisions, as applied informal logic, as an interplay of techniques necessary for effective problem solving, and as thinking that is purposeful, reasoned, and goal-directed. The word "critical" derives from the Greek word for judgment, *kritikos*, and one common element in all notions of critical thinking is good judgment in assessing information about the world and assigning value to that information. Matthew Lipman, for instance, defines critical thinking as "skillful, responsible thinking that is conducive to judgment because it relies on criteria, is self-correcting, and is sensitive to context." The teaching of critical thinking focuses on making judgments in problematic situations—that is, open-ended or unstructured situations that challenge us with uncertainty, offer multiple options or potential solutions, and require multiple criteria for determining the effectiveness of solutions. Joanne Kurfiss defines critical thinking in this context as "a rational response to questions that can't be answered definitively or solutions that can't be verified empirically." When we teach critical thinking, we are, in Bacon's words, training students to "weigh and consider." We are cultivating judgment.

Critical thinking is oriented toward decision and action. John McPeck, in *Critical Thinking and Education*, rightly says that critical thinking "involves a certain skepticism, or suspension of consent, towards a given statement, established norm or mode of doing things," but this skepticism is a condition of critical thinking, not its aim. The ancient Greeks valued good judgment not as an end in itself but as a means toward effective and justifiable action. Reflection is essential to critical thinking—one can't think critically without a willingness to reflect on and critique one's own biases and misconceptions—but, as John Dewey wrote, the primary goal of critical thinking is good judgment in making and acting on decisions. Dewey's emphasis is shared by George Polya, who wrote that "solving problems is the specific achievement of intelligence," and by Howard Gardner, who has defined intelligence as the potential for finding and creating problems and the ability to resolve them. A physician making a diagnosis and determining treatment in a complex case, a jury sorting through conflicting pieces of evidence to arrive at a fair and reasoned verdict, a community evaluating alternative solutions to a waste disposal problem—these are paradigms of critical thinking in action.

Ethical considerations are fundamental to critical thinking. The "good" in good judgment includes a serious effort to find solid ethical grounds for decisions and actions. In fact, a belief in the necessity of critical thinking is itself an expression of ethical value. Dewey and others have argued persuasively that a democracy depends on independent-minded critical thinkers, while psychologist Stanley Milgram, in his famous obedience experiments, has demonstrated all too clearly that failure to think critically can lead to blind obedience to authority, an obedience that can harm the innocent. One value of critical thinking, Marlys Mayfield says, is "providing protection from other people's manipulation."

Many scholars have tried to encapsulate critical thinking into a list of essential thinking skills. Richard Paul, Joanne Kurfiss, John Chaffee, Marlys Mayfield, and the critical thinking program at Alverno College all provide useful, detailed lists of skills and attitudes in profiling the ideal critical thinker. My own list, certainly not intended to be all-inclusive, would include the following elements

- getting relevant information to form a thesis or solve a problem
- determining which information is important and reliable
- distinguishing fact from opinion
- detecting slanting, bias, fallacies, and false assumptions
- detecting and analyzing the use of metaphorical language and analogies
- making well-founded inferences
- testing hypotheses in order to answer questions
- using specific, relevant evidence to support a thesis or claim
- using appropriate examples to illustrate definitions or generalizations
- examining issues from conflicting viewpoints
- evaluating alternative solutions to problems, alternative theories to explain phenomena, alterative interpretations of human behavior and artistic works
- foreseeing the probable consequences of decisions
- evaluating the effectiveness of strategies used in decision-making
- analyzing the process of making judgments and acting on those judgments

Yet scholars agree that teaching critical thinking can't be reduced to developing a set of demonstrable or measurable skills. "To the extent that critical thinking is a skill," writes John McPeck, "it is teachable in much the same way that other skills are teachable, namely through drills, exercises, or problem solving in an area," but he adds that teaching skills isn't sufficient. The teacher must also cultivate an attitude, a habitual mental disposition—the disposition of a Socratic learner who is a probing, systematic questioner of ideas. Richard Paul says that critical thinking has two basic components: "(1) a set of skills to process and generate information and beliefs (2) the habit, based on intellectual commitment, of using those skills to guide behavior." John Dewey believed that critical thinking originates with childhood curiosity and desire to learn, a belief which echoes Francis Bacon's idea that we must become as little children to enter the kingdom of science. The goal of formal education, Dewey said, is "the formation of a logical disposition" as students develop opinions, and he argued that any opinion not based on evidence and reflection is literally a "prejudice." Critical thinking includes thinking about thinking, curiosity about and sensitivity to our own thinking processes. Critical thinkers are willing to question the justifiability of their own ideas, brave enough to risk being wrong, and wise enough to realize that much can be learned from errors and failed solutions. We must also remember that critical thinking itself has its limits, that it is not the only mode of learning and responding to the world. I've yet to meet anyone whose aim in life is to become strictly and absolutely reasonable.

At the heart of critical thinking is open-mindedness. Otherwise, the development of thinking skills may become a cynical exercise in using reasoning to rationalize self-serving behavior or hold on to entrenched, unexamined beliefs. John Stuart Mill has eloquently expressed the reasons we place confidence in those who demonstrate the good judgment born of open-mindedness:

> In the case of any person whose judgment is really deserving of confidence, how has it become so? Because he has kept his mind open to criticisms of his opinions and conduct. Because it has been his practice to listen to all that could be said against him; to profit by as much of it as was just, and expound to himself, and on occasion to others, the fallacy of what was fallacious. Because he has felt that the only way in which a human being can make some approach to knowing the whole of a subject, is by hearing what can be said about it by persons of every variety of opinion, and studying all modes in which it can be looked at by every character of mind. No wise man ever acquired his wisdom in any mode but this; nor is it in the nature of human intellect to become wise in any other manner.

I could wax on forever about the value of critical thinking, but, as every teacher knows, the proof is in the classroom. As John McPeck says, "Clarifying what critical thinking is may not guarantee an answer to the question of whether it is teachable, let alone how to teach it." Despite Mill's claim that "to draw inferences has been said to be the great business of life," our students may feel that they have more compelling business to be about. Learning to be a critical thinker is hard work. It takes time, effort, persistence, and patience—qualities that students may not possess in abundance. One form of resistance to critical thinking was demonstrated by a student of mine who was making up an essay exam. I gave her an hour to complete the essay; she turned it in fifteen minutes later. When I suggested that she might use the remaining time to edit, revise, reconsider, she responded, "You mean, I have to worry about the writing?" The essay was for a composition course.

Some students may not perceive the need to learn critical thinking skills. As LaRochefoucauld said, "Everyone complains of his memory, and no one complains of his judgment." Students may become frustrated, discouraged, or bored by activities that require them to analyze complex arguments or answer highly problematic questions. In fact, Richard Paul claims that resistance to learning critical skills is a "natural" response, since the human mind has no built-in drive to question "its innate tendency to believe what it wants to believe." Or, as Francis Bacon put it, "Man prefers to believe what he prefers to be true." Howard Gardner contends that all of us, as adults, retain a strong loyalty to false "intuitive" ideas developed in childhood, and students may feel threatened if challenged to question entrenched beliefs—such as the conviction that punishment is the most effective way to change certain types of behavior. Critical thinking can also raise serious doubts about whether some problems, such as the rapidly increasing depletion of the earth's natural resources, can ever be adequately solved. The most important decisions in life may appear more problematic than students (or their teachers) would like them to be. We must challenge our students, but we must also offer both academic and moral support.

Students may also enter our courses lacking any interpretive framework or vocabulary with which to discuss thinking skills. Some formal tests of critical thinking require knowledge of terms from logic (premises, assumptions) that are unfamiliar to many students, and I have found, in using an assignment on testing a hypothesis, that many students struggle to grasp both the concept of a scientific hypothesis and the process of testing one. It's also difficult to teach students to transfer thinking skills from one activity to another, seemingly related activity. Gardner has found that many college graduates, who have supposedly proven their proficiency on physics or math exams, flounder when asked to transfer concepts from these disciplines to practical, everyday problems that differ from the types of problems they encountered on their exams.

Given these obstacles to teaching critical thinking, what is the teacher's role in developing students' thinking skills? First, I think, we must believe that critical thinking can be taught, that judgment can be cultivated. We must have faith in our students' curiosity, their potential for intellectual development, and their desire to train their minds, whatever the obstacles. Without this leap of faith—and with many students it does require a leap—we defeat our students and ourselves by communicating the expectation that some students could not possibly rise to meet the challenges we put before them.

Next, we must practice what we preach—that is, we must exemplify the skills we teach. As Aristotle said, "We are what we repeatedly do." As teachers, we naturally assume we are critical thinkers, but some research suggests that many college teachers don't think much about how to model critical thinking skills or whether they are in fact demonstrating these skills in their interactions with students. Thomas Gilovich notes a survey indicating that 94% of college professors think they're better at their jobs than their average colleagues—a figure which, at the least, suggests that we should not take inordinate pride in our objectivity.

Finally, we must try to nurture attitudes of inquiry, reflection, and the freedom to be creative, for, as Paulo Freire says, "education is the practice of freedom." Freire contrasts this spirit of inquiry to the "syllabus-to-be-completed" approach to teaching. He emphasizes the need for praxis, "action based on critical reflection," and he opposes critical thinking to the passing along of what Alfred North Whitehead called "inert ideas" that are "merely received into the mind without being utilized or tested or thrown into fresh combinations."

One way to nurture this spirit of inquiry is through activities like the ones presented in this sourcebook—activities that challenge students with what Harry Wade of Alverno College calls "problematic situations that are not understandable in terms of their existing frameworks." We should also be vigilant in observing, reflecting on, and responding to student demonstrations of thinking. This may include recognizing and addressing students' frustration or reluctance to question beliefs, discussing how personal beliefs (of students or others) are related to social conditioning and cultural values, or merely reminding students at appropriate moments that, as Edmund Burke put it, "to read without reflection is like eating without digesting." In short, we must engage our students—as mentors and guides, critics and coaches. Wade points out that we should be careful not to overstate the coherence, certainty, or completeness of human knowledge. Or, as Francis Bacon said, "The human understanding supposes a greater degree of order and equality in things than it really finds." Artemus Ward put the idea a little differently: "It ain't so much the things we don't know that get us into trouble. It's the things we know that just ain't so."

The ability to judge wisely and well is so fundamental to education that we can't afford not to nurture it. "Critical thinking," John McPeck says, "is a necessary condition for education." It is "not just a dietary supplement to be added to education, but is logically entailed by it." In the following pages you will find problems and puzzles, projects and experiments, and other adventures in the teaching of critical thinking, all presented with the hope that they will help you cultivate the judgment of your students.

ACTIVITIES BY DISCIPLINE

I have listed below the relevant disciplines for the 50 activity modules. Some activities could be used in any discipline, and many could be adapted for use in disciplines not specified here. Module #46 focuses on interdisciplinary activities.

Any discipline	1-4-10-46-47-48-49-50
Anthropology	16-24-38
Arts/music/humanities	19-44-46
Biology	3-13-15-16-21-23-44-45-46
Business	16-21-35-38-39-40-41-45
Chemistry	46
College success seminars	2-25-27-36-49
Composition	2-5-6-7-8-9-17-18-20-21-22-24-26-33-34-35-36-37-40-43
Computer-aided design	21-44
Computer science	19-44-45-46
Economics	21-40-46
Education	9-34-44-45-46
Engineering	3-42-46
Environmental science	15-21-22-36-45-46
Future studies	15-39
Gender studies	11-19-27
Gerontology	38-42
Health care professions	17-26-31-42-45
History	12-18-22-26-27-32-40-41

Human services	7-14-36-39-42
Journalism/media studies	5-6-7-9-18-33
Language/linguistics	5-6-7-19
Law/criminal justice	9-11-14-24-29-30-39-40-41-42-45
Library science	6-45
Literature	5-8-11-12-14-19-20-26-27-28-29-32-41-42-43-46
Mathematics	3-8-21-34-44
Nurse education	17-26-31-42
Philosophy/ethics	22-28-29-30-31-32-42
Physics	44-46
Political science	2-18-27-30-33-36-41
Psychology	2-8-11-13-16-19-25-27-29-31-36-38-44
Reading	2-5-6-7-18-35-45
Religion	18-28
Sciences	3-13-15-23-24-37-45-46
Social sciences	8-9-16-18-19-20-21-22-23-24-29-36-37-38-39-40-46
Sociology	9-24-29-39
Speech/drama	13-34-35-41-42
Statistics	8-21-40

Section One

Problems and Puzzles

ACTIVITY #1:
Thinking on Another Planet (Testing Critical Thinking)

APPLICATIONS: Any discipline

CRITICAL THINKING SKILLS: Evaluating evidence, distinguishing fact from opinion, making inferences, testing hypotheses, comparing alternative solutions

THE ACTIVITY

This activity involves administering the Level X ("Exploring in Nicoma") Test, a standardized test included in the set of Cornell Critical Thinking Tests. In taking this test, students are instructed to imagine themselves as part of the second group from Earth to land on the newly discovered (fictional) planet Nicoma. Nothing has been heard from the first group, which landed on Nicoma two years earlier, and the second group has been sent to write a report about what happened to the first group. Each student, working alone, must evaluate the importance and reliability of numerous statements about what has happened on Nicoma. Then the student must decide on what to report and determine a plan of action, choosing from a number of possible alternatives. The test consists of a series of multiple-choice questions. To answer these questions correctly students must make well-founded inferences, form a plausible hypothesis about the history of Nicoma, and determine whether certain conclusions follow logically from previous statements. Students are generally given 50 minutes to complete the test.

PURPOSES AND BENEFITS

To begin a book about teaching with the issue of assessment may seem like putting the cart before the horse, but the fact is that many students will first encounter the concept of critical thinking by taking some sort of diagnostic test that purports to measure such thinking. Furthermore, the benefit, for students, of any instructional method cannot be divorced from the question of how we as teachers plan to assess that benefit. If the essence of critical thinking is good judgment and sound evaluation, then for teachers, a good place to start is with a critical look at the tools we intend to use in trying to judge and evaluate the skills we hope to cultivate

The idea of testing critical thinking through any standardized test is highly problematic. As John McPeck argues in *Critical Thinking and Education*, critical thinking is always "critical thinking about X," and it makes little sense to attempt to teach critical thinking—or to measure critical thinking skills—in isolation from specific disciplines. "One cannot think critically about X," McPeck says, "until one knows something about X." He also contends that many existing standardized tests don't differ substantially from general intelligence tests or even reading comprehension tests, and that they are too restrictive to address all the complexities of processing and interpreting information that are involved in critical thinking.

Furthermore, McPeck claims, some existing tests are flawed in their designs. For instance, in examining the Watson-Glaser Critical Thinking Appraisal, he argues persuasively that some supposedly "self-contained" questions in fact require "application of general knowledge" or depend on the personal beliefs of those being tested. He also points out that the directions are sometimes confusing or self-contradictory: "Thus, the directions to judge whether a conclusion 'logically follows beyond a reasonable doubt from the information given in the paragraph' is systematically ambiguous." The Cornell Level Z test, he says, provides clear, straightforward directions and presents tasks that "manifest the instructions," but the test is limited by its standardized multiple-choice format, and some questions come with one than one plausible "correct" answer. I would add that some tests, such as Watson-Glaser and the California Critical Thinking Skills Test, require some familiarity with terms and concepts from logic (premises, syllogisms) or rely too much on prior knowledge to be fair indicators of students' ability to demonstrate critical thinking.

These caveats notwithstanding, standardized tests can have some value as assessment tools or as exercises in training students to apply reasoning skills. The Cornell Level X Test is the easiest of the tests I've examined—it was originally designed for high school students—but it has three features that make it useful in working with a wide range of college students: (1) It uses a narrative approach that engages student interest in solving well-defined problems within a specific context. (2) The vocabulary is accessible, and the test does not require knowledge of concepts or terminology from logic. (3) The test focuses on student demonstration of such important skills as making well-founded inferences, evaluating alternative solutions to problems, and foreseeing the probable consequences of decisions.

USES, ADAPTATIONS, AND RESOURCES

The Level X Test could be used to assess some (but not all) reasoning skills or to initiate a class discussion of critical thinking processes. It could be used to introduce key concepts in critical thinking—inference, hypothesis—or after students have already studied and gained experience with the process of making sound inferences, distinguishing facts from opinions, and evaluating evidence. Once the test has been administered and scored, the instructor might spend some class time reviewing answers and asking students to explain why they think that particular inferences or conclusions are more valid than others, especially in regard to test questions that may seem to have more than one plausible answer. I would use the scoring only for diagnostic or self-assessment purposes—certainly not as any kind of exit exam in a course on critical thinking.

In addition to the tests mentioned above, the International Center for the Assessment of Thinking (ICAT) has developed a "Critical Thinking Essay Examination" that requires students to identify the elements of reasoning used within a written piece and then compose an essay providing a critical analysis of that reasoning. Essay examinations, in contrast to multiple-choice tests, can be beneficial assessment tools because they require students to articulate the reasons for their judgments, to be precise in using language, and to marshal specific evidence in developing a line of reasoning that is relevant, coherent, and persuasive. Such written examinations are also harder to evaluate, since evaluation depends on both well-defined criteria for assessing the essays and the instructor's judgment in scoring each individual piece of writing. To be judged fairly, students taking an essay test like the ICAT exam need to be familiar with the terminology used to identify and critique "elements of reasoning," and they should have experience—classroom practice—in applying this terminology to defend their opinions about the strengths and weaknesses of the reasoning in specific written passages.

In *Critical Thinking and* Education, McPeck offers some sound guidelines for developing tests within the context of specific disciplines:

- That the test be subject-specific in an area (or areas) of the test taker's experience or preparation. This is required because knowledge and information are necessary ingredients of critical thinking.
- That the answer format permit more than one justifiable answer. Thus an essay might better fit the task, awkward and time-consuming as this might be. (This recognizes that there is usually more than one good way to pluck a goose.)
- That good answers are not predicated on being *right*, in the

sense of *true*, but on the *quality of the justification given for a response*.

- That the test results should not be used as a measure of one's capacity or innate ability, but as a learned accomplishment—which is usually the result of specific training or experience.

Also, in *Engaging Ideas*—an excellent source for examples of how to design writing assignments across the curriculum—John Bean devotes a chapter to constructing essay exams to test critical thinking within specific disciplines. He discusses some of the reasons why essay exams can be problematic as fair tests of students' thinking—questions may be too ambiguous; the standards by which answers will be judged may be too vague—and he offers suggestions on how to compose good essay questions, how to establish consistent grading criteria, and how to train students to write exams that exhibit their grasp of concepts.

To examine the Cornell Level X Test, contact the Critical Thinking Press & Software at P.O. Box 448 in Pacific Grove, CA 93950 (800-458-4849).

ACTIVITY #2
Who Killed Harry Skank? (Solving Problems and Puzzles)

APPLICATIONS: Reading and writing courses, college success seminars, psychology, political science, other disciplines

CRITICAL THINKING SKILLS: Problem-solving, using evidence, making inferences, testing hypotheses

THE ACTIVITY

Learning, John Dewey wrote, "originates in the learner's engagement with problems." In this engaging problem-solving exercise, which was passed along to me through a chain of other teachers, students use evidence to solve a murder mystery. Students are given 26 randomly arranged clues about a fictional murder. They use these clues to determine: (1) the murderer (2) the weapon used to commit the murder (3) the time of the murder (4) the place of the murder (5) the motive for the murder. Each clue is relevant in solving the problem, and the clues as a whole provide sufficient information to arrive at the answers. Students may carry out the exercise individually or in collaborative groups, in which case the clues are evenly distributed among group members and the group members must (orally) share and discuss clues in order to arrive at answers. Once each individual or group has determined the five points above, the answers are shown to the instructor, who indicates whether they are correct. If any answer is incorrect, the instructor tells the individual or group to continue with the exercise until are answers are correct.

PURPOSES AND BENEFITS

This simple, straightforward exercise is useful in introducing students to basic ideas about processing and organizing information (e.g. chronology), using evidence to reach conclusions, and collaborating effectively within a small group. Each student or group must form a hypothesis about the murder and then test the hypothesis against the available evidence. The exercise is also a way to prompt students to analyze and reflect on the strategies they use in solving problems. It illustrates the necessity of being methodical and persistent in problem solving, and, if used as a group activity, it requires active participation by all group members. Most students enjoy the challenge of resolving the mystery, and the exercise can be a good icebreaker at the start of a course. The exercise does have potential drawbacks: (1) Though it's not intended to be competitive, some students will approach it as a competition, and some may become frustrated or discouraged when others get the correct answers before they do. (2) Some students may never take a stake in the exercise, or they may become bored or impatient and lose focus on the task, which can annoy other group members—as well as the instructor.

USES, ADAPTATIONS, AND RESOURCES

I've used this activity as both an individual and group warm-up exercise in Composition I classes. Most students, working individually, arrive at correct answers within 15 to 30 minutes; most groups arrive at correct answers within 20-45 minutes. When classes work in groups, I cut up the list of clues so that I can distribute them among group members. Group members may not pass clues around; they must share their information orally. After the exercise, we discuss strategies used to organize information and arrive at answers, and I use the exercise to illustrate basic critical thinking concepts such as inference and hypothesis, and to examine why a particular inference (e.g. about which weapon caused the fatal injury) is more valid or persuasive than another. If some students became frustrated or annoyed by other group members during the exercise, we also talk about ways to overcome discouragement and to collaborate effectively in problem solving.

Bransford and Stein's *The Ideal Problem Solver*, Rubinstein's *Patterns of Problem Solving*, Stice's *Developing Critical Thinking and Problem-Solving Abilities*, and Wicklegren's *How to Solve Problems* all offer an abundance of problems, puzzles, and brain-teasers that can be used as warm-up exercises, collaborative projects, tests of reasoning ability, or illustrations of such problem solving approaches as lateral thinking and inductive reasoning. In her abstract "The 12 Ball Problem, or How I Stopped Hating the Assignment and Learned to Love Thinking," social science professor Carolyn Wright describes a problem solving assignment she uses in an introductory psychology course: "There are 12 balls, identical in appearance, but one is either heavier or lighter than the others. Using only a balance scale, and using it only three times, isolate the odd ball, and be able to say in which way it differs." Wright requires students to solve the problem, explain the techniques they used in solving it, and discuss how they responded to the obstacles they encountered. The assignment, she says, has been "enlightening" for many students in leading them to reflect on the psychology of problem solving. She mentions one student who "said that as he was forced to examine his thinking processes he could see a problem that affected many areas of functioning. He noted that he often clung to unworkable methods. 'Even when I knew I couldn't get to the solution by weighing six against six, I couldn't let it go. That happens to me a lot, not just on the 12 Ball Problem.'"

Douglas Hofstadter's *Metamagical Themas: Questing for the Essence of Mind and Pattern* is a wonderful source of stimulating, challenging, and sometimes highly abstract puzzles and problems. Hofstadter brings together the perspectives of mathematics, computer science, linguistics, art, and music in exploring "certain central riddles about how minds work." In one section he examines structures that are capable of replicating themselves, including genes, memes (self-replicating cultural ideas), and grammatical structures such as "viral" and "self-referential" sentences. The most famous self-referential sentence, known as the "Epimenides paradox" or "liar's paradox," is named after Epimenides the Cretan, who said, "All Cretans are liars." Hofstadter uses concepts like self-replication to explore the broader question of how information, and misinformation, is transmitted or in some cases not transmitted—an issue central to the process of critical thinking, which entails an ongoing analysis of where information comes from, how it is passed along, and how the form and content of information can change as it is transmitted. A focus on information transmission can also enable teachers and students to make connections between widely varying disciplines: Why are some mutations replicated, while others die out? How does a myth—say, a rumor circulated via the Internet—become widely accepted as fact? Why is one meme—a belief in the divinity of Jesus—passed on for thousands of years—while another meme—a belief in the divinity of Zeus—becomes culturally obsolete? Does some form of natural selection govern the survival of memes? How do distinctive musical styles develop in different cultures, and how do these styles change as they are spread from one culture to another? Are there general laws that govern the transmission of information? Robert Wright, in *The Moral Animal*, applies the idea of self-replication to both genes and memes (in this case, the meme of moral judgment) in his assertion that people tend to pass on the kind of moral judgments that help to move their genes into the next generation.

In his applications of game theory, Hofstadter offers another kind of conceptual tool that can be useful in problem solving and the critical evaluation of both mental and institutional patterns. In one section of his book, where he looks at the processes by which governments change their rules, Hofstadter explains the rules of the game Nomic, a "self-modifying" game based on a system of rules—both "mutable" and "immutable"—for changing the rules of the game. One practical application of such a game model—and a good assignment for students— would be a problem-solving analysis of gerrymandering, or, more generally, the means by which legislators establish rules to determine how legislators are elected. What are the best alternative methods of establishing these rules? Is there an optimal method—for instance, a computer model—to ensure that electors are fairly represented? Is it possible to establish "immutable" rules that would prevent anyone from unfairly altering the rules themselves?

The term "problem solving" is often used loosely to refer both to well-defined (often mathematical) problems with a single correct answer and to more open-ended problems with a multitude of possible solutions. SEE **Activity #36: What Are the Alternatives?** for more assignments on the second type of problem solving. For the Harry Skank murder exercise, SEE the following handout. The correct answers—or, I should say, the most reasonable inferences—are:

MURDERER: Mr. Rude
WEAPON: knife in back
TIME: 12:30
PLACE: Mr. Rude's room
MOTIVE: confrontation over affair between Mr. Skank and Mrs. Rude

PROBLEM-SOLVING EXERCISE:
Who Killed Harry Skank?

DIRECTIONS: This is a problem-solving mystery about the murder of Harry Skank. Below are 26 clues that will help you solve the problem. You must determine the following:

THE MURDERER————————————————

THE WEAPON USED TO COMMIT THE MURDER———

THE TIME OF THE MURDER————————————

THE PLACE OF THE MURDER—————————————

THE MOTIVE FOR THE MURDER———————————

- When he was discovered dead, Mr. Skank had a bullet hole in his thigh and a knife wound in his back.
- The elevator operator said that Miss Sleaze was in the lobby of the apartment building when he went off duty.
- Mr. Lout shot at an intruder in his apartment building at 12:00 midnight.
- The elevator operator reported to police that he saw Mr. Skank at 12:15 a.m.
- The bullet taken from Mr. Skank's thigh matched the gun owned by Mr. Lout.
- When the elevator operator saw Mr. Skank, Mr. Skank was bleeding slightly, but he did not seem too badly hurt.
- A knife with Mr. Skank's blood on it was found in Miss Sleaze's yard.
- Mr. Skank had destroyed Mr. Lout's business by stealing all his customers.

- The elevator operator said that Mr. Skank's wife frequently left the building with Mr. Rude.
- Mr. Skank's body was found in the park at 1:30 a.m.
- The knife found in Miss Sleaze's yard had Mr. Rude's fingerprints on it.
- Only one bullet had been fired from Mr. Lout's gun.
- Mr. Skank had been dead for one hour when his body was found, according to medical experts working with police.
- The elevator operator saw Mr. Skank's wife go to Mr. Rude's apartment at 11:30 p.m.
- It was obvious from the condition of Mr. Skank's body that it had been dragged a long distance.
- Miss Sleaze often followed Mr. Skank.
- The elevator operator went off duty at 12:30 a.m.
- Mr. Skank's wife disappeared after the murder.
- Miss Sleaze saw Mr. Skank go to Mr. Lout's apartment building at 11:55 p.m.
- Mr. Lout had told Mr. Skank that he was going to kill him.
- The elevator operator saw Mr. Skank go to Mr. Rude's room at 12:25 a.m.
- Police were unable to locate Mr. Rude after the murder.
- Miss Sleaze said that she saw nobody leave the apartment building between 12:25 a.m. and 12:45 a.m.
- When police tried to locate Mr. Lout after the murder, they discovered that he had disappeared.
- Mr. Skank's bloodstains were found in Mr. Rude's car.
- Mr. Skank's bloodstains were found on the carpet in the hall outside Mr. Lout's apartment.

ACTIVITY #3
Do Bees Build It Best? (Solving Mathematical Problems)

APPLICATIONS: Mathematics, engineering, biology, other disciplines

CRITICAL THINKING SKILLS: Getting relevant information, testing hypotheses, evaluating solutions to problems, analyzing relationships among problems

THE ACTIVITY

In this activity students answer the question: "Do bees build it the best?" In other words, is a regular hexagonal prism—the honeycomb of bees—the most efficient design for a structure that stores honey? In solving the problem, students use the Pythagorean theorem and basic trigonometric formulas to calculate the volume and surface area of a given structure, and they must compare the honeycomb design to other possible designs for a structure to store honey. Students might also apply the design principles they're learning in mathematics or engineering courses to other formats such as geoboard patterns, tessellation shapes, rug and patchwork quilt designs, and garden plots. Students may work individually or in groups. They explain their answers to the question—and the processes they went through in solving the problem—in written reports and/or classroom presentations.

PURPOSES AND BENEFITS

"You cannot understand science," Martin Gardner says in his introduction to Harold Jacobs' *Mathematics: A Human Endeavor*, "without knowing some mathematics, and if you know nothing about science you are as much a Philistine as a person who never read a line of Shakespeare." And, adds W.

W. Sawyer, quoted in Jacobs' book, "You can claim to be a mathematician only if you can solve problems that you have never studied before. That is the test of reasoning." One of the fundamental critical thinking skills—for prospective mathematicians, scientists, and students generally—is the ability to tackle unfamiliar problems that require the problem solver to consider and test a number of possible solutions.

Critical thinking also requires active learning—assignments that call upon students to use their resourcefulness in solving problems. This activity—passed along to me by Mike Frantz, chair of the math department at Brookline High School in Massachusetts, and included in *Interactive Mathematics Program: Year 2*—is part of the Interactive Mathematics Program (IMP), a four-year curriculum of problem-based mathematics now widely used in high schools. IMP emphasizes the application of mathematics to everyday problems and the connections between mathematics and other disciplines—in this case, both engineering and biology. Some problems, like this one, involve geometry and measurement; other parts of the program deal with statistical analysis, probability, and algebraic equations. The bee problem, in addition to being inherently fascinating, illustrates a key element of critical thinking—the systematic comparison of alternative solutions—while leading students to seek out evidence of mathematical principles in the designs of the natural world. The IMP approach also stresses group collaborations and students' presentations of their thinking processes; students become more attuned to their own problem solving strategies by articulating their reasoning. Though IMP was developed for high schools, many elements of the program, as well as specific problems, could be used effectively in college developmental math courses or in college math courses designed for liberal arts students.

USES, ADAPTATIONS, AND RESOURCES

In her abstract "Overcoming Roadblocks to Learning Math," Nancy Dorff-Pennea, of Palm Beach Community College in Florida, explains the approach she uses to help developmental math students understand the practical applications of algebraic principles while developing skills in solving problems and generalizing the strategies needed to solve problems in different contexts. Each student in her course must "construct a problem that occurred, or might occur, in life and solve it algebraically—such as a uniform method problem to determine how fast someone had been driving or a simultaneous equation and substitution problem to determine the money owed for a pizza party with various pies and different toppings." In another assignment, students must "pick four homework problems from a chapter we have just completed, show how they are solved, and describe the different skills (learned in an *earlier* chapter) that were required to complete each problem." Developmental math students often struggle in learning and applying analytical skills, and, regarding the second assignment, Dorff-Pennea says, "It often takes most of the semester for some of the students to realize that what I want is *not* a description of the problem-solving steps learned in the current chapter, but a reference to an *earlier* topic that had to be mastered in order to learn and to execute the new steps." Yet she reports that the assignments help students not only to approach problems logically but also to see how they might use—or have used—algebra in everyday situations.

John Bean's *Engaging Ideas* also presents assignments in which students apply new mathematical concepts—in this case from vector algebra—to everyday experiences. He especially recommends assignments, both in mathematics and in other disciplines, that create cognitive dissonance by challenging the "settled beliefs" or assumptions of students. He offers this example:

In class yesterday, 80 percent of you agreed with the statement: "The maximum speed of a sailboat occurs when the boat is sailing in the same direction as the wind." However, that intuitive answer is wrong. Sailboats can actually go much faster when they sail across the wind. How so? Using what you have been learning in vector algebra, explain why sailboats can sail faster when the wind blows sideways to their direction of travel rather than from directly behind them. Make your explanation clear enough for the general public to understand. You can use diagrams if that helps.

Johnson and Herr's *Problem Solving Strategies: Crossing the River with Dogs and Other Mathematical Adventures* is another text that focuses on "the strategies people in the real world use to solve problems." The book is organized by types of strategy—proof by contradiction, matrix logic, working backwards, Venn diagrams—and stresses the importance of exploring different avenues in arriving at solutions. Some exercises require solving the same problem with different strategies—many of them drawn from George Solya's classic *How to Prove It*—and one section demonstrates ways to shift one's point of view in problem solving by using different forms of organization or different modes of representation (e.g. numerical, spatial). Many assignments incorporate collaborative work or student presentation of problems—an approach also advocated by Theodore Panitz in *Learning Together* through his exercises on solving word problems and then presenting the guidelines best suited for solving such problems. Johnson and Herr offer useful advice about addressing student frustration and include several "student dialogues" to illustrate the process students go through in solving problems. Their book, like IMP, was designed for high schools, but many problems would be appropriate for developmental math courses, and some of the Set B problems are difficult enough to challenge many college students. The following problem, from which their title is taken, bent my poor brain for a while:

The five Family members and their five dogs (each family member owned one of the dogs) were hiking when they encountered a river to cross. They rented a boat that could hold three living things: people or dogs. Unfortunately, the dogs were temperamental. Each was comfortable only with its owner and could not be near another person, not even momentarily, unless its owner were present. Dogs could be with other dogs, however. The crossing would have been impossible except that Lisa's dog had attended a first-rate obedience school and knew how to operate the boat. No other dogs were that well educated. How was the crossing arranged and how many trips did it take?

"Puzzles," says Edward Kasman in Harold Jacobs' *Mathematics: A Human Endeavor*, "are made of the things that the mathematician, no less than the child, plays with, and dreams and wonders about, for they are made of the things and circumstances of the world he lives in." Jacobs' book is an excellent source of mathematical puzzles, problems, games, and what Martin Gardner calls "other forms of recreational mathematics," many of them well-suited for students in liberal arts math courses. Chapters cover such topics as inductive and deductive reasoning, symmetry (with some fascinating diagrams), functions and their graphs, the mathematics of chance, and statistical applications. Jacobs demonstrates the value of mathematics by explaining how mathematicians have used statistical analysis to break ciphers and codes, and how they've applied Descartes' method of coordinates in studying the structures of living things. He provides a wide range of stimulating problems for students: how to determine the path of a billiard ball, including a ball on an elliptical table; how to determine the relationship between the head shape and pitch of a kettledrum; how to establish the odds in a horse race; how to predict the results of genetic crossbreeding; and how to calculate the effects of a plan to redistribute wealth in an imaginary sheikdom. One problem, with some interesting historical implications, involves the Native Americans who allegedly sold Manhattan Island for $24 in 1626: students must figure out what the $24 would be worth now if the Native Americans had invested the money in a savings account paying 5% interest compounded annually.

Other challenging and sometimes mind-wrenching mathematical problems can be found in Douglas Hofstadter's *Metamagical Themas*. "Mathematics, more than any other discipline," Hofstadter writes, "studies the fundamental pervasive patterns of the universe," and his book is an attempt to discover the "inner mental patterns underlying our ability to conceive of mathematical ideas." Topics he covers range from the information-processing of the genetic code to the concept of "strange attractors" in theoretical physics to the use of psychological numbers game (with names like Flaunt and Mediocrity) to "provide models by which to understand evolutionary processes." In his chapter "On Number Numbness" he also offers "a lamentation of the general low level of people's understanding of the vast numbers that describe our society's population, consumption, budgets, weaponry, and so on, including some suggestions for helping increase 'numeracy.'"

Alan Schoenfeld's *Mathematical Problem Solving*, a book addressed to math teachers, presents some interesting ideas about how to train students to become resourceful, flexible, and efficient problem solvers. Schoenfeld begins with two general questions: "What does it mean to 'think mathematically'? How can we help our students to do it?" To answer these questions, he conducted research in his problem solving courses at the University of California in Berkeley, including the videotaping of students who solved problems out loud. He wanted to discover what actually takes place during solution attempts: how solutions evolve, how students respond to "typical roadblocks" in implementing strategies, and what accounts for success or failure. From the results of his research—and from his use of methodologies in decision theory, artificial intelligence, and information-processing psychology—Schoenfeld has developed a "framework for the analysis of complex problem solving behavior." One element of the framework is resources, or "the ways that competent problem solvers make the most of the knowledge at their disposal." Another element is heuristics, the mathematical "rules of thumb" and basic problem-solving strategies presented in the work of George Polya. A third element is "belief systems"—"the set of understandings about mathematics that establish the psychological context within which individuals do math." Unsuccessful students, he says, often "did not perceive their mathematical knowledge as being useful to them, and consequently did not call upon it." Schoenfeld describes the "results of instruction that does, and does not, focus on problem solving," and he argues that math teachers—as well as teachers in other disciplines—must cultivate effective problem-solving strategies, and communicate the value of these strategies, instead of merely laying out facts, definitions, theorems, and procedures. His book includes a number of specific problems that could be used with college students at different skill levels.

For a related activity, SEE **#36: What Are the Alternatives?**

Section Two

Analyses and Critiques

ACTIVITY #4
Is the Earth Hollow? (Distinguishing Fact from Opinion)

APPLICATIONS: Any discipline

CRITICAL THINKING SKILLS: Distinguishing fact from opinion, evaluating evidence, determining the reliability of information

THE ACTIVITY

This basic activity requires students to distinguish between statements of fact and statements of opinion. A statement of fact is a "report on reality." It isn't necessarily true—it is a statement that can be proven, definitively, to be either true or false. A statement of opinion is a "judgment or conclusion." It can be supported by facts and reasoning, but it can't be proven to be true or false. In this activity, students are given a list of 25 statements. They must mark each statement as **O** (statement of opinion) or **F** (statement of fact). Once students have finished marking all statements, the instructor guides a discussion in which they share their answers, explain the means used at arriving at answers, and consider the reasons why distinctions between fact and opinion may be problematic.

PURPOSES AND BENEFITS

Critical thinking involves an ongoing investigation into the means by which we gain information about the world. Before we can form opinions, or take action based on those opinions, we must first believe that certain information is true or factual. In *Critical Thinking and Education*, John McPeck discusses the senselessness of "purporting to teach critical thinking in the abstract" or removing "knowledge of facts and information from the domain of critical thinking." At the same time, students must use critical skills in judging whether "facts" are factual and whether information is reliable.

This activity is designed to develop students' ability to distinguish between types of statements in analyzing information. Class discussion of the exercise, especially of any disagreement in labeling statements, focuses on factors that must be considered in making valid distinctions: the phrasing of statements, the kind of evidence that could be used to prove statements, the possible sources of that evidence, and the nature of knowledge and proof—how we know, or think we know, that certain ideas (e.g. the earth is hollow) are true or not. The exercise can especially benefit those students who most resist it—that is, those so accustomed to true-false quizzes that they insist, at least initially, on marking statements **T** or **F**. It's also a way of showing students that education goes far beyond the mere accumulation of information. It requires critical thinking—the ability to evaluate the reliability and importance of information, as well as a willingness to reflect on the processes by which knowledge is obtained, demonstrated, and verified.

USES, ADAPTATIONS, AND RESOURCES

I use this exercise as students begin a major research-argument essay in Composition I. It helps them focus on finding and evaluating evidence in the argumentative essays they are reading as research, and it illustrates the necessity of using specific, reliable evidence to support claims they will make in arguments of their own. The exercise also prods students to see the value of that old dictum about conducting research: "consider the source" in judging your information. The choice of statements is virtually arbitrary, as long as the exercise contains some statements that are clearly **O**, some that are clearly **F**, and some that are problematic and difficult to categorize. I've used some simple statements about intelligence—Jill scored higher than Jack on an IQ test; Jill is more intelligent than Jack; women are more intelligent than men—that have led to heated, yet thoughtful debates about such questions as the definition of intelligence, the measurement of intelligence, the significance (or insignificance) of intelligence tests, and the validity of generalizations about gender differences. The statements in the exercise may also arouse curiosity about how professionals in certain fields know what they claim to know. How do geologists determine that the earth isn't hollow? How do historians arrive at a figure for the number of innocent people who were killed by Stalin's regime? I like to include a few statements that are humorous, provocative, or mystifying. The activity can easily be tailored to any discipline—history, for example—in which it's essential for students to distinguish between factual information (or information presented as factual) and interpretations of that information.

In *Critical Thinking: Reading and Writing in a Diverse World*, Rasool, Banks, and McCarthy include an excellent chapter on analyzing different types of statements. They provide alternative definitions of the term "fact" and use a number of examples, readings, and suggested activities to guide students through the process of distinguishing among observations, interpretations, facts, and conclusions. In her chapter "Facts: What's Real" from *Thinking for Yourself*, Marlys Mayfield discusses the standards used to determine facts—the process by which information "can be objectively demonstrated and verified"—and she examines the difficulty of establishing the "certainty" of any information. "*Certainty* in science," she writes, "usually means probability that approaches certainty." Mayfield also explores the relationship between facts and feelings, and she cites experiments by psychologist Solomon Asch to illustrate how social pressure may influence—or override—our interpretations of what is factual. We may actually come to believe that something is true because we want others to think that we believe it is true. One experiment, Mayfield writes, makes "a significant demonstration of the power of consensus to bring about conformity and to make a person invalidate his or her own perception."

S. J. Hayakawa's *Language in Thought and Action* also examines the differences between reports, inferences, and judgments. In analyzing the wording of statements—and how we judge others based on the wording of statements—he offers a useful distinction between sentences phrased as reports ("John committed a crime.") and those phrased as labels ("John is a criminal.").

For the exercise that I use, SEE the following pages. For related activities, SEE **#5: From the Known to the Unknown** and **#18: Who Fired the First Shot?**

FACT VS. OPINION EXERCISE

DIRECTIONS: Read the definitions below and then mark each statement as an **F** (statement of fact) or an **O** (statement of opinion).

Statement of Fact: a report on reality. A statement of fact isn't necessarily true; it's a statement that can be proven to be either true or false.

Statement of Opinion: a judgment or conclusion. A statement of opinion may be supported by facts, but it can't be proven to be true or untrue.

_____ 1. Columbus discovered America in 1492.

_____ 2. Columbus discovered America in 1942.

_____ 3. Jill scored higher than Jack on an I.Q. test.

_____ 4. Jill is more intelligent than Jack.

_____ 5. Women are more intelligent than men.

_____ 6. The earth is hollow.

_____ 7. The United States Marines invaded the Dominican Republic in 1965.

_____ 8. President Clinton engaged in a sexual act with Monica Lewinsky.

_____ 9. President Clinton engaged in a sexual act with Hillary Clinton.

_____ 10. There will be 400,000,000 people in the United States in the year 2050.

_____ 11. Stalin and Hitler were both mass murderers.

_____ 12. Human beings evolved from other primates.

_____ 13. All men are created equal.

_____ 14. During World War II, thousands of innocent Japanese-Americans were imprisoned in concentration camps in the United States.

_____ 15. Jazz is the only uniquely American form of music.

_____ 16. Most bacteria are not harmful to humans.

_____17. To succeed in college, students must attend class and be punctual.

_____18. Six million Jews were murdered during the Holocaust.

_____19. If there are two alternatives, choose the third one.

_____20. The sum of the squares of the lengths of the sides of a right triangle is equal to the square of the length of the hypotenuse.

_____21. Two wrongs don't make a right.

_____22. History repeats itself.

_____23. Incest is not always emotionally harmful to children.

_____24. Americans' current rate of consuming natural resources will eventually bring about the extinction of many animal species.

_____25. Any person can get a good education at North Shore Community College.

ACTIVITY #5
From the Known to the Unknown (Making Inferences)

APPLICATIONS: Reading and writing courses, literature, linguistics, journalism and media studies, other disciplines

CRITICAL THINKING SKILLS: Determining the importance of information, making inferences, using evidence, evaluating alternative interpretations

THE ACTIVITY

Begin by giving students a definition of "inference" and some examples to illustrate the concept. One definition I like is "a statement about the unknown based on what is known." Then provide students with the following letter, from Bill to his friend Jill:

> Remember Sally, the person I mentioned in my last letter? You'll never guess what she did this week. First, she let loose a team of gophers. The plan backfired when a dog chased them away. She then threw a party, but the guests failed to bring their motorcycles. Furthermore, her stereo system was not loud enough. Sally spent the next day looking for a "Peeping Tom" but was unable to find one in the yellow pages. Obscene phone calls gave her some hope until the number was changed. It was the installation of blinking neon lights across the street that finally did the trick. Sally framed the ad from the classified section and now has it hanging on her wall.

Give students about ten minutes to study the letter and answer these questions: (1) What was Sally trying to accomplish through her various tactics? (2) What did the classified ad say, and why did this ad indicate that Sally had succeeded in her plan? After students share their answers, discuss the following questions: In what ways do their answers illustrate the concept of inference? Do their answers account for all the details in the letter? Are there correct answers to the two questions, or are there several inferences that are equally plausible?

PURPOSES AND BENEFITS

Inferences are a way of interpreting the world. They are a means of moving from what we know—observed behavior, words on a page—to what we don't know or don't know for sure—the motives behind the behavior, the intended meaning of the words. Making well-founded inferences is one of the essential critical thinking skills, and this exercise, taken from *The Ideal Problem Solver* by Bransford and Stein, is a simple, engaging way to introduce the concept of inference to students. The exercise illustrates the role of inference-making in solving problems: it requires each student to consider the relevance of all the evidence, to form a hypothesis, and to test the hypothesis against the evidence. It also demonstrates the importance of persistence in problem solving. Typically, students have no trouble generating possible explanations of Sally's behavior, but these explanations are often far-fetched or unrelated to much of the evidence. The students who arrive at satisfactory answers are those who continue to focus on the problem, to generate new hypotheses and to test their hypotheses against the evidence. In a comparison of alternative interpretations of an event or a written work, the most persuasive interpretation is generally the one that, as John McPeck says, makes "intelligent use of all the available evidence."

Sally, by the way, was trying to drive out a neighbor. The classified ad indicated that the neighbor's apartment or house was now up for rent or sale. But is that the only plausible explanation of her motive?

USES, ADAPTATIONS, AND RESOURCES

I use this exercise in Composition I, in leading students to become more conscious of the potential pitfalls of making inferences when interpreting language and behavior. I reinforce the lesson with brief written exercises which present students with scenarios—an apparent argument between two people in a hallway, a student who thinks that a professor has spoken sarcastically to her—and then require the students to specify possible inferences and to distinguish between warranted and unwarranted inferences. Bransford and Stein provide other inference puzzles and assignments, as do many bibliographical sources. In one simple exercise, described in *de Bono's Thinking Course*, students must infer the possible reasons why a person is pouring fluid from a beer car into a car's gasoline tank, and Alverno College's *Teaching Critical Thinking in Psychology* presents a "My Dear Watson" exercise in which students make observations and inferences while pretending to be Sherlock Holmes. In *Critical Thinking, Thoughtful Writing* Chaffee, McMahon, and Stout suggest this analytical writing assignment, which focuses on the moral or social consequences of making false or unfounded inferences:

> Describe an experience in which you made an incorrect inference that resulted in serious consequences. For example, it might have been a situation in which you mistakenly accused someone, an accident based on a miscalculation, a poor decision based on an inaccurate prediction, or some other event. Analyze that experience by answering the following questions: (1) What was (were) your mistaken inference(s)? (2) What was the factual evidence on which you based your inference(s)? (3) Looking back, what could you have done to avoid the erroneous inference(s)?

For students of the media, Diane Halpern's *Critical Thinking Across the Curriculum* and Marlys Mayfield's *Thinking for Yourself* both examine the ways in which those who disseminate information may try to control the inferences made by those who receive it. Halpern quotes Jerome Bruner's definition of thinking as "going beyond the information given" and illustrates the techniques that writers use, in advertising and other fields, to direct or misdirect thinking so that readers will draw the desired inferences. One example she cites is that of a pro-life advocate who claims that the best way to win a debate on abortion is the frequent use of the words "kill" and "baby" in the same sentence. Mayfield, in her chapter on inference, uses examples from different media—cartoons, photographs, graphs, charts, scenarios, historical accounts (e.g. a measurement problem solved by the ancient Greek mathematician Archimedes), and short stories—to illustrate how to evaluate inferences and to distinguish between facts and interpretations. "When we infer," Mayfield writes, "we bring in our imagination or reasoning power to explain something. When we infer, we make a guess; we seek explanations to bridge what we know with what we don't know." She provides examples of inference chains (in which each inference leads to another), a collaborative inference-making assignment with steps and criteria for peer review, an assignment on analyzing inferences in a newspaper article (with a sample student composition), and another assignment on working from facts to inferences to hypotheses.

For basic reading or introductory literature courses, I've found that short poems, such as Theodore Roethke's "My Papa's Waltz" and Robert Hayden's "On Winter Sundays," are effective in introducing the process of inference-making in interpreting literature. In interpreting the Roethke poem, students must draw inferences from the details and language of the poem—such as the use of "papa" rather than "father" than "dad"—in deciding whether the dancing father is being playful or abusive, or both. Susan Glaspell's one-act play *Trifles* is also an excellent introduction to inferences, in this case inferences about apparently insignificant details ("trifles") that enable two women to figure out the motive for a murder. Short stories that work well in focusing on inference include Ernest Hemingway's "Hills Like White Elephants," Kate Chopin's "The Story of an Hour," Rabindranath Tagore's "Punishment," Eudora Welty's "The Worn Path" and Gina Berriault's "The Stone Boy" (in Mayfield's book), as well as more challenging stories such as Charlotte Perkins Gilman's "The Yellow Wallpaper," William Faulkner's "Barn Burning," and Albert Camus' "The Guest." And Montaigne's classic essay "Of the Inconsistency of Our Actions" contains some wise reflections on the hazards in the minefield of interpreting human behavior. He concludes by saying: "A sound intellect will refuse to judge men simply by their outward actions; we must probe the inside and discover what springs set men in motion. But since this is an arduous and hazardous undertaking, I wish fewer people would meddle with it."

In discussing literary works, I like to present students with an analogy between reading literature and "reading" the behavior of people, and we discuss why "readers" in both cases may make unsound inferences because of false assumptions, cultural stereotypes, or failure to consider all the evidence. We also look at what happens when stories are retold, again and again, as people share experiences with one listener after another, especially if the tellers feel compelled to justify their own behavior. The line between facts and interpretations becomes more and more blurred. What was once recognized as inference assumes the status of The Truth.

Finally, in *The Language Instinct*, linguist Stephen Pinker examines the astonishing process by which children, on their own, learn to decipher the meaning of complex sentences, make plausible inferences, and interpolate assumptions into the stories they hear. He also evaluates claims about the ability of animals to learn language, and he notes some of the difficulties involved in getting computers to mimic the linguistic capabilities of humans. Consider, Pinker says, the challenge of programming a computer to interpret the inferences made in the following dialogue:

A woman: "I'm leaving you."

A man: "Who is he?"

For related activities, SEE **#6: I'm Taking Medication—You're on Drugs, #8: Weighing the Evidence** and **#9: Eyewitness.**

ACTIVITY #6
I'm Taking Medication—You're on Drugs
(Detecting Slanting)

APPLICATIONS: Reading and writing courses, journalism, library science, other disciplines

CRITICAL THINKING SKILLS: Distinguishing fact from opinion, detecting slanting and bias, making well-founded inferences, analyzing the process of forming opinions

THE ACTIVITY

Begin this activity by giving students a definition of "slanting" and some brief examples to illustrate the concept. Then provide students with several longer examples of slanted written passages such as editorials or argumentative essays, or assign students to find and analyze examples of writing that contain slanted passages. Ask them to: (1) identify instances of slanting (2) describe the techniques used to slant information, and (3) determine the purposes of the slanting in these passages.

PURPOSES AND BENEFITS

Language can be an instrument of power, a tool used to influence or manipulate attitudes and behavior. In a highly literate society, those who don't grasp how this instrument can be used will remain powerless. We must often form opinions, make decisions, and take action in situations in which our primary knowledge comes, not from any first-hand experience, but from our evaluation of the language used to report and analyze the situation, whether it be a war in Southeast Asia, an anthrax scare, or controversy over an oil pipeline in Alaska. Critical thinking depends on critical reading— the ability to judge sources of information, to distinguish between objective information and information slanted to promote a particular point of view, and to understand the techniques writers use to sway public opinion. To develop thoughtful, well-informed opinions, students must not only be encouraged to be open-minded but must also be trained to evaluate the reliability of information, to detect bias, and, in particular, to recognize when information has been slanted to fool or mislead the reader. The point is not that slanting is wrong—any opinionated writing is slanted—but that there is a distinction between slanting through sound reasoning and supporting evidence and slanting through distortion or deception. It's a writer's obligation not to lie or distort; it's the reader's job to detect when a writer is lying or distorting. Students also need to reflect on the use of slanting in their own writing: how to support their opinions effectively through their choice of words and selection of facts, without resorting to deception or evasion.

USES, ADAPTATIONS, AND RESOURCES

I use this activity in Composition I, in conjunction with an argumentative composition based on research. I begin with a Sydney J. Harris article, "Diction and Point of View," which contains short examples of slanting through word choice, or connotation:

- I am taking medication; you are on pills; he takes dope.
- I vote on principles; you vote on ideology; he votes on dogmas.
- I am a social drinker; you tend to overindulge; he is a drunk.
- I am warm and affectionate; you are loose; she is a slut.

I ask students to analyze the slanting in these examples and to write examples of their own that follow the same model. Next, I ask them to generate a list of adjectives to describe X in the following sentence—"X does not like to spend money"—and we discuss how writers could slant their views of X by choosing words with positive or negative connotations (cheap, frugal, stingy, etc.). Then students must identify and analyze the use of slanting in three accounts of a labor-management dispute: one, a strictly factual report of the dispute; two, an account slanted to support the workers' point of view; and three, an account slanted from management's point of view. We discuss the motives of the writers in the three accounts and the techniques used in slanting to influence public opinion. From there we move on to analysis of longer readings.

In another exercise, designed to illustrate slanting through selection or omission of information, I give students a list of facts on some controversial topic—say, welfare reform or anti-terrorism security—and divide the class into groups of four or five, with each group assigned to advocate a particular position in the controversy. Each group, working collaboratively, must select ten facts that it would use to support its position, as well as five facts it would deliberately omit. Each group explains to the rest of the class its rationale for selecting and omitting information, and we discuss how the same information can be used to support or criticize different points of view. In *Engaging Ideas*, John Bean describes a similar "data-provided" assignment: "In this strategy, the teacher provides the data; students must determine what thesis or hypothesis the data might support. This strategy is particularly useful in the sciences for teaching students how to write the 'findings' and 'discussion' sections of scientific reports." Bean also offers many practical suggestions to help students "interact" with texts and overcome the obstacles that keep them from being critical readers. He discusses, for instance, how to "show that all texts reflect the author's frame of reference and thus are subject to interrogation and analysis" and how to "show students the importance of knowing cultural codes for comprehending a text." Using a concept taken from Peter Elbow, he recommends the "believing and doubting game" in which students, as critical readers, play the "double role or being simultaneously open to texts and skeptical of them."

George Orwell's classic essay "Politics and the English Language" discusses some of the motives behind deceptive slanting—in particular, the idea that writers fudge their language when they are trying to justify things that can't be justified—and many sources include sections on detection and analysis of slanting. The poet Donald Hall, in *Writing Well*, offers exercises to help students become more sensitive to shades of meaning. He explains, among other things, that, because of differences in connotation, no two words are truly synonymous. Marlys Mayfield, in *Thinking for Yourself*, suggests exercises on "recognizing evaluations conveyed by connotative words" and illustrates how evaluations (slanting) may be hidden or disguised in propaganda. And, to illustrate that the techniques of slanting are independent of anyone's actual opinion, S. J. Hayakawa, in *Language in Thought and Action*, recommends assignments in which the student writes: "(a) reports heavily slanted *against* persons or organizations he *likes*, and (b) reports heavily slanted *in favor of* persons or organizations he *dislikes*." He also gives examples of how to "conjugate" a series of three slanted sentences like those in the Sydney J. Harris article.

The Internet presents some special challenges in detecting slanting and, more generally, determining the reliability of information, and many available sources focus specifically on critical evaluation of Internet material. H. Eric Branscomb's *Casting Your Net*, for example, provides both a list of common slanting "tricks" or fallacies (either/or reasoning, begging the question) and the following checklist for evaluating Internet sources:

- Does this website/posting fit with how you want to appear in your research project?
- Does this website/posting commit any of the logical fallacies discussed earlier?
- When was the website last updated?

- Can you find the sources of information that the website/poster uses?
- Does this website/posting contain an unacceptable number of grammatical or spelling mistakes?
- Does real, concrete, and specific information appear on this website/posting, or is it vague and generalized?
- Who is the audience for this website/posting? Is the information slanted one way or the other to fit that audience's expectations?
- What do you know (or what else can you find out) about the source of the information (the poster or the website's creator)?
- What can you point to in the website/posting that makes you inclined to believe or not believe the information?
- Can you find corroborating information in other sources on the Internet or in print? How reliable are those sources?
- Find opposing points of view in the thread, other threads, or other websites. How can you reconcile these opposites?

SEE the following page for some selected online sources that provide more in-depth guidance in evaluating Internet information.

For related activities, SEE **#7: For the Semantically Challenged, #18: Who Fired the First Shot?** and **#33: In this Writer's Opinion.**

ONLINE SOURCES FOR EVALUATING INTERNET INFORMATION

Checklist for Evaluating Web Sites
http://www.canisius.edu/canhp/canlib/webcrit.htm
  (Canisius University Library)

Evaluating Internet Information
http://milton.mse.jhu.edu:8001/research/education/net.html
  (Johns Hopkins University)

Thinking Critically about World Wide Web Resources
http://www.library.ucla.edu/libraries/college/instruct/critical.htm
  (UCLA)

Critically Analyzing Information
http://www.library.cornell.edu/okuref/research/skill26.htm
  (Cornell University—guidelines for evaluating sources in general)

Evaluating Quality on the Net
http://www.tiac.net/users/hope/findqual.html
  (Babson College)

Criteria for Evaluation of Internet Information Resources
http://www.vuw.ac.nz/dlis/courses/847/m2resevl.html
  (online course at Victoria University, New Zealand)

ACTIVITY #7
For the Semantically Challenged
(Deciphering Euphemisms)

APPLICATIONS: Reading and writing courses, media studies, human services, other disciplines

CRITICAL THINKING SKILLS: Detecting slanting and bias, making inferences, distinguishing fact from opinion, using examples to illustrate concepts

THE ACTIVITY

This activity goes hand in hand with the previous exercises on slanting. Begin by giving students a definition of the term "euphemism," an explanation of its derivation (from the ancient Greek *euphemizein*, to speak with good words), and some examples to illustrate the definition. Then ask students to identify the euphemisms in assigned reading passages or to find euphemisms in their own reading, in public speeches, or in everyday conversations. You might also require students to create some euphemisms of their own. Class discussion might focus on the following topics: euphemisms as examples of slanting through connotation, euphemism as a form of deception, the motives for using euphemisms in various contexts, or, more generally, the use of language in labeling people and as a means of influencing public opinion.

PURPOSES AND BENEFITS

To be critical thinkers, students must grasp the nuances of language, the motives behind word choice, and the effects of language on readers and listeners. They should also be able to tell when someone is lying to them, and one way to lie, and make a lie sound true, is to use a euphemism—a vague and sometimes deliberately evasive term substituted for one that is more explicit; a sugar-coated phrase; or, in some cases, a nice way of saying something nasty. The idea that the name is not the thing is one of the basic tenets of semantics, and one of the challenges in studying language is that so many names, including euphemistic ones, may be used to refer to the same thing. Analyzing euphemisms is one effective way to illustrate concepts such as inference and slanting, and to examine how the choice of language reflects the values or intentions of both individuals and a whole society. Many euphemisms are intentionally or unintentionally humorous, and this subject engages students as they try to decipher examples of especially outrageous euphemisms. A nuclear explosion becomes an "energetic disassembly." Death on the operating table is a "negative patient outcome." A man in an ugly sweater is "aesthetically challenged." A gas station attendant is transformed into "a retail service representative for a major energy conglomerate." Slums are upgraded to "substandard dwellings," lies are disguised as "disinformation," and wars are minimized as "police actions." And that annoying ringing you hear as you sit down to supper is a "courtesy call." In the end, thankfully, we don't die—we receive our final marching orders, tee up our souls for the Great 19th Hole, and pass on from this life to ride the Highways of Heaven on our celestial Harley-Davidsons. After studying euphemisms, students should become more sensitive to their own choice of words as writers or speakers and more alert to the use of slanting in their reading and in everyday conversations.

USES, ADAPTATIONS, AND RESOURCES

I use this activity in Composition I as part of our study of semantics, propaganda, and slanting in argumentative writing. I provide examples from sources such as George Orwell's "Politics and the English Language," a taped George Carlin comedy routine satirizing the widespread use of euphemisms in our society, and Nancy Mairs' essay "On Being a Cripple,"

---

in which she explains why she prefers the term "cripple"—"a clean word, straightforward and precise"—to such euphemisms as "handicapped" or "differently abled." We discuss the various reasons why people use euphemisms—to spare others' feelings, to appear polite, to create the illusion of status, to avoid blame and accountability—and I use the concept of euphemism to initiate an analysis of the different forms deceit may take. One may tell a flat-out lie (a lie of commission). One may deliberately leave out essential parts of the truth (a lie of omission). Or one may deceive by using a misleading label with the desired connotations (a euphemism). As Orwell wrote: "Defenseless villages are bombarded from the air, the inhabitants driven out into the countryside, the cattle machinegunned, the huts set on fire with incendiary bullets: this is called 'pacification.'" After our discussion I assign students an in-class essay in which they must discuss two deceptive euphemisms, explain how these euphemisms mislead or deceive, and analyze the motives behind the deception.

This activity can be tailored to any field—human services, education, business, health care—in which euphemisms are used as labels or a means of influencing perceptions or attitudes. Almost any political speech will provide examples, and examples can be found in many books about semantics or the media, such as Gary Goshgarian's *Exploring Language*, but I also like to remind students that any of us, in a given situation, might have reasons to evade, to obfuscate, to avoid stating the facts explicitly. We may not exactly lie—I wouldn't call it dissembling—but we might feel compelled to expand or modify the parameters of truth.

ACTIVITY #8
Weighing the Evidence (Evaluating Evidence and Statistics)

APPLICATIONS: Composition, statistics, mathematics, psychology, literature, other disciplines

CRITICAL THINKING SKILLS: Getting relevant information, distinguishing fact from opinion, testing hypotheses, evaluating evidence, examining issues from opposing viewpoints

THE ACTIVITY

This activity comes in many varieties. In one exercise the instructor presents students with a written claim or assertion. For example: "A research study of Jamaican marijuana users has proven that long-term regular use of marijuana does not impair intellectual function or cause significant health problems" (a claim taken from a student essay with, I must add, dubious documentation). The instructor then asks students to list all the relevant information and supporting evidence that would have to be provided to them before they would agree that the claim has been adequately supported. For instance, who conducted this study? How was "intellectual function" measured? What constitutes a "significant" health problem? How many Jamaican marijuana users were studied? Was a control group used? Students share responses with their classmates, and the instructor uses the exercise as a take-off point to guide a discussion about the criteria for using evidence effectively to support claims and assertions.

In a variation on this exercise, the instructor provides students with a written claim—e.g. "Jack has been diagnosed as suffering from the behavior disorder known as Poor Impulse Control Syndrome"—and a list of statements used as

---

evidence to support the claim. The instructor then asks students to provide written responses to questions about the reliability, relevance, and sufficiency of the supporting evidence In class discussion, students share responses, and the instructor guides a discussion about the criteria for adequate evidence and the possible flaws or limitations of supporting evidence, such as the bias of an observer, the vagueness of a definition, or an inadequate sample in a research study.

PURPOSES AND BENEFITS

We should read, Francis Bacon wrote, in order to "weigh and consider," and one fundamental critical thinking skill is the ability to weigh and evaluate the use of evidence to support a claim or thesis. This activity focuses student attention on the process of determining criteria for effective use of evidence, the need to consider both the nature and extent of supporting evidence, and the importance of judging the reliability of evidence. I use the activity when my Composition I students write argumentative essays based on research. The exercises help them both in analyzing the evidence in their research sources and in marshalling evidence to support their theses in their own essays.

USES, ADAPTATIONS, AND RESOURCES

Exercises like these can be used in any course in which students are presented with assertions supported by evidence, and they can be carried out as in-class activities, collaborative projects, or longer written assignments. To approach the issue of evidence in more depth, the instructor might guide an in-class analysis of argumentative essays that use supporting evidence from research. I often assign essays in pairs: either two well-supported essays that argue the same issue from opposing viewpoints, or two essays that argue the same thesis—one chosen because it presents solid supporting evidence, the other chosen because its evidence is inadequate, unreliable, or otherwise flawed. The *Opposing Viewpoints* and *Taking Sides* series of books on current controversial issues provide many good examples of paired essays arguing the same issue from opposing perspectives. The instructor might also ask students to evaluate the evidence used in argumentative essays written by classmates. In this case it's especially important to remind students to distinguish between criticisms of the use of evidence and criticisms that merely indicate disagreement with opinions expressed in the essays. When I grade argumentative essays, I stress that students are entitled to their opinions and that my job is to evaluate their use of reasoning and evidence to support the opinions.

I also raise the issue of evidence with students when we discuss standards for analytical essays in literature courses. I provide students with several model essays by former students to illustrate the effective use of evidence in supporting literary interpretations, and I use examples to illustrate how to select and incorporate relevant examples and quotations from their readings to support thesis statements or points of interpretation in literary analysis.

The analysis of statistical evidence is a field in itself, covered both in statistics courses and in liberal arts-oriented math courses, but students may be introduced to some basics of statistical analysis in other courses and contexts. In their abstract "Collaborative Writing: English and Math," English instructor Barbara Murray and math instructor Jennifer Walsh, from Daytona Beach Community College in Florida, describe a collaborative English/statistics research project in which students conduct surveys and graph the statistical data they obtain: "We both explained the tools to be used for the project and discussed the types of surveys, and the students developed a hypothesis that could be used for both classes. Statistics placed heavy emphasis on learning sampling techniques and designing the questions to facilitate numerical analysis."

In Composition I, my students evaluate the use of statistics in a cause-and-effect essay about the negative effects of being raised in large families. I use the essay to illustrate not only the misleading use of statistics but also the necessity of defining terms ("large family") and the purpose of documenting sources. Since I wrote the essay myself, using phony but plausible sounding statistics from a nonexistent source, this activity also teaches students to beware of the tricks of their professors. I am, by the way, the youngest of seven children.

Many sources include worthwhile sections on evaluating evidence. Alverno College's *Teaching Critical Thinking in Psychology* provides some well-designed assignments on judging the validity and reliability of evidence in the social sciences (one of which, in modified form, is the Poor Impulse Control Syndrome exercise described above). The evidence chapter in Sally DeWitt Spurgin's *The Power to Persuade* categorizes types of evidence, provides guidelines for incorporating evidence in research papers, and demonstrates how to evaluate evidence in terms of whether it is recent, primary, unbiased, representative, and sufficient. *Critical Thinking: Reading and Writing in a Diverse World* by Rasool, Banks, and McCarthy discusses how to evaluate both quantitative and qualitative evidence, while Daniel McDonald's *The Language of Argument* contains arguments based on statistical evidence, including one entitled "Crime Higher in Gun Control Cities." McDonald quotes Daniel Huff's *How to Lie with Statistics* to illustrate how statistics may be manipulated to create a misleading impression:

> There are often many ways of expressing any figure. You can, for instance, express exactly the same fact by calling it a one percent return on sales, a fifteen percent return on investment, a ten million-dollar profit, an increase in profits of forty percent [compared with figures from a decade earlier], or a decrease of sixty percent from last year. The method is to choose the one

sounds best for the purpose at hand and trust that few who read it will recognize how imperfectly it reflects the situation.

Thomas Gilovich's *How We Know What Isn't So*—a fine source for cultivating numerical literacy—also includes various examples of misinterpreting numerical and statistical data, both in research and in everyday life. One instance he cites is the tendency of researchers, whether students or professional, to look for confirmatory evidence—evidence that reinforces their own positions—while paying insufficient attention to the absence or insufficiency of information or the presence of non-confirmatory evidence. Focusing exclusively on the search for confirmatory evidence is one of the most common problems in student research, and when I ask my composition students to write argumentative essays based on research, I require that they summarize, address, and, if possible, refute opposing arguments based on non-confirmatory evidence.

SEE the following page for the exercise on Jack's alleged Poor Impulse Control Syndrome (no such syndrome exists—it was invented for the purposes of this assignment). For related activities, SEE **#9: Eyewitness, #23: Dissecting Words Instead of Frogs, #24: What Did That Prove?** and **#37: Does a Dog Know Its Name?**

COURSE: Composition I

INSTRUCTOR: John Nelson

SUBJECT: Evaluation of Evidence

Claim: Jack has a behavior disorder known as Poor Impulse Control Syndrome (PICS).

Evidence

- Ms. Smith, Jack's second-grade teacher, reports that he is hyperactive and should probably be medicated.
- Two lunchroom monitors independently reported to the principal that Jack suddenly hit two female students for no reason during the lunch hour.
- Jack scored in the lowest five per cent on the Cullowhee Test of Impulse Control.
- Jack admits that he often blurts out things and acts without thinking.
- Jack finds it hard to suppress his resentment of his stepmother.
- Jack often has trouble following the rules when he plays organized games.
- Jack rarely expresses feelings of guilt.

Questions to Answer

1. Is this evidence sufficient to support the claim?
2. Is the evidence reliable? Is all the evidence relevant?
3. What are the possible sources of error in this evidence?
4. If you answered "yes" to question one, explain why the evidence is relevant and sufficient. If you answered "no" to question one, what else would you need to know in order to determine whether the claim is well-founded?

DIRECTIONS: Answer the four questions on a separate sheet of paper. Be specific.

ACTIVITY #9
Eyewitness (Observing, Remembering, Describing)

APPLICATIONS: Criminal justice, sociology, journalism, composition, early childhood education, other disciplines
CRITICAL THINKING SKILLS: Evaluating reliability of information, distinguishing fact from opinion, detecting bias and false assumptions, making inferences

THE ACTIVITY

I've used a simple form of this scenario activity in Composition I, when students are writing narrative and descriptive papers. First, the instructor finds a volunteer assistant or accomplice (perhaps a student from another class), and together the instructor and accomplice work out a scenario. The instructor coaches the accomplice on what to wear (something with distinctive details), what to say, and what to do in playing the role of Intruder. Then, at a prearranged time, the Intruder (accomplice) barges into the instructor's classroom, frantically seeking some lost item such as a bookbag. The instructor asks and then orders the Intruder to leave, but the Intruder rudely refuses and continues to move around the room, desperately searching for the lost item, while insisting that it contains something valuable and must be somewhere in the classroom. Finally, after a prearranged signal from the instructor—"If you don't leave now, I'll have to call Security"—the Intruder indignantly leaves. Then the instructor asks the students in class to describe everything that just transpired—what the Intruder wore, what anyone in the classroom said and did—in as much detail as possible. Afterwards, students share their descriptions and discuss the accuracy and completeness of their observations. To test their memories of the event, the instructor might ask students to write a new but equally detailed description of the event during the next class meeting.

PURPOSES AND BENEFITS

Observation may not commonly be identified as a critical thinking skill, but being a good observer—one who is able to gather reliable data from direct experience—is at the least a prerequisite for more abstract or more analytical reasoning skills. This exercise demonstrates the importance of being careful observers and accurate, thorough reporters of events, while raising critical questions about the trustworthiness of memory. The activity encourages students to reflect on their behavior as observers and reporters, and it can be used to lead into an in-depth discussion of the reliability of eyewitness testimony. The exercise definitely gets students' attention. The staged intrusion almost always fools them, and it illustrates the idea that eyewitnesses to crimes are generally reporting events in situations in which they are not expecting or prepared to be careful observers.

USES, ADAPTATIONS, AND RESOURCES

In his *New Yorker* article "Under Suspicion," Atul Gawande explores questions about the reliability of eyewitnesses and the significance of these questions for our judicial system. Gawande describes a similarly staged scenario, carried out in 1901 by a criminal law professor at the University of Berlin, in which two students engaged in a nasty, apparently spontaneous argument during a lecture—one threatened the other with a gun. After the professor had restored order and the two students had left, the professor explained to the class that the incident had been staged, and he asked students to describe exactly what they had seen. "The results were dismal," writes Gawande. "The most accurate witness got twenty-six per cent of the significant details wrong; others up to eighty per cent. Words were put in people's mouths. Actions were described that had never taken place. Events that *had* taken place disappeared from memory." This scenario has been reenacted on many subsequent occasions, sometimes before audiences of judges, with similar results.

Gawande relates this experiment to wrongful convictions based on eyewitness testimony in criminal cases, and he applies the idea of "empirical scrutiny" to other "understudied factors" that influence the results of criminal trials, such as the number of jurors, the instructions given to jurors, and prosecutorial discretion. "The law," he says, "has balked at submitting its methods to scientific inquiry," and he argues persuasively that, if the judicial system examined itself more critically, "surprisingly simple changes in legal procedures could substantially reduce misidentification" in criminal cases. He sums up the views of sociologist Lawrence Sherman in stating that "the process of bringing scientific scrutiny to the methods of the justice system has hardly begun." This type of "empirical scrutiny" is a good example of critical thinking in action.

Sharon Begley's *Newsweek* article "Memory's Mind Games" also looks at the unreliability of both eyewitness testimony and memory. In illustrating "the mind's drive to infer cause," Begley describes one experiment in which subjects were shown a video of groceries being spilled. 68% reported seeing the cause of the spill (a ripping bag) even though it was not part of the video. In another experiment, subjects were shown a number of snapshots, which did not include a picture of the perpetrator of the crime they'd witnessed, and they became more confident in their overall recall of details after they had been (falsely) told that they did identify the actual suspect. As Jonathan Miller says in *The Body in Question*, what the mind sees is not what there is, but what it supposes there might be.

Vincent Ruggiero's *The Art of Thinking* includes a section on memory's malleability and the demonstrated ability of researchers to "plant" details in the memories of experimental subjects. He cites a report from the Columbia Associates in Philosophy, which concludes that "eyewitnesses have a tendency both to perceive and to remember things, first according to their expectations, second, according to their emotional bias, and third, according to their private notions as to what would be the natural or reasonable way for things to happen." Gary Lane Hatch's *Arguing in Communities* contains two argumentative essays with opposing views on the value and reliability of eyewitness testimony, while John Chaffee, in *Critical Thinking*, uses a hypothetical criminal case to set forth questions that can be asked to evaluate the credibility and relevance of eyewitness testimony: "What information is the witness providing? Is the information *relevant* to the charges? Is the witness *credible*? What *biases* might influence the witness's testimony? To what extent is the testimony accurate?"

The investigative work of students and professors at Northwestern University—particularly law professor James Marshall and journalism professor David Protess— demonstrates both the urgency of questioning eyewitness evidence and the value of applied critical thinking. Faculty-student investigative teams researched cases of men convicted of capital crimes in Illinois and were able to prove that some of these death row inmates had been wrongfully convicted because of dubious eyewitness testimony. Their work not only saved the lives of innocent men but also persuaded Governor George Ryan to announce a moratorium on executions in Illinois. These investigations have since led to the formation of the Center on Wrongful Convictions, a joint project of Northwestern's School of Law and its Medill School of Journalism, dedicated to rectifying wrongful convictions and formulating critical strategies to improve the criminal justice system. This kind of "wrongful conviction" research recalls an article I read some time ago, about a black man on trial in a criminal case. The defendant's lawyer was given permission to replace his client at the defense table with the defendant's friend, a black man of about the same age and size, in order to challenge the credibility of eyewitnesses. A series of witnesses identified the friend as the wrongdoer, and the friend, who had no connection whatsoever to the crime, was ultimately convicted by a jury on the basis of eyewitness testimony.

Another activity, sometimes called the "spread a rumor" game, can be used to illustrate the unreliability of information conveyed orally. In the version I use, the instructor asks five students to leave the classroom. One student is brought back in, and the instructor (or another student) reads to that student a narrative, containing some detailed information. The second student is then brought in, and the first student must convey the information orally to the second student. The process is repeated with the remaining three students, and the final student retells the narrative to the whole class. By this point most of the information has been lost or distorted, including the point of the narrative and the motives of any persons therein. On a related point, Thomas Gilovich, in *How We Know What Isn't So*, suggests that fictitious or inaccurate stories are frequently told and retold, as factual, merely because they make such good stories. He cites the widely disseminated false rumor that singer Bobby McFerrin committed suicide shortly after the huge success of his upbeat song "Don't Worry, Be Happy."

If observational skills lay the groundwork for critical thinking, then it makes sense to nurture these skills as early as possible, an approach recommended in Mary Rivkin's "Discovery: Taking Critical Thinking Outdoors," an article aimed at early childhood education teachers. "Because there is so much information outdoors," Rivkin writes, "children can sharpen their critical thinking skills by: (1) making observations (2) making connections (3) communicating their discoveries (4) evaluating those discoveries along with those of their peers." For adults, Diane Ackerman's *A Natural History of the Senses* is a lively source of descriptions and reflections on how we take in the world through our senses. "The latent findings in physiology," she writes, "suggest that *the mind* doesn't really dwell in the brain but travels the whole body on caravans of hormone and enzyme, busily making sense of the compound wonders we catalogue as touch, taste, smell, hearing, and vision."

One method of cultivating observational skills—observation logs—is explained in Kathleen Bell's *Developing Arguments*, with sample logs from such sources as Charles Darwin's *Voyage of the Beagle* and Jane Goodall's description of chimpanzees making and using tools to feed on termites. In *Thinking for Yourself*, Marlys Mayfield suggests some "discovery exercises" to help students learn to "observe how you observe," as well as writing assignments on observing both familiar and unfamiliar objects. Mayfield also discusses factors that distort perception—such as the tendency to turn the unfamiliar into the familiar—and act as barriers to reliable observation.

For related activities, SEE **#17: Incident Report, #18: Who Fired the First Shot?** and **#42: Suddenly You're Old.**

ACTIVITY #10
Asking the Right Questions (Asking Questions, Getting Information)

APPLICATIONS: Any discipline

CRITICAL THINKING SKILLS: Getting relevant information, distinguishing fact from opinion, detecting slanting, evaluating evidence, testing hypotheses

THE ACTIVITY

Students carrying out this activity write, distribute, and collect responses to a questionnaire, and/or they write a series of interview questions and then arrange and conduct an interview using these questions. Before the actual interview or distribution of the questionnaire, the instructor reviews the questions and suggests revisions in the phrasing of questions, the sequencing of questions, or the inclusion of omitted questions that could help students get the information they seek. Students then revise their questions and proceed with the interview or questionnaire. They present their results in an in-class report, a written report, or as part of a larger research paper.

PURPOSES AND BENEFITS

"Learning to think critically," writes John McPeck in *Critical Thinking and Education*, "is in large measure learning to know when to question something, and what sorts of question to ask." This activity addresses one basic element of the critical thinking process: getting relevant, reliable information. Students must think about: (1) the nature of the information they seek to obtain (2) the possible sources of information (the respondents to their questionnaires, the people they will interview) (3) the wording of questions to elicit relevant, useful responses—for instance, how to phrase clear, unslanted questions, and (4) the means by which they will conduct their interviews or distribute their questionnaires. They must take the initiative to arrange and conduct interviews and/or distribute the questionnaires. The activity also gives students experience that may prove useful when they are interviewed for jobs or interview others as part of their jobs. Finally, if students are conducting interviews as a part of a larger research project, their subjects often lead them to other valuable sources of information.

USES, ADAPTATIONS, AND RESOURCES

This activity could be used in any discipline, for various purposes: determining public opinion on an issue, developing an argument, learning about careers in a given field, and so on. I use both elements in Composition I—the questionnaire when students write reports on testing hypotheses (SEE **Activity #37**), and the interview when students are seeking information for their required research papers. Students often need help in coming up with questions, phrasing questions, and sequencing questions, and we discuss these issues both in class and in individual consultations. We also discuss how students should present themselves, how to take notes, and how to select and incorporate relevant information for use in their papers.

Many composition and speech texts include sections on interviewing. Alverno College's *Teaching Critical Thinking in Psychology* includes a "Job Hunting" interviewing exercise with a list of suggested questions. Kathleen Bell's *Developing Arguments* discusses the issue of establishing objectivity and inhabiting a confidence-inspiring persona during interviews, and she includes sample interviews on controversial issues such as disposal of nuclear waste, corporate responsibility for acid-rain pollution, and the Miranda ruling. Christine Hult's *Researching and Writing Across the Curriculum* examines the overall process of inquiry and how it varies from discipline to discipline. She cites a business survey used to determine the causes of occupational stress in a workplace situation, and she discusses how to gather and analyze the kind of data that is typically used in social science research. In her section on life histories, Hult uses an excerpt from a Studs Terkel interview to show how he edited the taped version of the interview, and gave it narrative form, for inclusion in *Hard Times: An Oral History of the Great Depression.*

William Rivers' *Finding Facts* provides a more in-depth view of gathering information, including common interview questions, guidelines for conducting interviews and taking notes, and common errors in interviewing, such as the "single interview" error. To limit oneself to a single interview with the subject of a report, he writes, is "to invite imprisonment in the subject's perspective." He adds: "Additional interviewing and careful research in documents enables the reporter to triangulate: Here is what he says, here is what others say, here is what the record seems to show. The probable truth is more likely to emerge from this process than from a single interview." Rivers also illustrates how the choice of a single word in the phrasing of a question—"should" instead of "might" or "could"—can significantly influence responses to the question.

In discussing the conduct of interviews, Rivers suggests techniques both to encourage response and to probe when responses are not forthcoming. "Most often," he says, "the interviewer should ask questions in a way that indicates that there are no right or wrong answers," but he also quotes psychologists Eleanor and Nathan Maccoby on the unavoidability of assuming a role, or persona, during an interview: "The interviewer must occupy some role, whether he wishes it or not, and therefore the research worker must be conscious of the various roles possible . . . and attempt to establish a role which will best further the purposes of this study." John Bean, in *Engaging Ideas*, extends this idea of defining roles to the actual writing of a research paper: "Teachers might consider discussing with students the various roles they might play in their research writing—or even specifying the role as part of the assignment. Often the writer's role and purpose depend on the nature of the research question posed." Bean describes some typical roles such as "problem-solving detective and analyst," "original field or laboratory researcher," and "advocate in a controversy."

For a related activity, SEE **#11: The Guiding Light.**

ACTIVITY #11
The Guiding Light (Using Study Guides Collaboratively)

APPLICATION: Literature, criminal justice, psychology, gender studies, other disciplines

CRITICAL THINKING SKILLS: Analyzing metaphorical language, making inferences, evaluating alternative interpretations of artistic works

THE ACTIVITY

In this activity students collaborate, working in class in groups of four or five. Before the class, the instructor provides them with a study guide consisting of problematic questions about assigned reading material—questions that require reflection, interpretation, and/or application of concepts previously covered in class. Students in each group discuss the material and answer questions assigned to that group, then report their answers to the class as a whole. The class proceeds to discuss the assigned material in more depth.

PURPOSES AND BENEFITS

The primary benefit of this activity is that it promotes active learning by all students in a class. In a course with 25 or 30 students, or more, it's difficult to guide a class discussion that allows or encourages everyone to participate. Here, all students interact and discuss their viewpoints with classmates in small, non-threatening groups. I've used the activity in literature courses as a way of breaking up the task of interpretation when we're discussing especially difficult works. I encourage students to reflect on all questions in the study guide, but they are directly responsible only for reporting answers to the specific questions assigned to their groups.

I assign roles—recorder, monitor—to insure that each group keeps focused and organized, or I designate one individual within each group to be primarily responsible for reporting the group's answer to one particular question. The objective is to get everyone involved in discussion.

USES, ADAPTATIONS, AND RESOURCES

This activity can be used effectively in almost any discipline, and many textbooks provide study questions or ready-made study guides that can be used with collaborative groups. The approach does have its drawbacks. Developing a study guide is time-consuming, and, though the activity can stimulate in-depth analysis and develop cohesion among students, it involves spending significant class time on one particular work. Depending on the length and complexity of the material, I allot anywhere from 20 minutes to an entire class for groups to meet. I pass out the study guide and set up groups at least one class period before the groups actually meet; groups may flounder if students are absent or unprepared. Also, when they report to the class as a whole, some students are neither articulate nor very forthcoming, and they may look to more proficient or more vocal group members to rescue them and elaborate for them. I try to set up groups and guide class discussions in ways that anticipate and minimize these problems—for instance, by giving the role of recorder/ reporter to a student who seldom participates in discussion or by posing a series of follow-up questions to a student who isn't forthcoming.

In *Engaging Ideas*, John Bean devotes a chapter to the use of small groups in coaching students to demonstrate critical thinking. The "goal-directed" method he recommends has, he says, "a consistent rhythm: the teacher presents a disciplinary problem requiring critical thinking; students work together in small groups to seek a consensus solution to the problem; and the teacher coaches students' performance by observing their process and critiquing their solutions." Bean discusses how to design and implement group tasks, how to set up groups so that they work effectively, and how to get groups focused on specific types of strategy (e.g. the problem-posing strategy, the evidence-finding strategy, the case strategy, the metacognitive strategy). He also responds to both pragmatic and philosophical objections to the use of small groups as a teaching technique. Small groups can be effective in eliciting participation and giving students a stake in a discussion; they don't work well if the instructor's primary goal is to disseminate information.

SEE the following pages for a stanza-by-stanza guide to John Keats' poem "Ode to a Nightingale" and a chapter-by-chapter guide to Patricia Pearson's *When She Was Bad*, a nonfiction psychological study of female aggression and crime, which I've used both in my course "Criminals in Literature" and as an example of a researched argument in Composition I.

STUDY GUIDE
Patricia Pearson's
When She Was Bad

As you read each chapter, reflect on the following questions in preparation for class discussion. Terms in **boldface** may be topics on the in-class essay on the book.

Girls Will Be Girls (Chapter #1)
- What is the "myth" the author refers to on p.7, and why does the author believe that this myth is false? Why, according to the author, do people believe in this myth?
- What does the author mean when she says on p.22 that "aggressive gestures are directed by cultural expectations"? What examples could illustrate this idea?
- What does the author mean when she claims on p.23 that we don't view women as "responsible actors"? How would you define a "responsible actor"? What evidence does she use to support this claim?
- Paraphrase the following quotation from p.32: "How do we affirm ourselves to be as complex, desirous, and independent as men without conceding the antisocial potential in those qualities?"

Maybe You Mistook Me for an Angel (Chapter #2)
- What is meant by the phrase "**the vocabulary of motive**" on p.40? What are some examples of this "vocabulary"? In what ways is this vocabulary "different for male and female offenders"?
- What is "**learned helplessness**"? Why does the author believe that learned helplessness is not a valid homicide defense?
- What evidence does the author use to challenge the idea that "violence on the part of women is usually in response to abuse"(p.55)? Are you convinced by her evidence?

- What points or ideas does the author illustrate through the stories of Karla Homulka, Francine Hughes, and Guinevere Garcia?

The Problem That Still Has No Name (Chapter #3)
- Why is the author skeptical about the use of "syndromes" to explain or excuse violence committed by mothers?
- Why is the difference between the "baby blues" and "**postpartum psychosis**"?
- According to the author, what are some of the main reasons why women kill their children?
- What does the author mean when she says on p.91 that "infanticide, like any act of violence, is profoundly idiosyncratic"?

Medea in Her Modern Guise (Chapter #4)
- Who is Medea, and why is she famous?
- What points or ideas does the author illustrate through the story of Marybeth Tinning?
- What is **Munchausen syndrome by proxy**? How does this concept relate to violence committed by women? Why does the author believe that this syndrome is often a "hugely misleading" label?
- What is the "anomie theory" (p.103), and how does it relate to violence committed by women?
- Does the author believe that victims of abuse are destined to become abusers?

Balancing the Domestic Equation (Chapter #5)
- What points or ideas does the author illustrate through the story of Peter Swann?
- According to the author, why do people refuse to consider the abuse of husbands a serious problem? Does the author persuade you that this problem is common and serious? Do you agree with the idea that a "real man" cannot be abused?
- On p.134 the author quotes an anger management teacher:

"Violence is a learned behavior." How is violence learned?
- What is **shadowboxing**, and how does this concept relate to aggression in relationships?

Woman as Predator (Chapter #6)
- What points or ideas does the author illustrate through the stories of Dorothea Puente and Aileen Wournos?
- On p.154 the author quotes a psychologist who says that male and female serial killers differ in modus operandi, not in motive. What does this statement mean? What evidence does the author use to support this statement?
- What does the author mean on p.175 when she says that violent women are "human first, and gendered second"?

What's Love Got to Do with It? (Chapter #7)
- On p.181 the author quotes Allison Morris: "Learning crime includes not only techniques but also rationalizations, justifications, and attitudes." Think of examples that would illustrate this statement.
- What is meant by the concept of **"compliant victims"** on p.185, and why does the author question this concept?
- What is a "folie a deux"? How does this concept relate to violence committed by women?

Island of Women (Chapter #8)
- What are some of the main differences between male and female inmates?
- What accounts for these differences?

Let the Gun Smoke (Chapter #9)
- What is the **"liberation hypothesis"** (p.229)? Do you think that this hypothesis is valid?
- What is the "culture of victimhood"? Why does the author believe that this culture is harmful to both women and society as a whole?

- Why does the author believe that the rights of victims are demeaned by "our refusal to concede female contributions to violence"?

Epilogue
- What points or ideas does the author illustrate through the story of Karla Faye Tucker?

STUDY GUIDE for IN-CLASS GROUPS: "Ode to a Nightingale" by John Keats

STANZA #1
1. What is the speaker feeling in this stanza? Why?
2. To whom is the speaker speaking?
3. What do "hemlock" and "opiate" signify, and what is their relevance here?

STANZA #2
1. What does the speaker want to do, and why does he want to do it?
2. What do "Flora" and "Provencal" signify, and what is their relevance here?
3. What images are used in this stanza? What feelings do you get from these images?

STANZA #3
1. What are some of the things the nightingale "hast never known"?
2. Why hasn't the nightingale known these things?
3. Why does the speaker want to forget these things? Is it possible to forget these things?

STANZA #4
1. How will the speaker "fly" to the nightingale?
2. Who is Bacchus, and why does the speaker refer to him here?
3. What is meant by the phrase "the dull brain perplexes and retards"?

STANZA #5
1. What is the speaker feeling in this stanza? Why?
2. What images are used in this stanza? How do these images make you feel?

3. Why can't the speaker see the flowers or the incense?

STANZA #6
1. What is the poet feeling in this stanza? Why?
2. Why does the speaker say: "Now more than ever seems it rich to die"?
3. What is personified in this stanza, and why?

STANZA # 7
1. What is the speaker feeling in this stanza? Why?
2. What does the speaker mean when he says that "thou wast not born for death"?
3. What do the emperor, the clown, and Ruth all have in common?

STANZA #8
1. What is "the fancy," and why is it called a "deceiving elf"?
2. What is "the plaintive anthem," and why does it fade?
3. What is the meaning of the questions in the last two lines?

QUESTIONS FOR ALL
1. What is the main theme of the poem?
2. What is an ode? Why is this ode addressed to a bird, and why this particular bird?
3. Has the speaker arrived at any resolution, or gone through any change in feelings or attitude, by the end of the poem? If so, what is the nature of this change or resolution?
4. What feelings or questions remain unresolved at the end of the poem?

ACTIVITY #12
What Do Men Want? (Comparing Student Opinions)

APPLICATIONS: Literature, history, other disciplines

CRITICAL THINKING SKILLS: Examining issues from opposing viewpoints, evaluating alternative solutions to problems

THE ACTIVITY

In this simple exercise the instructor surveys student opinion on some question relevant to assigned readings or topics of class discussion. The instructor poses the question and asks students to express their opinions in brief written responses (a paragraph or so). The instructor then asks students to share their responses with the whole class, or the instructor collects the responses and types up excerpts to be presented to the class. Students discuss the various responses and compare them to viewpoints presented in the assigned readings.

PURPOSES AND BENEFITS

This activity, like the previous one, is a way to involve everybody in class discussion so that a task of critical analysis becomes a group effort. It's intended to encourage the precise written expression of opinions, to elicit student reactions to themes in assigned readings, and to engage students in dialogues and critical analyses of issues they have a stake in debating. I've used the exercise in literature courses when we've discussed stories of forbidden love in Ovid's *Metamorphoses*. I pose a question implicit in all the stories we read: "Can sexual desire, especially desire for someone forbidden, be controlled? If so, how? If not, why not?" Students provide a variety of responses, ranging from, "Yes. We can suppress lustful thoughts and use reason to foresee the consequences of our actions," to, "No. If we could control our desires, people wouldn't cheat so much." I collect the responses, type and distribute excerpts from all responses, and in class discussion ask all students to indicate both the responses closest to their own opinions and the responses most contrary to their opinions. Students are intrigued, sometimes surprised, and sometimes appalled by their classmates' views, and they get involved in lively discussions on such points as the nature of desire, the relationship between reason and self-control, and the definition of "control" in the question. Though it's time-consuming, I generally use typed excerpts because some students might be embarrassed if asked to read responses in class. I leave it up to the students to claim responses as their own. We relate the discussion to Ovid's stories, and the exercise has helped to sharpen students' perceptions of the dilemmas faced by Ovid's characters (or dilemmas of their own) and to find thematic continuity in stories that might seem unconnected.

USES, ADAPTATIONS, AND RESOURCES

This exercise is one way to establish a framework for a critical analysis of an issue raised in a text. Its purpose is not merely to generate a list of opinions but to provide students with a range of alternative interpretations or alternative solutions to a problem, and the activity can help to pinpoint why a particular issue is problematic. This type of exercise can be carried out in almost any discipline, and textbooks for many courses include study questions that could be used to conduct class surveys. Can pedophiles be rehabilitated or "cured"? Do terminally ill patients have a right to assisted suicide? Should we educate the children of illegal immigrants in our public schools? I've used this approach with a variety of readings in literature and composition classes. For instance, when we've discussed the prologue and story by Chaucer's Wife of Bath, I've posed the question that is raised and answered in the story itself: What do women what? We compare each student's response to other class responses and to the various answers provided within the text. The exercise has, among other things, helped students focus on the significance of the setting and context in Chaucer's story: what a woman wants depends on who the woman is, when and where she lives, and what her circumstances are within a particular culture. In one class, our discussion prompted a number of students to request class responses to another question: What do men want?

In a related activity, I sometimes ask students, either individually or in groups, to submit several questions about an assigned literary work—any questions they would like the whole class to discuss—and then I select some questions for general discussion or debate. This approach may seem haphazard—the questions are all over the map and may be big or small, crucial or trivial—but through careful selection and organization of the selected questions, an instructor can use them to frame a coherent critical analysis of the text and to bring out connections between seemingly disparate questions. Students often raise questions I've never considered, or questions that lead to detailed examination of problematic passages, and this exercise can be effective in getting students to articulate—and getting instructors to understand— the reasons why they are either puzzled by or resistant to texts.

In *Engaging Ideas*, John Bean describes a similar question-generating approach used by a history professor, who says: "As the semester continued, students came to class with their favorite questions already in mind . . . The wealth of questions helped to reinforce the intended impression that learning about the seventeenth century, or any other historical topic, can never be finished and over with. There is always more of interest to investigate." Bean's book contains an abundance of ideas on how to use brief "exploratory writing" assignments, both in and out of class, to stimulate critical thinking. Recommended assignments include guided journals, reading logs, imaginary dialogues between fictional or historical characters, thesis statement writing, and "writing during class to refocus a lagging discussion or to cool off a heated one."

ACTIVITY #13
At First Blush (Analyzing Behavior)

APPLICATION: Psychology, biology (physiology), speech, other disciplines

CRITICAL THINKING SKILLS: Testing hypotheses to answer questions, using evidence to support a claim, evaluating alternative interpretations of behavior

THE ACTIVITY

This activity comes from Atul Gawande's article "Crimson Tide," originally published in *The New Yorker* and included in his book *Complications: A Surgeon's Notes on an Imperfect Science*. Gawande describes the exercise as follows: A teacher announces to a class that he/she will randomly point at a student and explains that the pointing is meaningless and reflects no judgment whatsoever about the person pointed at. The teacher then closes his/her eyes and points. Everyone in class looks toward the student that the teacher is pointing at. Invariably, that person is embarrassed and blushes. The teacher then repeats the exercise by pointing randomly at several other students. Afterwards, the teacher conducts a class discussion that raises questions like the following: What is blushing? What function does it serve? Why do we blush when we're praised or when people merely look at us? Why do dark-skinned people blush? Can blushing be controlled?

PURPOSES AND BENEFITS

Knowledge begins with curiosity, and this activity is a vivid way to appeal to students' curiosity. Its purpose is to illustrate a phenomenon and then raise critical questions about it—in this case, the physiology and psychology of blushing. The exercise could be carried out in conjunction with specific readings about blushing and embarrassment or broader readings about the physiology of emotion or our perceptions of how others view us. The exercise is also a way to demonstrate the concept of a scientific hypothesis. Here's a phenomenon, blushing, that needs explaining. How can we formulate and test a hypothesis to explain it?

USES, ADAPTATIONS, AND RESOURCES

This exercise may make students uncomfortable—indeed, it is intended to—and I can imagine reasons why an instructor might wish to fudge the randomness of the experiment and avoid pointing at a particular student. However, I think that instructors can easily convey that students are being made to suffer minor embarrassment purely in the spirit of scientific inquiry. To ease any tension, the instructor might first offer to be pointed at by the entire class.

Another interesting slant on the physiology of emotion—and the attempt to study this physiology empirically—comes from Malcolm Gladwell's *New Yorker* article "The Naked Face." Gladwell begins with the question: "Can you read people's thoughts just by looking at them?" He goes on to discuss research intended "to create a taxonomy of facial expression" and to determine whether the emotional signals carried by different facial expressions are universal. "The face," he writes, "is such an extraordinarily efficient instrument of communication that there must be rules that govern the way we interpret facial expressions. But what are those rules? And are they the same for everyone?" One result of this research has been the Facial Action Coding System (FACS), a catalogue of virtually every possible minute variation in facial expression—the lips, for example, may "elongate, de-elongate, narrow, widen, flatten, protrude, tighten, and stretch"—with an interpretation of each expression. Gladwell also touches on such topics as the distinction between voluntary and involuntary expressions, the application of FACS in fields ranging from psychotherapy to counter-terrorism training, and the uncanny face-reading skills of some aphasics who have lost their ability to understand language. In one anecdote he tells, FACS expert Paul Ekman remembers the first time he observed Bill Clinton, during the Democratic primaries in 1992: "I was watching his facial expressions, and I said to my wife, 'This is Peck's Bad Boy.' This is a guy who wants to be caught with his hand in the cookie jar, and have us love him for it anyway. There was this expression that's one of my favorites. It's that hand-in-the-cookie-jar, love-me-Mommy-because-I'm-a-rascal look. It's A.U. twelve, fifteen, seventeen, and twenty-four, with an eye roll." Students might carry out a face-reading project by researching FACS and then using the system to interpret the expressions of people in various contexts. Children, lovers, bosses, George W. Bush—the possibilities are endless. Students might also conduct a critical evaluation of FACS itself to determine how expressions are assigned meaning as signals in this system, how reliable the system is as a tool for the analysis of behavior, and whether there is in fact a scientific basis for the interpretation of specific expressions.

One practical use of face-signal analysis is in speech classes, in which students could watch videotapes of speeches they presented in class and then, with the instructor's help, compare the facial signals (or body signals) they actually sent during their speeches to the signals they had hoped to send, or the personas they had hoped to inhabit. More generally, analysis of the physiology and display of emotion is a fruitful area for the application of critical thinking skills—and for an interdisciplinary approach to understanding human behavior—and recent studies by Joseph LeDoux, in *The Emotional Brain*, and Jean-Didier Vincent, in *The Biology of Emotions*, explore the subject in depth.

"There's a blush for won't," wrote John Keats, "and a blush for shan't, and a blush for having done it."

For a related activity, SEE **#37: Does a Dog Know Its Name?**

ACTIVITY #14
The State vs. Rumpelstiltskin (Using Evidence, Applying Principles)

APPLICATIONS: Criminal justice, children's literature, human services (drug and alcohol rehabilitation), other disciplines

CRITICAL THINKING SKILLS: Determining the relevance of information, using evidence to support a claim, applying generalizations to specific situations, examining issues from conflicting viewpoints

THE ACTIVITY

Professor Robert W. Peetz, Coordinator of Criminal Justice at Midland College in Texas, presents this assignment in his abstract "Criminal Law—the 'Grimm' Truth." Each student reads one fairy tale from a select group of tales and then applies the Texas Penal Code to the acts described in the tale. Peetz explains: "The basic premise of the assignment was that the story represented a police report, prepared by an officer and submitted to the student, acting as a supervisor. The goal was to have the student/supervisor recommend all charges to the prosecutor." Students may work individually or collaborate in groups, but each student must submit an individual report for grading. The instructor meets individually with students to guide the project. Peetz uses this assignment toward the end of the semester in a criminal justice course, after he has introduced students to the principles of criminal law and the Texas Penal Code.

PURPOSES AND BENEFITS

This activity is a creative way to teach principles of criminal law and the application of these principles to specific situations. Professor Peetz reports that students "found the law less intimidating when there was an objective to achieve," and that improvement in critical thinking was demonstrated by students' increased "concern over accuracy and comprehensiveness of stories/reports" in criminal law cases. The students who completed the assignment showed more confidence and more knowledge of the Texas Penal Code when they took their final exams in the course. The assignment also stimulated their curiosity about the reasons why fairy tales contain so much violence.

Aside from its direct benefits for criminal justice students, this assignment illustrates how critical thinking can be enhanced by activities that bring together radically different perspectives or disciplines—in this case criminal justice and the study of fairy tales. I remember the sense of revelation I felt when, in an undergraduate folklore course, I read a Freudian analysis of the phallic symbolism and Oedipal conflict in *Jack and the Beanstalk*. The idea for my own course "Criminals in Literature" was inspired by the realization that many famous literary works, including fairy tales, are in fact stories about crime. Literary works that we may not think of as crime stories, ranging from the story of Jesus in *The New Testament* to *The Adventures of Huckleberry Finn*, can take on new dimensions when approached as narratives of criminal behavior—or behavior judged to be criminal.

USES, ADAPTATIONS, AND RESOURCES

This activity could easily be modified to use the penal codes of other states. A different interdisciplinary approach to crime is illustrated by a project I carried out as part of a grant-funded "curriculum infusion" program designed to involve different disciplines in studying the impact of alcohol and drug abuse. In my World Literature II course, students analyzed Robert Louis Stevenson's *The Strange Case of Dr. Jekyll and Mr. Hyde* as a novel about addictive behavior. The project's purpose was to increase student awareness of the effects of drug abuse and the nature of addiction, while raising ethical and legal questions about individual responsibility for drug-influenced behavior. Students were given two options as writing assignments:

1. Discuss Dr. Jekyll as an addict—addicted to becoming Mr. Hyde. What causes the addiction? What are the symptoms of the addiction? What pleasure, if any, does Dr. Jekyll derive from his addiction? Why is he unable to cure himself of his addiction?

2. Assume that, before his death, the mystery of Mr. Hyde's identity is revealed, and Dr. Jekyll is brought to trial for the murder of Sir Danvers Carew. Assume, also, that you are a member of the jury, in possession of all the facts in the story. Would you convict Dr. Jekyll of murder? If so, what sentence would you give him? If not, why not? Explain your reasoning, and address the arguments that might be raised against your position.

Before this project, most students were familiar with the story in one of its many film versions, but they had viewed it primarily as a horror story. Approaching it as a study of addictive behavior, with serious moral and psychological implications, brought a new perspective to the story and gave students a deeper understanding of the nature of addiction. A number of students wrote thoughtful compositions on the topics, and some related Dr. Jekyll's addiction to their own experiences with drugs and alcohol abuse.

For related activities SEE #30: Crimes and Punishments and #41:Trying Jekyll for the Crimes of Hyde. SEE **Activity #46: My Aquatic Uncle for a fuller discussion of interdisciplinary approaches.**

ACTIVITY #15
It's a Bird, It's a Bootie Bird (Defining Terms, Applying Definitions)

APPLICATIONS: Biology, environmental science, future studies, other disciplines

CRITICAL THINKING SKILLS: Distinguishing fact from opinion, testing hypotheses to answer questions, using examples to illustrate definitions, evaluating alternative theories to explain phenomena

THE ACTIVITY

In this activity the instructor provides students with descriptive details about real or imaginary organisms: physical characteristics, habitats, ranges, means of reproduction, behavior, and so on. Students must then place each organism within a biological system of classification and provide rationales for their placements. The activity is used after students have examined the process of classification, become familiar with terminology used in classification, and discussed potential pitfalls in classifying organisms. The instructor might use examples to illustrate the difficulty in determining whether two closely related organisms are separate species or subspecies, or to illustrate how differences in defining speciation can lead to differences in classifying organisms or in viewing relationships among organisms.

PURPOSES AND BENEFITS

The purpose of this activity to help students understand how scientists, biologists in particular, operate: how they arrive at definitions, how they apply definitions to specific cases, and how they use critical thinking skills to evaluate different possible solutions to a problem. The activity also demonstrates that the process of defining and applying scientific concepts can be problematic. Biologists, for example, may share a belief in a basic concept—species—but may differ in their definitions of the concept, in their analyses of the mechanics of speciation, or in their views of the best way to apply the concept to actual organisms. For instance, as Colin Tudge explains in *Last Animals at the* Zoo, by one standard means of defining a species—the ability to "breed together sexually and produce fully viable offspring"—the fire-bellied toad and the yellow-bellied toad of Europe would be classified as one species, but the two toads have different mating calls, live in different habitats, and produce hybrids that are not quite as "viable" as parents of either type and that live in a distinct "hybrid zone" between the ranges of the two parent types. "So biologists in general," Tudge writes, "are content to leave the two as separate species." The concept of species is used to distinguish between different kinds of organisms, but biologists may disagree about what constitutes a "distinct difference" or the means of determining the nature or degree of differences. In *The Diversity of Life*, biologist Edward O. Wilson writes:

> Still, the biological-species concept has deep problems. From the beginning of its first clear formulation at the turn of the century, it has been corroded by exceptions and ambiguities. The fundamental reason is that each species defined as a reproductively isolated population or set of populations is in some stage or other of evolution that makes it different from all other species. It is moreover a unique individual, not merely one unit in a class of identical units such as a hydrogen atom or a molecule of benzene. This qualification makes it different from a concept in physics or chemistry, which is a summary term for a set of measurable quantities.

USES, ADAPTATIONS, AND RESOURCES

My personal interest in this topic arose from my enthusiasm for the study of bird life. I once considered the idea of a species a fairly clear-cut concept that could be applied without great difficulty. Now that I've studied birds in some detail, I've learned that it's not so easy to apply our man-made constructs to the complex, elusive and sometimes unknown intricacies of actual bird life or the lives of other organisms. Speciation is dynamic and ongoing, and increased knowledge of DNA in birds has led to reclassifications of bird species. Some birds that were once viewed as close family members are now seen as more distant relatives, while other birds that appear highly dissimilar may have common ancestors. Wood storks, for instance, may seem to resemble cranes or herons, but they are more closely related to vultures. Among taxonomists of birds, some are "lumpers"—more likely to lump similar birds as subspecies of a single species—while others are "splitters"—more likely to classify these similar birds as distinct species. I've also learned that many common names for birds are misnomers. Worm-eating warblers don't eat worms. Tennessee Warblers breed in soggy spruce woods in Canada, not in Tennessee.

Another way to apply critical thinking to the problem of biological classification is to have students construct a cladogram, a classification instrument in which branching diagrams are used to show the relationships among species in regard to their shared, derived characters. In her introductory text *Biology*, Sylvia Mader defines the field of cladistics—"a school of systematics that determines the degree of relatedness by analyzing primitive and derived characters"—and she provides both a model cladogram and guidelines that students can follow in constructing cladograms of their own. She cautions that a cladogram is one of several possible means of showing biological relationships and "should be regarded as a hypothesis that can be tested and either corroborated or refuted on the basis of additional data."

The process of defining and applying concepts is fundamental to all fields, and this kind of definition/classification activity could be carried out using terms from many other disciplines. How is "addiction" best defined and applied?

How do philosophers define and use the concept of "natural rights"? What's the distinction between "masculine" and "feminine," and how does this distinction apply to specific acts or viewpoints? What do "natural" and "organic" signify? What are the essential elements of "jazz"? When my Composition I students write definition-example essays, I provide them with readings from authors who define terms precisely and use examples effectively to illustrate their definitions and to indicate potential problems in applying definitions. In one essay we discuss, "Dirt," chemist Terence McLaughlin uses vivid and amusing examples to explain what dirt is and what it isn't: "Lipstick on a girl's lips may make her boyfriend more anxious to touch them with his own lips; lipstick on a cup will probably make him refuse to touch it." The anthology *Writing About Science* contains some excellent essays showing how scientists—J. B. S. Haldane in "On Being the Right Size" and Lewis Thomas on "Germs"—use examples to illustrate definitions and scientific concepts.

Stuart Hirschberg's *Strategies of Argument* and Sally DeWitt Spurgin's *The Power to Persuade* both offer frameworks on the uses and purposes of definitions, particularly in argumentative writing. Hirschberg defines various forms of definition—lexical, synonymous, etymological, figurative, stipulative, negating, and exemplary—and illustrates how to use these types of definition in setting up and developing lines of argument. Spurgin provides exercises on identifying types of definitions and evaluating their uses in persuasion. Both sources include short definition essays for analysis.

A different and highly creative approach to teaching biological principles, evolution in particular, is presented by biologist Dougal Dixon in his illustrated book *After Man: A Zoology of the Future.* Dixon describes his work as "an exploration of possibilities" that is "set, arbitrarily, 50 million years in the future," after human beings have become extinct. He begins by summing up basic principles of evolution and the history of life on Earth. Then, using different habitats as his mode of organization (e.g. tundra, tropical grasslands), he describes and illustrates various species that might evolve after human extinction. Dixon explains: "The future world is described as if by a time-traveler from today who has voyaged the world of that time and has studied its fauna. Such a traveler will have some knowledge of today's animal life and so can describe things with reference to the types of animals that will be familiar to the reader." As a bird lover, I'm particularly fond of his large, shaggy, predatory Bootie Bird. Students using this book might be asked to describe or illustrate imaginary future species of their own and then provide rationales to explain why these species might evolve. Such an assignment would be beneficial in demonstrating ecological principles and the process of evolution over time—including the idea that the vast majority of all species that have ever lived are now extinct—as well as in testing students' understanding of the relationship between various habitats and the adaptive features of the organisms that live in those habitats. Also, the idea of a bestiary has a long literary tradition, and, in a more whimsical approach, students might be asked to use a scientific method to classify fictional or hypothetical animals, such as those in Jorge Luis Borges' *The Book of Imaginary Beings*.

For related activities, SEE **#16: The Pecking Order, #23: Dissecting Words Instead of Frogs,** and **#46: My Aquatic Uncle.**

ACTIVITY #16
The Pecking Order (Applying Concepts, Using Examples)

APPLICATIONS: Psychology (interpersonal dynamics, conflict resolution), anthropology, biology, business, other disciplines

CRITICAL THINKING SKILLS: Getting relevant information, making inferences, using evidence, analyzing behavior, applying concepts and theories to specific situations

THE ACTIVITY

In biology, a pecking order is a hierarchy within a flock of poultry, in which stronger or more aggressive members peck and otherwise dominate the weaker members. Biologists have observed and described similar hierarchies in other birds and other species, and anthropologists and other social scientists have extended the pecking order concept to human behavior within hierarchical groups in which some members dominate and exert power, while other members defer or submit to those who are more influential. A human pecking order may be formalized—a military chain of command—or it may develop informally in groups or associations without explicit rules or assigned roles that grant some members authority over others.

This activity requires students to study the informal pecking order within a specific group—e.g. a group of friends, siblings, co-workers, an athletic team. Students must observe, describe, and analyze the pecking order within the group. They should consider questions like the following: In what ways do some group members dominate or exert power or influence over others? What qualities enable some group members to dominate others? Why do some group members defer or submit to others? What are the advantages and disadvantages of both dominance and submission? How rigid or flexible are roles within the hierarchy—that is, do roles of dominance and submissiveness vary from one situation to another? The group studied might be one, such as an office staff, which has both a formal hierarchy (i.e. some members supervise others) and an informal pattern of influence and deference that diverges from the formal structure. In this case students could analyze the reasons for the divergence.

PURPOSES AND BENEFITS

This activity promotes active learning by students while giving them experience in applying concepts to specific situations. Students must observe the group behavior carefully and record and describe this behavior as accurately and objectively as possible. They must reflect on and apply the definitions of "dominance" and "submission"—that is, what exactly constitutes the exertion of influence or deference to another's influence in the context of this particular group? They must make thoughtful inferences and use analytical skills in understanding the motives of group members: what do group members gain or lose by being dominant or submissive? The instructor might caution students not to assume that a dominant role is necessarily preferable. Ornithologists have discovered that, in monogamous bird species, there is little evidence to show that dominant individuals are more likely to survive than subordinate individuals.

USES, ADAPTATIONS, AND RESOURCES

This activity could be used as the basis for a composition assignment and/or carried out as a collaborative project. Taking the idea literally, biology instructors could ask students to analyze a pecking order by observing an actual group of birds—and perhaps relating the pecking order to success at procreation—or the pecking order concept could be used in any course, such as Business Management, in which students are trying to understand the interpersonal dynamics of group behavior. One difficulty in implementing this activity is that students might find it hard to gain access to groups that do not include themselves as members. If they study groups to which they belong, they could certainly not be objective observers; however, this drawback could be outweighed by the insights students might gain in reflecting on the roles they play in relating to others within groups.

More generally, the approach illustrated by this activity—applying specific concepts in the critical analysis of behavior—can be carried out using concepts from a variety of disciplines, in projects of varying degrees of complexity. For instance, in *Engaging Ideas*, John Bean suggests this brief assignment on applying the concept of conditioning in a psychology course: "In the morning, when Professor Catlove opens a new can of cat food his cats run into the kitchen purring and meowing and rubbing their backs against his legs. What examples, if any, of classical conditioning, operant conditioning, and social learning are at work in this brief scene? Note that both the cats and the professor might be exhibiting conditioned behavior here." And in *Language: Introductory Readings*, editors Clark, Eschholz, and Rosa suggest the following exercise as a study of territorial behavior:

> Prepare a report in which you describe the reactions of another person when you do some or all of the following: (a) after a class has been meeting for at least three weeks, deliberately sit in a seat that you know has regularly been occupied by someone else; (b) in your library or snack bar, move someone else's books or food and sit down while the person is temporarily away; (c) in an uncrowded library or classroom, deliberately sit right next to another individual; (d) in your dorm room or at home, deliberately sit (in a chair, at a desk, etc.) where you know someone else "belongs."

Instructors might add a disclaimer freeing them of responsibility for any injuries that might befall students who carry out this exercise.

More elaborate analysis of interpersonal dynamics could

focus on concepts such as the reasons for *subgroup formation*, the use of *emotional intelligence* in establishing and maintaining alliances, or the most effective means of *conflict resolution*. Students analyzing conflict resolution might try to answer questions like the following: What kinds of conflicts occur within this particular group? What means are used to resolve these conflicts? Who initiates attempts to resolve conflicts? Do some members tend to benefit more than others from the resolution of conflicts? How might these conflicts be resolved more quickly, more effectively, or more equitably? Once conflicts are resolved, do they stay resolved, or do they reoccur under other guises?

For related activities **SEE #17: Incident Report, #25: Coping 101** and **#38: Anthropology Comes Home.**

ACTIVITY #17
Incident Report (Reporting Events, Making Decisions)

APPLICATIONS: Nurse education, other health care fields, technical writing, other disciplines

CRITICAL THINKING SKILLS: Distinguishing fact from opinion, detecting slanting, foreseeing consequences of decisions, evaluating decision-making strategies

THE ACTIVITY

An incident, as defined by one Massachusetts hospital in its instructions for filing incident reports, is "any occurrence which is not consistent with the routine care of the patient, visitor, or employee or the routine operation of the institution." In this activity designed for nurse education, the instructor provides students with a series of narratives about specific events (real or hypothetical) that have occurred in the workplace, each event involving at least one nurse. In each case the student must decide whether the event constitutes an "incident" (as defined above) and warrants the filing of a report. If an incident report is warranted, the student writes one from the nurse's point of view. The instructor then responds, either in writing or in class discussion, to the students' decisions (whether to file a report or not) and their composition of incident reports. The instructor leads a discussion of guidelines for both the language of reports and the appropriateness of filing reports in specific situations.

PURPOSES AND BENEFITS

This activity is designed to help students anticipate and understand actual workplace situations and to reflect on the types of choices they may one day be called upon to make. It also prompts students to think critically about the purpose of incident reports (sometimes called "variance reports") as well as what constitutes the "routine operation" of an institution. Incident reports are part of a problem-solving process in health care institutions. They are intended to be a way to identify problems and develop strategies to resolve or prevent them, not a means of determining blame or culpability for a problem. Under certain circumstances, such as "fetal deaths" or a "procedure performed on the wrong patient or body part," many institutions mandate the filing of a report. In other situations, however, decisions about whether to file reports are left up to individual employees. These decisions may be problematic, both practically and ethically, for a number of reasons: concerns about relationships with fellow workers, errors or mistakes in judgment by the nurse or other employees, ambiguity about responsibility in a situation, doubts about the wisdom of calling attention to situations in which no apparent harm was done, and so on. The language used in incident reports also deserves critical consideration. Reports are meant to be brief and strictly factual, but, in any situations in which errors have been made, there's a natural tendency to slant information—through word choice of omission of details—to present one's own behavior in the best light.

USES, ADAPTATIONS, AND RESOURCES

The idea for this activity grew out of conversations with my wife, Mary Nelson, a nurse. The activity could be used with students entering a variety of health care fields as well as other fields, such as law enforcement, in which workers within institutions may have to file incident reports or something comparable in problematic situations. For instance, in her abstract "Surprise! Something a Little Different Today," English instructor Janet Cook, from Clatsop Community College in Oregon, describes an assignment in which technical writing students watch an Emergency Medical Services training video about a simulated accident and then write factual, accurate incident reports about the details of the accident.

Another activity designed for both nurses and potential nurses, "Using Chautaugua to Explicate Nursing Values," was presented by Pamella Stoechal, a nursing professor at the Community College of Denver, during the 1999 NISOD (National Institute for Staff and Organizational Development) conference at the University of Texas. The Chautaugua method uses role-playing to examine values and to think critically about the satisfactions and conflicts experienced by people, in this case nurses, within a profession. This particular presentation focused on the question of why so many nurses were leaving the profession. Actors played three roles—a staff nurse, a nurse practitioner, and a nurse administrator—as a way of dramatizing the values held by nurses (caring, excellence of service, professional image, security, compensation), the conflicts they faced in their work, and their means of resolving conflicts.

Peter Horn's *Clinical Ethics Casebook* poses a wide variety of ethical questions in the health professions, ranging from confidentiality issues to interpretations of professional codes to the ethical complexities of obtaining informed consent. Horn uses numerous brief case studies to raise questions about situations that present ethical dilemmas, to "provide guidance for structuring possible answers" to these dilemmas, and to look at ways in which health care professionals may try to "escape" from ethical difficulties. One case study, entitled "A Hateful Patient," involves Mr. O, "a patient who requires frequent attention, makes many unreasonable demands, insults the staff, and generally makes life miserable for them. They try to provide a high level of professional care for him but increasingly find themselves tempted to do the minimum necessary." Another case involves a nurse on a hematology/oncology unit who is frequently asked the question "What would *you* do?" by cancer patients and their family members evaluating treatment options. Horn raises questions like the following: (1) "Should health workers offer their opinions in situations of this sort? Does it risk improperly influencing patients' decision making?" (2) "Is there a difference between saying, 'What would you recommend for me?' and 'What would you do if you were in my situation?'" (3) "Should health workers be completely nondirective, mostly nondirective, somewhat directive, or very directive toward patients' decision making? Why? Might it depend on the sort of situation?" Horn also presents a "Dosage Error and an Incident Report" case similar to the exercise explained above. He includes a "Clinical Ethics Glossary" and what he calls a "moral workup," a model used to synthesize clinical decision making and ethical problem solving.

Ethics at the End of Life, an anthology edited by Ralph Baergen, focuses on ethical decision making by health professionals and others in situations involving such issues as the refusal of life-sustaining treatment, surrogate decision making, resuscitation of dying patients, assisted suicide, and caring for seriously ill newborns. In his introduction Baergen provides a useful overview of different approaches to addressing ethical issues in medicine. He defines basic moral principles (respect for autonomy, justice) that can be applied to clinical decisions, grapples with the problem of defining the "moral rights" of patients, and examines the moral dilemmas involved in making "allocation decisions" in rationing medical resources.

Finally, as an example of clinical writing at its best, I'd recommend Oliver Sacks' *The Man Who Mistook His Wife for a Hat and Other Clinical Tales*, a series of enlightening and often heart-rending case studies about patients with severe neurological disorders.

For a related activity, SEE **#42: Suddenly You're Old.**

ACTIVITY #18
Who Fired the First Shot? (Analyzing Historical Accounts)

APPLICATIONS: History, political science, journalism, religion, reading and writing courses

CRITICAL THINKING SKILLS: Determining the reliability of information, distinguishing fact from opinion, detecting bias, examining issues from conflicting viewpoints

THE ACTIVITY

Begin by providing students with a number of conflicting published accounts of the same historical event. Ask students to: (1) find points of similarity and difference in the accounts (2) distinguish between verifiable statements of fact and statements of opinion (3) look for signs of slanting or bias, and (4) evaluate the use of evidence presented to support any claims or interpretations. After students have studied the different accounts, they can share their analyses in class discussion and/or present them in a writing assignment.

PURPOSES AND BENEFITS

"It is all too common," John McPeck says in *Critical Thinking and Education*, "for specific subject-oriented courses to permit information and authority to rule in the place of reason, and where authority reigns, unreflective obedience will follow. Critical thinking, by contrast, requires knowledge of the reasons behind the putative facts and various voices of authority." This activity is valuable because some students are apt to view the study of history merely as an accumulation of facts arranged in chronological order—that is, one damn thing after another. Truth, says the old adage, lies in the eyes of the beholder, and the activity promotes a critical view of history—and historical "truth"—by leading students to evaluate the sources of historical information, to consider the motives or aims of those who provide historical accounts, and to realize that accounts may differ not only in interpretations of facts but also in their claims about what the facts are. Students must also demonstrate critical thinking in detecting signs of slanting or bias in the reporting of events and in evaluating the use of evidence to support interpretations of events.

USES, ADAPTATIONS, AND RESOURCES

This assignment builds on and brings together some of the skills developed by previous activities, including #4 (distinguishing fact from opinion), #6 (detecting slanting), and #8 (weighing evidence). I've used this activity in Composition I in a unit on semantics and propaganda, when students analyze conflicting accounts of a fictitious labor-management dispute. I've also used conflicting reports of current events. The activity is ideally suited to history or journalism courses but could be modified to fit any course in which students study the significance of specific events and need to evaluate the reliability of accounts. The assignment can be restricted to class discussion or expanded to include an essay or (perhaps collaborative) research project. Richard Paul's *Critical Thinking* includes five conflicting reports of who fired the first shots in the Boston Massacre, while John Chaffee's *Thinking Critically* presents conflicting accounts of the assassination of Malcolm X, the Battle of Lexington, and the 1989 confrontation at Tiananmen Square. Chaffee also provides a set of questions for analysis, including: "How reliable is the source? What are the author's perceiving lenses, which might influence his or her account? Is the account consistent with other reliable descriptions of this event?" Other examples can be found in various history and journalism texts.

"But how reliable are the relics of the past as clues to what was really there?" This question is raised by historian Daniel Boorstein in his article "The Historian: 'A Wrestler With an Angel'," a discussion of "the universal obstacles to recovery of the past" and the reasons why existing documents may give us a distorted or incomplete record of historical events. Boorstein takes his title from J. M. Huizinga's description of a historian as "a wrestler with an angel," the angel of death, who, Boorstein says, makes the historian's work "necessary yet destined never to be definitive." Boorstein uses examples from his own research to illustrate "how partial is the remaining evidence of the whole human path, how casual and how accidental is the survival of its relics." He goes on to delineate about ten "biases of survival"—all relating to the preservation and accessibility of historical records—that make it difficult for historians to determine whether "relics" are reliable or representative. For instance:

- *Survival of the Collected and the Protected:* "We emphasize political history and government in the life of the past," Boorstein says, "partly because governments keep records, while families and other informal groups seldom do." Yet the experience of informal groups, such as, "the anonymous wagon trains that crossed the continent," may tell us more about what has been characteristic of American experience.

- *Survival of the Academically Classifiable and Dignified:* "Teachers," Boorstein writes, "teach the subjects in which they have been instructed." Traditional notions about geography and a dismissal of works stigmatized as "subliterary" but often important in revealing the cultural values of the past.

- *Survival of the Victorious Point of View:* The Success Bias: In studying the history of innovations, Boorstein says, we focus on the success stories–Thomas Edison, Henry Ford–while tending to ignore the complexity of culture innovation and the anonymous experimenters whose near successes or flawed theories made these later successes possible. A more insidious form of the success bias–the idea that the most widely promoted version of events often comes from those who, through whatever means, triumphed in conflict with others–has been noted by Simone Weil, who wrote, "Official history is believing the murderers at their word."

Boorstein concludes by saying that, while historians should be chastened by the knowledge that they will never discover the full truth of history, "The historian-creator refuses to be defeated by the biases of survival. For he chooses, defines, and shapes his subject to provide a reasonably truthful account from miscellaneous remains."

In *Engaging Ideas*, John Bean suggests a related assignment in which students rewrite a first-hand historical account from a different point of view, an approach that helps students to understand how any account by a participant in an event may be subjective, slanted, incomplete, or self-justifying. I've used this assignment in an American literature class when teaching Mary Rowlandson's narrative of her captivity during a 17th century war between Massachusetts colonists and a native American tribe. I ask students to narrate the same events from the perspective of Weetamoo, one of Rowlandson's captors. Bean also recommends the approach used by a colleague, who "gives his students a series of controversial theses that bring the course's subject matter into problematic focus." One sample thesis is the following: "The ultimate victors in the English Revolution of 1688, the American Revolution, and the French Revolution were the economically conservative property-owning classes." The writing assignments based on these theses all follow the same model: "Present an argument that supports, rejects, or modifies the given thesis, and support your response with factual evidence."

Another, and highly controversial, approach to the issue of historical accuracy is the critical Biblical scholarship of the Jesus Seminar, an international group of scholars who are trying to determine the actual words and deeds of Jesus. Seminar founder Robert Funk explained the purpose of the Seminar in his address to assembled scholars in 1985: "We are going to inquire simply, rigorously after the *voice* of Jesus, after what he really said." Fellows of the Seminar meet twice a year to examine scholarly papers, debate points of contention, and vote on whether specific words or deeds can reasonably be attributed to Jesus. They employ a four-color voting system:

- RED: The historical reliability of this information is virtually certain. It is supported by a preponderance of evidence.
- PINK: This information is probably reliable. It fits well with other evidence that is verifiable.
- GRAY: This information is possible but unreliable. It lacks supporting evidence.
- BLACK: This information is improbable. It does not fit verifiable evidence; it is largely or entirely fictive.

The Rutgers University Department of Religion maintains a website "The Jesus Seminar Forum" (http://religion.rutgers.edu/jseminar/index.html) with an analysis of the "synoptic problem" in the Four Gospels, a discussion of criteria for evidence, critiques of the Seminar's work, and links to other web sites on historical interpretations of Jesus. The Westar Institute, the Seminar's sponsor and a self-described "advocate for literacy in religion," has it own web site (http://westarinstitute.org) dedicated to "scholarly research on issues of cultural importance in western religion."

In *Perspectives: Case Studies for Readers and Writing*, Joanna Gibson employs a case study method to compare and contrast historical accounts. In her overview for students, she defines a case study as a "problem—hypothetical or real—presented in narrative form or in a series of sources. The method you'll use to solve the problem in a case study is read, evaluate, analyze, and synthesize . . . You are an investigator weighing the evidence that supports a claim." Her studies focus on five individuals: Tokyo Rose, "jungle doctor" Tom Dooley, Dr. Martin Luther King, AIDS activist Jeff Getty, and Mexican artist Diego Rivera. "Their stories," she writes, "give students a narrowed focus they don't usually find in textbooks, and illustrate the very nature of research—that is, that sources are often contradictory, biased, and repetitive, and that information in print is not immune from inconsistent or outright erroneous information." In the chapter "Education.com: A Case Study for Practice," Gibson includes a case study of "Pickaprof," a web site developed by Texas A & M University students to give their fellow students a forum for evaluating and ranking faculty. She also provides an annotated reading assignment and a web site (www.ablongman.com/gibson) with resources to be used in conjunction with her book.

In another case method approach, historians Richard Neustadt and Ernest May, in *Thinking in Time: The Uses of History*, discuss "how to make practical use of history in day-to-day decision making and management." Their book, which is based on their course "Uses of History" at Harvard University, is primarily aimed at "those who govern—or hope to do so," but it is a valuable resource for anyone studying the process of decision-making in government or business. Topics they address include: (1) "how to draw sound historical analogies –and how to spot false ones—in order to clarify problems and isolate core concerns" (2) "how to think in terms of 'time-streams' by looking at the present as part of an unbroken continuum between past and present" (3) how to make "canny judgments about feasibility" or "the doability of contemplated courses of action," and (4) how to foresee the likely results of specific actions. One problem-solving technique they advocate is the use of "Alexander's question": "What fresh facts, if at hand, by when, would cause you to change your presumption?" They also recommend questions to ask in evaluating the process of making decisions: "Why did we believe *that*? Why did we expect *that*? What made us believe that he or she (or they) would do *that*?" More generally, they consider the value of critical historical analysis. "Seeing the past," they write, "can help one envision alternative futures." They add: "One of history's uses is to understand people whose age, sex, race, nationality, or beliefs are different from one's own." The appendices to *Thinking in Time* provide methods and steps for the use of historical case analysis in decision-making.

"It will be enough for me, however," wrote the ancient Greek historian Thucydides regarding his history of the Peloponnesian War, "if these words of mine are judged useful by those who want to understand clearly the events which happened in the past and which (human nature being what it is) will, at some time or other and in much the same ways, be repeated in the future."

For related activities, **SEE #22: Just Because, #32: How Will We Be Judged?, #36: What Are the Alternatives?** and **#40: Making the Case.**

ACTIVITY #19
You Write Like a Girl (Analyzing Literature, Detecting Stereotypes)

APPLICATIONS: Literature, psychology, linguistics, gender studies, computer science

CRITICAL THINKING SKILLS: Detecting bias and false assumptions, making inferences, evaluating alternative interpretations of artistic works

THE ACTIVITY

Provide students with a number of brief literary works by unidentified authors. The students must read the works and then speculate about the gender of each author. Students can be given two choices for each author (male, female), three choices (male, female, can't tell), or a range of choices (definitely male, probably female, etc.). After the class has completed the exercise, students share results, and the instructor leads a discussion on students' rationale for their choice and raises the following questions: Are some literary styles distinctively masculine or feminine? If so, what are the characteristics of these styles? Are some literary subjects inherently masculine or feminine? If so, which ones? On what basis did students make their choices? Did students use sex-role stereotyping in making choices? If so, what stereotypes were used? Finally, on what basis did the instructor choose the literary works for this exercise?

PURPOSES AND BENEFITS

This exercise involves a process of discovery for both instructor and students. In examining the rationale for their choices, students discover and reflect on their attitudes toward differences between genders, or gender stereotypes, and

---

the exercise can lead to a revealing discussion of such topics as historical changes in literary styles or the issue of whether a man—or, for that matter, a woman of a different race or culture—can tell an authentic story from a particular woman's point of view. Also, the selection of literary works is itself an excellent exercise in problem solving. Trying to pick a "representative" sample begs the question that the activity is designed to answer. Who's representing what exactly? Many factors might bias the sample of authors selected, including the subjects of the literary works, the time period of the works, and authors' use of first-person narrators of a gender different from their own.

USES, ADAPTATIONS, AND RESOURCES

It would be all too easy to set up this exercise as a kind of trap, in which students are fooled and then, through their explanations of their rationales, reveal the stereotypes that led them to be fooled. However, in the spirit of critical thinking, the exercise should be carried out with no preconceptions about whether there are in fact any significant differences in the ways that men and women use language. This question has been debated for centuries—by linguists, psychologists, feminists—and was recently the subject of a "gender detection experiment" by a team of three Israeli computer scientists (two men and a woman), who claim to have developed "a computer algorithm that can examine an anonymous text and determine, with accuracy rates of better than 80 percent, whether the author is male or female." In the article "He and She: What's the Real Difference?" Clive Thompson reports that the team examined 604 widely ranging texts from the British National Corpus, a collection of documents assembled by scholars for linguistic research. The main gender differences they found did not involve "important" words (nouns, verbs) but rather the use of pronouns and modifiers. Women were more likely to use personal pronouns; men were more likely to use determiners (that, these) and quantifiers (more, some). Moshe Koppel, one of the experimenters, and linguist Deborah Tannen both view these differences as support for the old idea that woman tend to talk about people, while men tend to talk about things. Critics have claimed that gender-detection experiments tend to exaggerate gender differences, and linguist Janet Bing argues that "this whole rush to categorization [of differences] usually works against women." Tannen also cites a classroom experiment she conducted in which students analyzed articles from men's and women's magazines. In comparing the writing styles found in these articles, Tannen says, "It didn't matter whether the author was male or female. What mattered was rather the intended audience was male or female."

The exercise I propose could be modified for use in various courses in which students are studying gender stereotypes or the issue of whether there are innate psychological or intellectual differences between genders. Useful sources for the study of gender differences in thinking and language include Robin Lakoff's widely anthologized essay "You Are What You Say" (which discusses "lady" and "girl" as euphemisms), *Critical Thinking, Thoughtful Writing* by Chaffee, McMahon, and Stout (with short essays defining "masculinity" and "femininity"), Susan Brownmiller's *Femininity* (a study of gender differences and cultural views of gender roles), and the section "Language, Gender, and Sexism" in Gary Goshgarian's *Exploring Language* (with numerous readings, including a "nonsexist" version of the Book of Genesis in the Bible compared to the Revised Standard Version). In *You Just Don't Understand: Women and Men and Conversation*, Deborah Tannen develops the thesis that women and men use language so differently, in both style and substance, that conversation between them often constitutes a form of "cross-cultural communication." Language differences between the genders, she claims, reveal profound differences in self-image, cultural values, and interpretations of behavior.

In *Metamagical Themas*, Douglas Hofstadter recounts his personal experiences with gender stereotyping in his chapter "on the deep, hidden, and oft denied connections between subconscious imagery and discriminatory usage in everyday language." He begins by describing the embarrassment he felt over not solving the following riddle more quickly:

> A father and his son were driving to a ball game when their car stalled on the railroad tracks. In the distance a train whistle blew a warning. Frantically, the father tried to start the engine, but in his panic, he couldn't turn the key, and the car was hit by the onrushing train. Am ambulance sped to the scene and picked them up. On the way to the hospital, the father died. The son was still alive but his condition was very serious, and he needed immediate surgery. The moment they arrived at the hospital, he was wheeled into an emergency operating room, and the surgeon came in, expecting a routine case. However, on seeing the boy, the surgeon blanched and muttered, "I can't operate on this boy—he's my son."

Hofstadter uses this riddle to illustrate the "default assumptions" that "permeate our mental representations and channel our thoughts." He defines a default assumption as what holds true in "the 'simplest' or 'most natural' or 'most likely' possible model of whatever situation is under discussion. In this case, the default assumption is to assign the sex of male to the surgeon." The key point, he says, is that default assumptions are "made automatically, not as a result of consideration of elimination." He uses examples to illustrate that "relying on default assumptions is extremely useful" in helping us to negotiate the complexities of the world, but then shows that these assumptions may involve stereotypes or assumptions—in this case about gender—that are demonstrably false. He also uses examples—such as the German term *Doctorvater*, literally "doctor father," for a dissertation advisor—to illustrate how assumptions based on gender stereotypes are embedded in different languages in the world.

Another way to examine unconscious stereotypes—about race, cultural differences, sexual preference, and body image as well as gender—is discussed in Craig Lambert's *Harvard Magazine* article, "Stealthy Attitudes," on the "social cognition" research of Mahzarin Banaji, a professor of social ethics in Harvard's psychology department. Banaji's work focuses on the discrepancies between people's claims about their own attitudes and the unconscious stereotypes that are "deeply embedded in both individuals and cultures." "People report holding neutral attitudes," Banaji says. "What people say *explicitly* is quite different from what the tool shows about their *implicit* attitudes. It's the dissociation or split between them that's interesting." Banaji's research tool, developed in collaboration with professor Anthony Greenwald of the University of Washington, is the Implicit Association Test (IAT), which requires subject to make rapid associations in reacting to words and pictures. One example she cites, which relates to unconscious linkages between race and weapons, involves "using photographs of old weapons like cannons and medieval axes that are not particularly associated with African-Americans. Nonetheless, 70 percent of white subjects associated weapons with blacks, while only 7 percent linked them with whites." Banaji has also found that situational factors—e.g. asking subjects beforehand to reflect on a question such as "What are strong women like?"—can influence responses to the test. The IAT is available online at www.i-a-t.com.

The "write like a girl" exercise could also be carried out using musical compositions, paintings, or works of art in other media, while the basic idea of a "blindfold experiment" could also be applied to race, or some other construct, instead of gender. The jazz trumpeter Roy Eldridge once claimed that, simply by listening to a recording, he could tell whether a given jazz musician was black or white. To test this claim the jazz magazine *Downbeat* invited him to take one of their "blindfold" tests and listen to recordings by unidentified musicians. Eldridge was not successful in identifying the musicians by race.

ACTIVITY #20
Can Shakespeare Be Trusted? (Writing Critically about Literature)

APPLICATIONS: Literature, composition, social sciences, other disciplines

CRITICAL THINKING SKILLS: Making inferences, using evidence, examining issues from opposing viewpoints, evaluating interpretations of artistic works

THE ACTIVITY

One example of this activity is the following writing assignment: "Various readers of *Othello* have claimed that the following points in the play are implausible—that is, difficult or impossible to believe: (1) that Desdemona would ever marry Othello, a Moor, in the first place (2) that Desdemona would fail to see that Othello has become jealous of Cassio (3) that Desdemona would not blame Othello for her murder at the end of the play (4) that Iago would succeed in fooling everybody in the play, including his wife, about the nature of his character. Discuss these points one by one, and explain why you consider each point plausible or implausible."

Students write their essays after these points—and the play as a whole—have been discussed in depth during class. The instructor evaluates the essays on the basis of the persuasiveness of their reasoning, their use of supporting evidence from the play, and their demonstrated understanding of the issues in the play and its context, not on whether students find the play plausible or implausible.

PURPOSES AND BENEFITS

"The most intensive and demanding tool for eliciting sustained critical thought," writes John Bean in *Engaging*

Ideas, "is a well-designed writing assignment on a subject matter problem." Bean adds: "When we make students struggle with their writing, we are making them struggle with thought itself."

This activity requires critical thinking in the written analysis of a literary work. Students must: (1) read the work carefully and thoughtfully (2) grasp the issues raised by the four points above, such as the significance of Othello's identity as a Moor (3) determine which passages are relevant to these points (4) consider the behavior of characters from a variety of perspectives, and (5) reflect on both their reactions to the play and their opinions on what is or isn't plausible in literature and life. They must also make and support a judgment on a problematic question—whether a work of literature is believable or not. Finally, they must demonstrate their thinking in writing, by using language precisely, by reasoning persuasively, and by marshalling relevant evidence to support a point of view.

USES, ADAPTATIONS, AND RESOURCES

In using this assignment, I refer students to some of the "various readers" who have criticized the play, while emphasizing that they must come to judgments of their own about its plausibility. More generally, as a teacher of literature in freshman and sophomore college courses, I allow students to use outside sources—e.g. literary criticism—when they write essays interpreting literature, but I encourage them to rely primarily on their own analysis and reactions to the literature itself. Literary criticism can be enormously helpful in guiding readers to understand literature, but some students become so dependent on outside sources, or so intimidated by critics more astute than they are, that they grow reluctant to express their own opinions and end up turning in essays with little original or critical thought. However, in many cases, such as the assignment above, criticism can be useful in framing issues for students or in raising questions of interpretation that students must answer for themselves. I like to use criticism that serves the function of a devil's advocate by questioning the plausibility of a literary work, the author's success in resolving issues raised in the work, or the work's ethical implications. I may refer students to specific critics or present them with a summary of criticisms. For instance, my students have responded to critics who find fault with the plot resolution in *Huckleberry Finn* and the presentation of homosexuality in Tennessee Williams' *Cat on a Hot Tin Roof.* When we discuss Ibsen's *A Doll's House*, I have students respond to a critique by Elizabeth Hardwick (in her book *Seduction and Betrayal*), who generally praises Ibsen's portrayal of women but faults him for allowing his heroine, Nora, to abandon her children too easily. Hardwick writes: "Ibsen has put the leaving of her children on the same moral and emotional level as the leaving of her husband and we cannot, in our hearts, assent to that. It is not only the leaving but the way the play does have not time for suffering, changes of heart. Ibsen has been too much the man in the end. He has taken the man's practice, if not his stated belief, that where self-realization is concerned children shall not be an impediment."

This activity could be modified for use in other disciplines in which students analyze controversial theories or research that makes debatable claims. In carrying out activities such as **#23: Dissecting Words Instead of Frogs** and **#24: What Did That Prove?**, students could refer to critics who question the methodology or reasoning in the articles and experiments they are studying. In the social sciences, for instance, some critics have targeted the methodology of Shere Hite's research on sexual behavior in America, claiming that her sampling is biased and unrepresentative, while others have challenged the ethics of Stanley Milgram's obedience experiments, in which student experimental subjects believed that they were inflicting pain on other participants in the experiments.

More generally, Bean's *Engaging Ideas* is an excellent source in helping faculty across the curriculum to design effective writing assignments and to guide students through the process of composition. Bean makes a persuasive case for the use of structured assignments, like the Othello topic, instead of broad, open-ended topics, especially for students who have not yet learned "the conventions of inquiry and argumentation in a discipline." He also illustrates how to set up assignments to give students a variety of options (the *Othello* topic above is one of several options I offer to students writing about the play). "My point," Bean says, "is that instructors can influence the thinking and writing processes of their students by varying such aspects of the assignment as the audience, the rhetorical context, the writer's assumed role, the purpose, or the format. When planning assignments, therefore, teachers need to consider not only the learning goals they have set for their courses but also the thinking and writing processes that they want to invoke in their students as learners." Bean's book contains a step-by-step model of the composing process and a list of specific suggestions for encouraging students to revise effectively. One technique I'd especially recommend is to have students read their rough drafts aloud, either in or outside of class. These readings can help students detect unclear passages, tortuous constructions, and grammatical errors, and, as Bean points out, students often unconsciously correct written errors when reading out loud.

For one more related activity, SEE **#43: Playing with Literature.**

ACTIVITY #21
The Prisoner's Dilemma (Using Cost-Benefit Analysis)

APPLICATIONS: Economics, computer-aided design, environmental science, biology, business, mathematics, statistics, composition, other disciplines

CRITICAL THINKING SKILLS: Getting relevant information, using evidence to support a proposal, evaluating alternative solutions, foreseeing consequences of decisions

THE ACTIVITY

In their abstract "Using a Cost-Benefit Proposal to Help Improve Teaching," professors Jim Hammons and Ken Turner of the University of Arkansas describe a procedure for writing a cost-benefit proposal, to be used by faculty in seeking funding for staff, supplies, equipment, or facilities. This procedure could easily be adapted for use as an assignment for students, who would define a need in their college or community, conduct research to support a proposal addressing that need, and then write the proposal including a rationale, an explanation of the expected benefits, and an accounting of the anticipated costs. Hammons and Turner provide guidelines for writing proposals, as well as a "cost-benefit table" for a proposal presented "to insure that Westark Community College continues to provide quality instruction in Computer-Aided Drafting and Design that meets current workplace needs."

PURPOSES AND BENEFITS

This activity teaches critical thinking through a tool—cost-benefit analysis—commonly used in problem solving. Students must: (1) define a problem (2) consider alternative

---

solutions (3) conduct research to get relevant information (4) carry out a cost-benefit analysis of a proposed solution, and (5) present a succinct, persuasively written proposal aimed at winning over a specific audience for a definite purpose. The assignment gives students experience in both analytical thinking and practical problem solving, and the proposal could actually be submitted in an effort to get funding to address a specific need in the college or community.

USES, ADAPTATIONS, AND RESOURCES

Students could carry out this activity individually or collaboratively, and the activity could be used as a research assignment, an in-class speech, a Power Point presentation, and/or in conjunction with the study of problem solving or the needs of specific institutions. During my research paper assignment in Composition I, we apply cost-benefit analysis to problematic situations in which both costs and benefits may be more abstract and harder to measure or quantify, such as social benefits or moral costs. Two essays we discuss—one pro, one con—analyze the costs and benefits of legalizing drugs. I also use a "project and predict" exercise in which students predict the probable costs and benefits, both personal and social, of a five-year increase in the average life expectancy of Americans.

Cost-benefit analysis requires methods of estimating probabilities, assessing risks, and foreseeing the likely consequences of specific decisions or proposals. Diane Halpern's *Critical Thinking Across the Curriculum* includes sections on probability evaluation and risk assessment, and she illustrates some common errors in assessment, such as the "conjunction error" of believing that the occurrence of two events is more likely than the occurrence of one of them. Thomas Gilovich's *How We Know What Isn't So* also explains common fallacies and biases—such as "the misinterpretation of

---

incomplete and unrepresentative data"—in assessing risks and estimating probabilities.

In his classic essay "The Tragedy of the Commons," biologist Garrett Hardin applies cost-benefit analysis to situations in which individuals in a group, each concerned with maximizing his/her own benefits, will act in such a way that the group as a whole incurs disastrous costs. Hardin uses the work of a 19th century mathematician who showed that, if each herdsman is allowed to determine the number of his cattle to graze in a common pasture, the pasture will ultimately become overgrazed. By carrying out a particular economic activity without limits, each individual appears to benefit while incurring no costs, but the result is ultimately "tragic" for everyone in the community. Hardin writes: "Ruin is the destination toward which all men rush, each pursuing his own best interests in a society that believes in the freedom of the commons." Hardin applies his "tragedy of the commons" idea to such social problems as waste disposal and population control.

A variation of the "tragedy of the commons" is the cost-benefit conundrum known as "the prisoner's dilemma." The dilemma can be formulated mathematically (not by me), but it is usually illustrated by a two-player game in which each player, through a process of trial and error, must calculate the shifting costs and benefits of cooperating with or competing against the other player. During my undergraduate days at Harvard University, I participated in a prisoner's dilemma game as a paid experimental subject (my motives included intellectual curiosity and beer money), and, after the experiment, the experimenters explained the nature of the dilemma:

> Two players each have two possible actions—to cooperate or to compete. If both cooperate, both do well. If both compete, both do poorly. The dilemma arises when one player competes and the other cooperates: the competitor does very well, and the cooperator

does very poorly. So rational analysis leads to only one conclusion—the same for each player—to compete. Yet that logic forces an outcome that is clearly worse than what is possible if both cooperate.

Gilovich illustrates the dilemma with a case of a district attorney pitting two suspects against each other by offering each a plea bargain at the other's expense, but it applies to any situation—nuclear arms negotiation, for example—in which two "players" could maximize their benefits by cooperating if only each could trust the other to be faithful to an agreement to cooperate.

In *Metamagical Themas*, Douglas Hofstadter provides further examples, examines attempts to formulate the dilemma mathematically, and considers the larger question of how cooperation has evolved in human societies. He asks: "How can [cooperation] get started at all?" "Can cooperative strategies survive better than noncooperative ones?" "Which cooperative strategies will do the best, and how will they come to predominate?" One conclusion he reaches is that "mutual cooperation can only emerge in a world of egoists without central control, by starting with a cluster of individuals who rely on reciprocity." Hofstadter also discusses attempts to resolve the dilemma through computer programs, one of which, TIT FOR TAT, uses this simple tactic: "Cooperate on move #1; thereafter, do whatever the other player did the previous move." In his chapters "Dilemmas for Superrational Thinkers" and "Irrationality Is the Square Root of All Evil," he presents other "cooperation" vs. "defection" cost-benefit dilemmas, some involving statistical analysis, that raise important questions about the ethics of behavior within groups or between competing groups. He defines a "defection" as "an action such that, if everyone did it, things would be clearly worse (for everyone) than if everyone refrained from doing it, and yet which tempts everyone, since if only one individual (or a sufficiently small number) did it while others refrained, life would be sweeter for that individual (or select group)."

In *Choice and Consequence*, economist Thomas Schelling also uses game theory to carry out cost-benefit analyses. He defines game theory as "the formal study of rational decision" in problematic situations: "Two or more individuals have choices to make, preferences regarding the outcomes, and some knowledge of the choices available to each other and of each other's preferences. The outcome depends on the choices that both of them make, or all of them if there are more than two. There is no independently 'best' choice that one can make; it depends on what the others do." Schelling provides a framework for estimating the consequences of choices, while considering such issues as the ethics of economic policy and the exercise of individual "self-command" in making rational choices. He applies game theory in what he calls "vicarious problem solving" to topics ranging from nuclear terrorism to organized crime.

The work of sociobiologists offers another illustration of cost-benefit analysis through the application of scientific principles. Sociobiology, as explained by Sylvia Mader in *Biology*, "applies the principles of evolutionary biology to the study of social behavior in animals. Sociobiologists develop hypotheses about social living based on the assumption that a social individual derives more reproductive benefits than costs from living in a society. Then they can perform a cost-benefit analysis to see if their hypotheses are correct." Sociobiologists explore such issues as the benefits of "altruistic" behavior and try to answer questions such as why certain birds help to raise offspring that are not their own, or what benefits are derived by human stepparents. Edward O. Wilson's *Sociobiology* and Robert Wright's *The Moral Animal* both demonstrate this approach in book-length studies.

One essential element of critical thinking is a willingness to subject the tools of thinking to critical examination.

In *Small Is Beautiful: Economics as if People Mattered*, economist E. F. Schumacher critiques cost-benefit analysis itself as
a methodological tool in economics. One problem, he claims,
is that cost-benefit analyses often don't consider the costs of
damage to the environment, while failing to make distinctions between renewable resources and resources that can
never be replaced. "This means, " he says, "that an activity
can be economic although it plays hell with the environment,
and that a competing activity, if at some cost it protects and
conserves the environment, will be uneconomic." Another
problem, Shumacher says, is that cost-benefit analysis is not
well-suited to accounting for values that can't be quantified:
"In fact, however, it is a procedure by which the higher is
reduced to the level of the lower and the priceless is given a
price." More broadly, Shumacher argues that it is "inherent
in the methodology of economics *to ignore man's dependence
on the natural world*," and he challenges some of the assumptions of economics that underlie cost-benefit analysis—for
example, the assumption that economic growth is inherently
good: "The idea that there could be pathological growth, un-
healthy growth, disruptive or destructive growth, is to him
[the economist] a perverse idea which must not be allowed to
surface."

Christopher Shea's article "Mad for Risk at Harvard"
examines both the value and the potential drawbacks of using cost-benefit analysis to set public policy. Shea focuses
on John D. Graham, founder of Harvard Center of Risk Analysis and the current "regulatory czar" at the nation's Office of
Information and Regulatory Affairs, who has "long argued
that regulations to, say, eliminate the last traces of toxins in
drinking water often aren't worth the cost—as much as bil-
lions of dollars per life saved, according to this calculations."
Graham's use of risk analysis has been challenged by Tufts
economist Frank Ackerman and Georgetown law professor
Lisa Heinzerling, who argue that "you actually lose informa-

tion" when you try to give monetary value to things like cancer or the loss of a species: "You lose clarity about how many deaths, how many diseases, how much damage to the ecosystem." Shea illustrates how risk analysis has been used both to limit governmental regulation and "as a tool for more aggressive regulation." At the heart of the debate lies the problem of assigning a number to the value of life. "With each slain being," wrote the Polish writer Stanislaw Lem in another context, "an entire world dies. For that reason arithmetic provides no measure for ethics. Irreversible evil can't be measured."

For related activities, SEE #22: **Just Because** and #36: **What Are the Alternatives?**

ACTIVITY #22
Just Because (Using Causal Analysis)

APPLICATIONS: History, philosophy (logic), composition, other disciplines

CRITICAL THINKING SKILLS: Getting relevant information, detecting bias, making inferences, using evidence, evaluating alternative theories to explain phenomena

THE ACTIVITY

This activity requires a written analysis of a causal relationship. Students could explain the causes of a specific event (an industrial accident, a medical epidemic), natural phenomena (the extinction of a species), a problem (the failure of a business, a legal dispute resulting in litigation, a state's budget crisis), the behavior of individuals in life or literature (a decision to get divorced), broader historical conflicts (warfare between two nations), and so on. Before writing their analyses, students conduct research on the topic, and the instructor may introduce conceptual tools such as causal chains or contributory causes, or terminology commonly used in analyzing causal relationships, such as the distinction between "sufficient cause" and "necessary condition." The instructor may also give students exercises in identifying examples of common fallacies in causal analysis, and the class may discuss more philosophical questions about the nature of causation and the difficulties in determining both proximate and ultimate causes.

PURPOSES AND BENEFITS

In this activity students must analyze information and make judgments about problematic situations in which effects may have multiple, complex causes. Students must evaluate sources that may provide different and conflicting explanations of causes, and they must demonstrate their ability to use reasoning, evidence, and precise language in supporting their judgments and demonstrating their understanding of causation. Causal analysis can be also be linked to problem solving assignments; the best strategies for solving a problem incorporate an analysis of what brought the problem about.

USES, ADAPTATIONS, AND RESOURCES

I've used this assignment in Composition I—several students always insist on calling it "casual analysis"—and we also discuss the process and pitfalls of causal analysis when students write problem solving or argumentative essays. The activity can be used in virtually any discipline with virtually any topic, ranging from specific events with relatively simple causes to historical processes in which causation is far more complicated and uncertain. The activity works best with some required research, though students may analyze causation in personal experiences, relying on first-hand knowledge rather than formal research. A common fallacy in student essays is to treat sequence as *de facto* proof of causation. They may write narratives to show causation—he did this, then he did that—instead of using analytical reasoning to establish that certain causes were instrumental in bringing about certain effects. In *Engaging Ideas*, John Bean recommends some strategies to help students get beyond this "and then" approach and other ineffective approaches to writing essays (such as "text parroting" and "data dumping") that result in compositions which manage to grow longer and longer while failing to exhibit any actual causal analysis or critical thinking.

Thomas Gilovich's *How We Know What Isn't So* discusses common fallacies in analyzing causation—and the general tendency of students and others to find order and coherence where none exist— while Bransford and Stein's *The Ideal Problem Solver* uses examples to illustrate how causal analyses may be tested. *Critical Thinking, Thoughtful Writing* by Chaffee, McMahon, and Stout provides a useful chapter on analyzing causation, including definitions, common

---

fallacies, sample essays for analysis, and guidelines for writing assignments. Causal analysis is also one of the rhetorical modes commonly covered in composition textbooks, such as Winterowd and Winterowd's *The Critical Reader, Thinker, and Writer*. They discuss the idea of a "writer-reader contract" and suggest questions that readers can reasonably expect writers to answer: Does the writer provide all the information the reader needs to understand the writer's explanation? Can the reader rely on the writer's knowledge and truthfulness? Is everything in the composition relevant to the point that the writer is explaining? Has the writer been as clear as possible?

In *Critical Thinking and Education*, John McPeck examines the teaching of informal logic through causal analysis, particularly the detection of fallacious reasoning. Too often, he says, instructors or textbooks merely list common fallacies with definitions or brief explanations. He characterizes this approach as the Charlie Brown Syndrome of "teaching" logic by "providing names for obvious mistakes in reasoning"—a reference to a *Peanuts* cartoon in which Lucy sits behind a "Psychiatric Help—5 cents" sign and says to Charlie Brown, "For five cents, if you tell me what is bothering you today, I'll give you a name for it." In reality, McPeck claims, it's not so easy for students, or others, to apply concepts such as the "irrelevant reason" fallacy. It's important for teachers not only to discuss why fallacies are fallacious—that is, to identify the elements that fallacies have in common—but also to explain and illustrate how fallacies differ from non-fallacious arguments.

Seeds of Change: Five Hundred Years Since Columbus, an anthology edited by Herman J. Viola and Carolyn Margolis (and nicely illustrated), offers a book-length example of causal analysis—in this case, an analysis of such causative factors as crop exchanges, exposure to new diseases, and slavery (all "seeds of change") in bringing about cultural and environmental changes, both positive and negative, in the Western

Hemisphere during the past 500 years. On a similar subject, a model of ambitious causal analysis at its best is Jared Diamond's *Guns, Germs, and Steel: The Fates of Human Societies,* "a short history of everybody for the last 13,000 years." Diamond—who has expertise in linguistics, physiology, and ornithology as well as history—frames his topic in this passage from his prologue:

> We all know that history has proceeded very differently for peoples from different parts of the globe. In the 13,000 years since the end of the last Ice Age, some parts of the world developed literate industrial societies with metal tools, other parts developed only nonliterate farming societies, and still others retained societies of hunter-gatherers with stone tools. Those historical inequalities have cast long shadows on the modern world, because the literate societies with metal tools have conquered or exterminated the other societies. While those differences constitute the most basic fact of world history, the reasons for them remain uncertain and controversial.

In accounting for these "historical inequalities," and in explaining the factors that have caused human societies to develop in different ways on different continents, Diamond examines the origins of crops, boats, writing, religion, guns, and empires. In his epilogue, "The Future of Human History as a Science," he discusses "the difficulties historians face in establishing cause-and-effect relations in the history of human societies," difficulties that arise from the complexity and unpredictability of historical systems, and he advocates the use of "the comparative method and so-called natural experiments" to give the study of history a stronger scientific basis. "I am thus optimistic," Diamond writes, "that historical studies of human societies can be pursued as scientifically as studies of dinosaurs—and with profit to our own society today, by teaching us what

---

shaped the modern world, and what might shape our future."

For a related activity, SEE **#36: What Are the Alternatives?**

ACTIVITY #23
Dissecting Words Instead of Frogs
(Analyzing Scientific Articles)

APPLICATIONS: Biology, other sciences and social sciences, other disciplines

CRITICAL THINKING SKILLS: Determining the importance of information, detecting slanting and bias, making inferences, testing hypotheses, evaluating evidence used to support claims, evaluating alternative theories and interpretations

THE ACTIVITY

In his abstract "Want to Cut Up Something Different in Biology? Try a Journal Article Dissection," Peter V. Lindeman, a biology professor at Madisonville Community College in Kentucky, discusses his use of this activity in the first semester of a majors-level Principles of Biology sequence. First, the instructor explains the use and purpose of scientific methodology, including basic principles of statistical inference, and students spend some laboratory time carrying out simple statistical tests. Then, after going over research terminology (e.g. "null hypothesis") and the steps commonly followed in standard journal articles, the instructor assigns a series of journal article dissections. Students are asked "to explicitly state the question and hypothesis of the research; to identify independent and dependent variables, and, if applicable, control variables and experimental and control groups of treatments; to formally state each null hypothesis and interpret, with statistical confidence levels, each null hypothesis test; and to identify in the discussion section any new hypotheses offered which might be tested in the future." Lindeman requires that student dissections include "a critical appraisal of the work they have dissected," and he includes guidelines for selecting the articles to be dissected.

PURPOSES AND BENEFITS

"Criticism without discipline is frivolity," John McPeck says in *Critical Thinking and Education*, and this activity is one effective way to introduce students to a disciplined from of criticism. Professor Lindeman uses the activity to help students understand that "science is not just a staid old body of knowledge, but rather a process, a means of acquiring and adding to our body of knowledge." He combines the dissections with laboratory exercises to give students an "abundance of examples" that illustrate the process of scientific inquiry. Although this activity is challenging, especially for students who struggle with either analytical reasoning or composition skills, Lindeman reports that it leads to "a dramatically increased understanding of scientific methodology" while preparing biology majors for more in-depth critical appraisals of journal articles. Students can better grasp both the potential benefits of scientific research and the kind of work that professional researchers actually do. They may better understand the development of scientific knowledge by being exposed to conflicting hypotheses that attempt to account for the same phenomena, or to experiments that help to clarify points of uncertainty even though hypotheses are not proven valid. The assignment also exemplifies the spirit of writing across the curriculum programs by giving students experience in applying their composition skills within the field in which they plan to specialize.

USES, ADAPTATIONS, AND RESOURCES

This activity can be modified to apply to the analysis of journal articles—or less formal articles—in other sciences, the social sciences, health care fields, and other disciplines. Various bibliographical sources, such as Alverno College's *Teach-*

ing Critical Thinking in Psychology, provide guidelines, evaluative criteria, and recommended methods for carrying out this type of assignment. In the "Thinking as Hypothesis Testing" chapter of her *Critical Thinking Across the Curriculum*, Diane Halpern examines the process of hypothesis testing, while explaining and illustrating such basic elements of methodology as the use of operational definitions in measuring concepts, the distinction between independent and dependent variables, the isolation and control of variables, the potential for bias in the sampling of populations, and the difference between "cause" and "correlation." Halpern also quotes scientist Wendell Johnson's point that scientific research is meant to be a rigorous search for knowledge, not merely an attempt to prove a theory, and that the purpose of established scientific methodology is to insure that any theory is fully and reliably tested: "To a scientist a theory is something to be tested. He seeks not to defend his beliefs, but to improve them. He is, above everything else, an expert at 'changing his mind.'" At the end of her chapter, Halpern provides a checklist for "thinking as an intuitive scientist," with questions like the following: "What was the nature of the sample? Was it large enough? Was it biased? Were extraneous variables controlled? What are other plausible explanations for the results? Is disconfirming evidence being considered? How could the experimenter's expectancies be biasing the result?"

Kathleen Bell's *Developing Arguments* and Stuart Hirschberg's *Strategies of Persuasion* both present frameworks and examples to help students distinguish between types of claims—factual claims, causal claims, claims of value—in journal articles and in argumentative writing generally. *Critical Thinking: Reading and Writing in a Diverse World* by Rasool, Banks, and McCarthy includes the article "Bystander Intervention in Emergencies: Diffusion of Responsibility" as an example of quantitative research in the social sciences, while explaining basic methodology in both ethnographic and qualitative research. Marlys Mayfield's *Thinking for* Yourself and Theodore Panitz's *Learning Together* both contain collaborative assignments for less formal analysis of periodical articles. And the *Writer's Guide* series—with books on the life sciences, political science, history, and psychology—offers chapters on writing article summaries and abstracts, reviewing the relevant scholarly literature, conducting policy analyses, and writing research proposals. Finally, for a broader view of scientific thinking, Gerald Holton's *Thematic Origins of Scientific Thought: Kepler to Einstein* and Thomas Kuhn's *The Structure of Scientific Revolutions* both examine the development of scientific knowledge within a historical context. Kuhn is best known for his concept of a "paradigm shift" to explain how scientists change their basic assumptions (paradigms) about the governing principles in their fields.

For related activities, SEE **#24: What Did That Prove?, #34: The Devil's Advocate,** and **#37: Does a Dog Know Its Name?.**

ACTIVITY #24
What Did That Prove? (Analyzing Experiments)

APPLICATIONS: Sociology, criminal justice, social sciences, sciences, composition, other disciplines

CRITICAL THINKING SKILLS: Distinguishing fact from interpretation, detecting slanting and false assumptions, making inferences, testing hypotheses, examining issues from opposing viewpoints, evaluating alternative theories and interpretations

THE ACTIVITY

This activity overlaps with the previous one but focuses more directly on the methodology and implications of experiments. I use one form of the activity when my Composition I and Criminals in Literature classes discuss the article "Pathology of Imprisonment," sociologist Philip Zimbardo's account of a role-playing experiment involving Stanford University students who volunteered to play the roles of guards and prisoners for two weeks in a mock prison. First, we review the basic facts Zimbardo provides about the experiment, which, he claims, produced such disturbing results that the experimenters had to close down the mock prison after six days. "In less than a week the experience of imprisonment undid (temporarily) a lifetime of learning," Zimbardo writes. "Human values were suspended, self-concepts were challenged and the ugliest, most base, pathological side of human nature surfaced." Then, we discuss the broader conclusions that Zimbardo draws from this experiment. "With regards to prisons," he writes, "we can state that the mere act of assigning labels to people and putting them into a situation where those labels acquire validity and meaning is sufficient to elicit pathological behavior." He goes on to generalize: "Many people, perhaps the majority, can be made to do almost anything when put into psychologically compelling situations—regardless of their morals, ethics, values, attitudes, beliefs or personal convictions." Finally, we critique both the methodology of the experiment and Zimbardo's claims about its implications. We discuss criteria for evaluating the validity of experiments generally, and we especially examine any factors that may have biased or influenced the results of Zimbardo's experiment, such as the selection of participants, the motives of participants, their expectations in entering the mock prison (based on the ways in which their roles were explained to them), and the expectations of those who set up the experiment. Students present their critiques of the experiment in writing.

Professor Zimbardo has developed on online slide show about his imprisonment experiment (www.prisonexp.org/).

PURPOSES AND BENEFITS

The main purpose of activities like this is to introduce students to the methodology used in conducting experiments in the social sciences and other disciplines. In addition to engaging student interest in the topic of the experiment, the assignment requires students to focus on criteria for evaluating the validity of experiments—for instance, whether the act of measuring something has affected the measurements. Students must then apply these criteria to a specific case. They must also evaluate the reasoning used to arrive at generalizations about the implications of an experiment, and they must determine whether the experiment provides sufficient, reliable evidence to make certain general claims about human behavior. After this activity, students write research papers and/or argumentative essays in both of my courses, and they are better able both to evaluate the experimental studies discovered in their research and to use experimental results as evidence in supporting assertions in their own arguments.

USES, ADAPTATIONS, AND RESOURCES

I've used this activity with other articles about experiments, including David Rosenhan's "On Being Sane in Insane Places," a well-known experiment from the 1970's in which "pseudopatients" (volunteer subjects not suffering from schizophrenia) entered mental institutions claiming to hear voices and were diagnosed as schizophrenics. For weeks, psychiatric professionals—but not, in most cases, fellow patients—continued to believe that the subjects were suffering from schizophrenia. After the subjects claimed that they no longer heard the voices, they were released from the institutions with the diagnosis "schizophrenia in remission." Rosenhan discusses the reasons for and consequences of the misdiagnoses as well as the more general issue of the effects of being labeled (in this case as a schizophrenic).

Introductory texts in various disciplines explain the fundamentals of scientific experimentation and summarize experiments that students could research in more depth and analyze in writing assignments. For instance, in *Psychology: An Introduction*, Jerome Kagan and Julius Segal explain fundamentals such as independent and dependent variables, the use of control groups, and the distinction between single-blind and double-blind experiments. They provide brief accounts of experiments on topics such as the neurological basis of sexual orientation, the susceptibility of children to revisions of memory, and the validity of lie detector tests. In her introductory text *Biology*, Sylvia Mader offers a number of examples to illustrate how experiments are used to make predictions and test hypotheses, such as the hypothesis that "the evolution of predation was a strong selection pressure, giving rise to the evolution of a much greater diversity of animals."

For a related activity, SEE **#37: Does a Dog Know Its Name?**

Cultivating Judgment

Section Three

Opinions, Decisions, Values

ACTIVITY #25
Coping #101 (Using Critical Thinking in Self-Examination)

APPLICATIONS: Psychology, college success seminars, other disciplines

CRITICAL THINKING SKILLS: Examining issues from multiple viewpoints, evaluating alternative solutions or interpretations, evaluating decision-making strategies, analyzing the process of making judgments

THE ACTIVITY

In this activity the instruct or gives students questions, as composition topics, to encourage reflection on the patterns of their lives, their self-concepts and values, their coping strategies, their relationships with others, ongoing changes in their personalities, and so on. Mark Libon, a psychology professor and a former colleague of mine in the Motivation to Education learning community at North Shore Community College, uses this activity in Psychology of Adjustment, a course designed to introduce basic principles of psychology and apply these principles to students' strategies of adjustment. Libon gives students a wide range of self-probing topics, including the following:

- Discuss an important belief you have modified or abandoned, indicating how this change came about and the effect of this change on your life.
- Suppose an anthropologist unobtrusively followed you around for a week, recording everything you said and did, with the intent of determining your philosophy of life—not from what you said it was but from what you showed it was. What would s/he report?
- How have you dealt with death and/or some great loss or misfortune in your life? What did you learn from this experience?

- What obstacles to growth have you found in yourself and how have they affected your life?
- Has there ever been a time in your life when you felt your life was aimless or senseless? If so, discuss this time and what you did or are doing in response to it.
- What do you value most in life? Why? How has your value system changed over the years? What accounts for this change?
- Describe a moral conflict or problem you face or have faced and indicate your resolution or response.
- Are you an optimist? A pessimist? Discuss this aspect of yourself and include examples and a consideration of how well your attitude serves you.

PURPOSES AND BENEFITS

This activity encourages critical thinking as a means toward personal understanding and academic growth. The range of topics allows students to focus on issues they care about, and the topics themselves emphasize the value of self-examination in coping with problems or resolving conflicts more effectively. The activity is especially beneficial for many students just entering college, such as the "at risk" students in our learning community, who may be undergoing a difficult process of transition, struggling with anxiety or low self- esteem, or grappling with personal problems that undermine their efforts to succeed in college. The topics may lead students to come up with helpful coping strategies, and Professor Libon's classes discuss how the topics connect to the principles of psychology that students encounter in their text.

USES, ADAPTATIONS, AND RESOURCES

Professor Libon also gives students a theoretical framework on "Coping Strategies and Their Personality Correlates" with explanations of strategies such as active coping, restraint, acceptance, seeking social support for instrumental or emotional reasons, turning to religion, venting of emotions, mental disengagement, and denial. He then asks students to apply the framework in a composition with these instructions: "To begin this exploration, recall the problems that you have faced in the recent past and the coping strategies you have used to deal with these problems. Then write the answers to these questions: (a) Which three or four of the fourteen coping strategies have you used the most? (b) Have those most-used strategies served you well? Why or why not?" In working with Professor Libon and other psychology instructors in our learning community, I've assigned other, informal self-probing compositions, such as letters by student-parents that their children will read at some point in the future, or letters from students to themselves—either as they were five years earlier or as they hope to be five years into the future. I've also assigned E. M. Forster's "What I Believe," anthologized in Penguin's *Fifty Great Essays*, to exemplify the lucid and thoughtful expression of personal beliefs.

Another colleague at North Shore Community College, psychology professor Jennifer Harris, assigns a student autobiography at the beginning of her Psychology of Women course. She asks students to explore what it means for them to be a woman or man and what has influenced their sense of themselves as women or men. At the end of the semester students revisit their autobiographies, applying principles they've learned during the course. Also, in the course Theories of Personality, her students write, then revisit autobiographies describing their personalities and their informal theories of personality development. Harris finds these assignments valuable in overcoming student resistance to examining themselves and articulating viewpoints about themselves within a theoretical context. In a more specialized activity, Alverno College's *Teaching Critical Thinking in Psychology* describes a "Mom Always Liked You Best" exercise, in which students are introduced to Adler's theory of birth order and then, working in small groups based on their birth order, apply the theory to their own personality characteristics.

In *Emotional Intelligence*, Daniel Goleman suggests other ways to explore what he calls "affective education," or schooling the emotions, in "Self Science" classes. To demonstrate the importance of emotional intelligence, Goleman quotes Aristotle: "Anyone can become angry—this is easy. But to be angry with the right person, to the right degree, at the right time, for the right purpose, and in the right way—this is not easy." Goleman's theory of the "domains" of emotional intelligence includes: (1) knowing one's emotions (2) managing emotions (3) motivating oneself (4) recognizing emotions in others, and (5) handling relationships. As an example of research on emotional intelligence, he cites a study of husbands and wives watching their videotaped arguments. The most "empathic accuracy" occurred, he says, in those spouses whose own physiology tracked the responses of the spouses they were watching rather than repeating their own physiological responses. Goleman discusses the value of applied emotional intelligence in coping with stress, resisting impulse, managing anger, and handling workplace relationships. His theory could be related to such topics as temperament types, parenting skills, and drug or alcohol abuse. He particularly emphasizes the value of writing—illustrated by the activities above—in getting people to express their most disturbing thoughts. He also offers advice on how to deliver an "artful critique" to a friend or co-worker. Finally, he illustrates the importance of seeing ourselves in perspective through W. H. Auden's remark that his private image of himself was "very different from the image which I try to create in the minds of others in order that they may love me."

For related activities, SEE **#27: A Personal Declaration of Independence, #28: Dealing with the Devil** and **#49: Time to Take Inventory.**

ACTIVITY #26
Tracing the Family Tree (Examining Family and Cultural Heritage)

APPLICATIONS: History, literature, composition, health care professions, other disciplines

CRITICAL THINKING SKILLS: Getting relevant information, relating general principles to specific examples, evaluating alternative theories to explain phenomena

THE ACTIVITY

Michele N. Costanza, a professor at Johnson County Community College in Kansas, describes this activity in her abstract "Tracing the Family Tree: Meeting the Research Aim in Composition." Students in her composition class write a genealogical research paper: "Students," Professor Costanza explains, "must trace their maternal or paternal side back three generations, counting themselves as one generation. They must cite sources and make connections between events in their families to events in history." Students conduct research, read about and analyze relevant historical events, and produce a final paper showing the relevance of these events in their family histories. Professor Costanza has developed a website that allows students to view a sample family tree and to link to other web site resources. She also notes her sensitivity to personal reasons—adoption, divorce, concerns about privacy, traumatic events in family history—that might make students reluctant to take on the assignment. She allows students "the option of choosing another assigned research topic of equal breadth and depth."

PURPOSES AND BENEFITS

This activity is an effective, engaging way to introduce students to research methodology and to develop the critical thinking skills necessary to relate personal family histories to historical events. The assignment sets in motion a process of discovery, encouraging students to go where curiosity takes them and study relevant research in some depth. Students may discover information that is valuable in helping them form or understand their own identities, and, as Professor Costanza points out, some students are inspired to carry out more advanced family research on their own.

USES, ADAPTATIONS, AND RESOURCES

Professor Costanza uses this assignment in a composition course, but it could certainly be used in history courses to examine the significance of historical events in individual lives. *Writer's Guide: History*, by Henry Steffens and Mary Jane Dickerson, includes a unit on oral history, with suggested procedures for interviewing elderly family members, or other elderly subjects, about historical events they have witnessed.

I've used a related assignment in literature courses, in conjunction with readings by Elie Wiesel, M. Scott Momaday, and Louise Erdrich that focus on the significance of one's cultural heritage. Students write essays discussing specific aspects of their personal heritage and explaining why their heritage is important to them. Some students write about values—a belief in family honor, a tradition of artistic expressiveness—that connect them to distant lands or generations past. Others focus on problems of cultural assimilation, divided loyalties, or generational conflicts that stem from conflicting cultural values. Students must also relate their cultural backgrounds to issues of cultural heritage that we've discussed in our analysis of readings, such as survivor guilt, the transmission of spiritual beliefs, the preservation of cultural values, ambivalence about cultural identity, or feelings

---

of cultural isolation or displacement The assignment requires students to seek out relevant information, to articulate their values, and to demonstrate critical thinking skills in making connections between their own cultural backgrounds and more global events or issues. Students have written thoughtful and sometimes eloquent essays about the relevance of cultural heritage to their own identities, and sometimes—as in the case of a student who compared his family's escape from Vietnam to Stephen Crane's story about surviving a shipwreck, "The Open Boat"—they connect their own lives to course readings in revealing and surprising ways. Many of our students have compelling stories to tell, and this assignment offers a chance to tell them.

Another twist on this assignment, one that can be used in courses studying human health and disease, involves the investigation of family medical histories. Here, students conduct interviews with family members or obtain death certificates or other medical records of family members (alive or deceased). This investigation can be carried out in connection with analysis of readings about the inheritability of diseases, patterns in longevity, and the importance of medical histories in diagnosis of disease. Students may discover valuable information about their families' medical histories, and the assignment engages their interest by relating general principles about medical histories to their own family situations. As with Professor Costanza's assignment, the instructor should address student concerns about privacy and sensitivity of personal information. In fact, the instructor might use the assignment to initiate a critical examination of the issue of privacy of medical records.

For a related activity, SEE **#32: How Will We Be Judged?**

ACTIVITY #27
A Personal Declaration of Independence (Making Decisions)

APPLICATIONS: Literature, psychology, history, political science, gender studies, college success seminars

CRITICAL THINKING SKILLS: Using examples and evidence, examining issues from conflicting viewpoints, evaluating solutions, foreseeing consequences of decisions

THE ACTIVITY

This activity is a writing assignment. Students are given the following directions for an essay of three to five pages: "Using 'The Declaration of Independence' as your model, write an essay in which you justify your decision to sever your relationship with an individual (e.g. parent, spouse, friend) or an organization (e.g. political party, religious institution). Explain and support the rationale for your decision."

PURPOSES AND BENEFITS

One value of critical thinking, Marlys Mayfield says in *Thinking for Yourself,* is "lessening the likelihood of making serious mistakes in important decisions." This activity encourages students to reflect on and articulate the ethical bases for their decisions, their means of solving personal problems, and the foreseeable consequences of their decisions. The topic has elicited some thoughtful, heartfelt compositions, as well as some lighthearted essays, including one about severing a relationship with a math class. Before my students write, we discuss the actual "Declaration" (reprinted in Penguin's *Fifty Great Essays*) as a model of argumentative reasoning. It makes a good model because it states its goals explicitly, presents specific and thorough rationale to support the position it advances, uses a variety of effective rhetorical devices, and addresses the *process* of problem-solving. One key idea in the "Declaration" is that the radical decision to sever ties with England has been made only after less drastic solutions have been tried without success. We also discuss the importance of foreseeing the consequences of severing a relationship and anticipating how one might rebut or respond to the rationale presented to justify the severance. In addition to applying critical thinking skills to their life situations, students gain a better understanding of both the specific political arguments presented in the "Declaration" and the more general issue of providing rationale and supporting evidence to justify positions in persuasive writing.

USES, ADAPTATIONS, AND RESOURCES

I've used this topic in literature courses as one of several essay options, not as an assignment for the entire class, since some students may not have had experiences that fit the topic. In grading any composition assignment, including this one, I evaluate both the overall writing skills demonstrated in essays and students' effectiveness in addressing the requirements of a given topic. This assignment can be difficult to evaluate because the subject matter is so personal. I focus on judging the clarity of the rationale, the specificity of evidence, and the logic of the reasoning. It's not for me to decide whether it is in fact wise for the student to sever the relationship in question. However, in most cases I speak individually to students about their topics, and in one situation I suggested counseling help to a student who was deeply troubled by a personal problem that she had resolved on paper but not in fact.

Because of its style, diction, and the rigor of its logic, the "Declaration" is a challenging piece of reading for some students, and the assignment works best with students who have prior experience in dissecting argumentative writing. Another use of the "Declaration" is Elizabeth Cady Stanton's "Declaration of Sentiments and Resolutions," presented to the Seneca Falls Convention on women's rights in 1848 (in *Fifty Great Essays*), in which Stanton follows the format of the original to argue, not for the severance of a relationship, but for the "immediate admission" of women "to all the rights and privileges which belong to them as citizens of the United States." Mary Wollstonecraft's *A Vindication of the Rights of Women*, published in 1792 and frequently excerpted in anthologies (including *Fifty Great Essays*), is a good companion piece for an analysis of either the original "Declaration" or Stanton's speech.

Other literary works, such as Franz Kafka's famous letter to his father, can be used in similar ways as examples of how to apply critical thinking skills to personal situations (and, in Kafka's case, of how reasoning can be self-serving). First, the class as a whole can analyze the literary work and focus on points such as rationale, evidence, tone, and response to opposing arguments. Then, students can use the literary work as a model to write personal essays on relevant topics of their own choice. One writing assignment I've used, in connection with a George Orwell story about imperialism, is the following: "Compare and contrast Orwell's experience in 'Shooting an Elephant' to an experience of your own in which you had to go against your own principles in order to maintain your position and/or the respect of other people. With both the Orwell story and your own experience, be specific in explaining the principles that have been violated and the motives for violating these principles." One student wrote about an experience, still etched in his mind twenty years after the fact, in which he was pressured by two fellow American soldiers to participate in the killing of three Vietcong prisoners by throwing them from a helicopter.

Critical Thinking, Thoughtful Writing by Chaffee,

McMahon, and Stout includes a framework for analyzing decisions, steps in the process of making decisions, and a writing assignment (with several examples of student essays) on "analyzing a decision to be made." They provide an excerpt from Amy Tan's novel *The Joy Luck Club* to illustrate the process of decision-making. Diane Halpern presents a worksheet procedure with multiple goals and alternatives in her useful chapter on decision-making in *Critical Thinking Across the Curriculum*, while *de Bono's Thinking Course* provides Consequence and Sequel exercises on anticipating the consequences of a course of action, as well as "decision preframes" and "decision postframes." For examples of essays about deciding to sever a relationship, consult *The God That Failed*, edited by Richard Crossman, in which international authors Andre Gide, Richard Wright, Ignazio Silone, Stephen Spender, Arthur Koestler, and Louis Fischer explain their decisions to sever their connections to the Communist Party.

Other sources present ideas for assignments that focus less on making specific decisions and more on evaluating entrenched beliefs John Chaffee's *Thinking Critically* offers these questions for evaluating beliefs: "(1) How effectively do your beliefs *explain what is taking place?* (2) To what extent are these beliefs *consistent with other beliefs* about the world? (3) How effectively do your beliefs help you *predict what will happen* in the future? (4) To what extent are your beliefs supported by *sound reasons and compelling evidence* derived from *reliable sources?*" To illustrate the process of changing beliefs, he includes the essay "Why I Quit the Klan" by C. P. Ellis. Howard Gardner, in *The Unschooled Mind*, examines the ways in which children form intuitive theories that may later prove to be false, and he discusses a variety of false beliefs held by adult students, ranging from misconceptions about evolution's "direction" to beliefs in "laws at variance with formal physical laws." He believes that most teachers place insufficient emphasis on challenging their students' preconceptions.

For a related activity, SEE **#36: What Are the Alternatives?**

ACTIVITY #28
Dealing with the Devil (Examining Personal Values)

APPLICATIONS: Literature, religion, ethics

CRITICAL THINKING SKILLS: Examining ethical beliefs, foreseeing the consequences of decisions, using language precisely

THE ACTIVITY

Here, the student writes a composition in the form of a pact or contract with the Devil. The pact must specify, as precisely as possible, the powers that the student will be given by the Devil, the price the student must pay for these powers, and other conditions of the contract, such as the time allotted for the student's life span and contingencies in case the conditions of the contract are not fulfilled. The assignment is open-ended in that the powers granted may be used for either self-serving or altruistic purposes, or both, but students must spell out how they intend to use their powers. The "price" paid for the powers need not be eternal damnation, but it must be some extremely undesirable consequence.

PURPOSES AND BENEFITS

Though one might argue that this activity says more about my Catholic upbringing than my goals as a teacher of critical thinking, I see the assignment primarily as an exercise in values clarification. Ethical considerations are fundamental to critical thinking, and this activity offers a different slant on the examination and expression of ethical beliefs. Students must reflect on their lives as a whole and articulate what they value or desire enough to place themselves in serious jeopardy. The assignment is also a good test of using language precisely.

When I evaluate student compositions I especially look for vagueness of phrasing, possible loopholes in the contract, or powers that (as specified in the pact) could easily backfire.

USES, ADAPTATIONS, AND RESOURCES

I've used this assignment when we've studied Goethe's *Faust* in World Literature II. I would never require the assignment of an entire class—some students might be offended or frightened by the notion of making a deal with the Devil, even as an exercise— but students may choose this topic as an alternative to a traditional literary analysis of *Faust*. Before students write their compositions, we discuss such issues as the conditions of Faust's pact with Mephistopheles, Faust's motives for making the pact, Faust's use of his powers, the relationship between God and Mephistopheles, and the literary tradition of characters making deals with the Devil.

The assignment could be modified to relate to other works of literature or philosophy—for instance, a genie-and-three-wishes composition as part of a study of the Arabic *1001 Nights.* In Composition I, I ask students to write short in-class essays explaining why they "want" or "fear" some particular thing. This assignment has elicited some reflective, sometimes poignant essays, as well as some humorous ones, in which students articulate what they desire or dread. One student was scared that he would succumb to the family tradition of alcoholism. Another was terrified by Christmas trees.

In a related activity, when we study Dante's *Inferno* in World Literature I, students write a brief in-class composition explaining whom they would send to hell (one person or group of people) and why they would send this person or group to hell. They share and discuss their responses as a lead-in to a discussion of the idea of hell in Dante. Students provide an interesting variety of responses. They may condemn individuals in their own lives (treacherous Aunt Sue), public figures (Saddam Hussein), and/or whole categories of sinners (murderers, child molesters). Some students refuse to send anybody to hell; others question whether hell exists or whether it should exist. When we discuss Dante directly, we consider the following questions: What is hell exactly? How did the idea of hell develop? Does hell really exist? If it doesn't, should it? What is the common element among all the various groups of sinners Dante consigns to hell? Is there a common element in the sinners that students have consigned to hell? When the students write compositions on Dante, they may choose either an analytical essay on Dante's idea of "symbolic retribution" or the following option: "Using Dante as your model, narrate your visit to your own version of hell. You must describe at least three circles of hell, and you must describe at least three distinct groups of sinners (e.g. seducers, hypocrites) that have been condemned to hell. Your description/explanation of their punishments should clarify or dramatize why these sinners are in hell and how their punishments symbolically fit their sins." Discussion of the idea of hell, and its role in the history of religious and ethical beliefs, can also be related to such works as *The Book of Job* in the Old Testament, Augustine's *Confessions*, Jonathan Edwards' "Sinner in the Hands of an Angry God," and James Joyce's *Portrait of the Artist as a Young Man*.

In another related activity, students write essays about one of the traditional Seven Deadly Sins: anger, envy, gluttony, greed, lust, pride, and sloth. Each student must define one of the sins, use examples to illustrate the sin, and explain why this type of behavior is sinful. Students must also explain why this sin has traditionally viewed as "deadly," and they may use examples to distinguish between sinful and non-sinful expressions of this human quality (e.g. "good" pride vs. "bad" pride). I've used this assignment in connection with studies of Hawthorne and Dante in literature courses, and it is, I think, an effective means of getting students to articulate their ethical values and judgments of human behavior. It provides a well-defined structure while allowing students latitude in expressing their viewpoints. The assignment also helps them learn how to use examples to illustrate generalizations—a key critical thinking skill. When I evaluate the compositions I may comment on their ethical beliefs, but I'm careful not to impose my own values. I judge compositions on the clarity of the definitions, the precision with which students make distinctions, and the specificity and relevance of their examples.

The Boston Globe Magazine devoted an entire issue (October 3, 1999) to a series of essays on the Seven Deadly Sins: "Seven: A Thousand Years of Deadly Sin." For one more related activity, SEE **#29: Defending the Indefensible.**

ACTIVITY #29
Defending the Indefensible (Examining the Ethics of Motive)

APPLICATIONS: Literature, ethics, psychology, sociology, criminal justice, other disciplines

CRITICAL THINKING SKILLS: Detecting slanting and bias, examining issues from conflicting viewpoints, analyzing the process of making judgments, relating behavior to ethical standards

THE ACTIVITY

In this activity, the student assumes the persona of someone trying to explain and justify an act that most people would consider morally reprehensible and impossible to justify. I've used the assignment in literature courses in conjunction with such works as Euripides' play *Medea*, in which the title character kills a king, the king's daughter, and her own children. First, we examine Medea's attempts to justify the murders both to herself and to others. Then, students may choose, as one of several options for a required paper, to write a composition following these directions: "Narrate a story which reveals why a character commits an act that most people would find morally indefensible, and show how the character tries to justify the act to himself/herself and to others."

PURPOSES AND BENEFITS

The title of this activity comes from George Orwell's essay "Politics and the English Language": "In our time, political speech and writing are largely the defense of the indefensible." In his essay Orwell analyzes the ways in which writers use language when they defend morally dubious actions that can be defended "only by arguments which are too brutal for most people to face, and which do not square with the professed aims of political parties." Robert Wright, in *The Moral Animal,* echoes Orwell when he discusses the use of techniques of persuasion to justify behavior that may have no ethical basis. "The proposition here," Wright says, "is that the human brain is, in large part, a machine for winning arguments, a machine for convincing others that its owner is in the right—and thus a machine for convincing its owner of the same thing. The brain is like a good lawyer: given any set of interests to defend, it sets about convincing the world of their moral and logical worth, regardless of whether they in fact have any of either. Like a lawyer, the human brain wants victory, not truth; and, like a lawyer, it is sometimes more admirable for skill than for virtue." Claude Levi-Strauss makes a similar point when he says that "one has to be very naïve or dishonest to imagine that men choose their beliefs independently of their situations."

The main purpose of this assignment is to focus student attention on the connection between reasoning skills and ethical considerations. More specifically, it's a way to consider how strategies of persuasion can be used toward unethical ends or divorced from ethical values. The assignment requires students to examine behavior from conflicting ethical perspectives and to consider what Wright characterizes as the human propensity for self-justification. Or, as E. M. Forster puts it, "A man does not talk to himself quite truly." I've long believed that one value of literature lies in its ability to dramatize our human capacity to delude both others and ourselves.

USES, ADAPTATIONS, AND RESOURCES

I've used similar assignments, in both essay and narrative forms, in my "Criminals in Literature" course, when we study why criminals in literature commit their crimes. The assignment could be used in any course, ranging from Abnormal Psychology to criminal justice courses, in which students seek to understand behavior that is considered criminal, deviant, or difficult to justify on any ethical grounds. I judge the compositions on the persuasiveness of the character's reasoning, the character's effectiveness in anticipating and addressing objections to his/her self-justification, and the plausibility of the character's motives. I tell students beforehand that papers will be judged according to these admittedly—and, I think, unavoidably—subjective criteria.

This assignment is related to others in this sourcebook—including class debates, mock trials, and other role-playing activities—that require students to play roles or assume personas as a means of viewing issues from conflicting viewpoints. With such assignments it's important to remind students that the value of the learning activity depends on strict adherence to their roles, since students may resist taking on roles that incorporate values radically different from their own, or they may have difficulty staying within their roles. I've also learned, through experience with this assignment, that the instructor must be quite explicit and provide sufficient examples in explaining what constitutes "an act which most people would find morally indefensible." Some students have written narratives in which no such act occurs.

In a related activity, Alverno College's *Teaching Critical Thinking in Psychology* provides a "Dear Diary" exercise in which the student writes diary entries from the perspective of a person who has been ostracized in some way. The novels *Flowers for Algernon* and *The Color Purple* are suggested as examples. John Bean's *Engaging Ideas* includes a psychology assignment in which students write poems from the perspective of a schizophrenic.

For an in-depth analysis of the motives that compel criminal or aberrant behavior, a good source is sociologist Jack Katz's *Seductions of Crime: Moral and Sensual Attractions in Doing Evil*, a study of "the dialectic process through which a person empowers the world to seduce him to criminality." To understand criminal behavior, Katz writes, we first need to consider the appeal of being bad, or at least behaving badly in particular ways. For each type of crime he considers, he examines a "set of individually necessary and jointly sufficiently conditions, each set containing (1) a path of action—distinctive practical requirements for successfully committing the crime (2) a line of interpretation—unique ways of understanding how one is and will be seen by others, and (3) an emotional process—seductions and compulsions that have special dynamics." He uses studies of street criminals and true crime stories such as Truman Capote's *In Cold Blood* to capture the subjective experience of "what it means, feels, sounds, tastes, or looks like to commit to particular crime" and to show how criminals explain their behavior to themselves and others.

Patricia Pearson's *When She Was Bad*, a study of violent crimes committed by women (SEE the study guide after **Activity #11**) also examines what the author calls "the vocabulary of motive"—the set of phrases, rationales, excuses, and self-justifications that criminals and others commonly use to explain the motives behind or the reasons for criminal behavior. "Although self-justification is universally human," Pearson writes, "the vocabulary of motive is different for male and female offenders. Because we won't concede aggression and anger in women, the language we use to describe what they do is much more limited, and much more exonerative." Criminals, she says, both male and female, often portray themselves as "putty in the hands of fate" or victims of "forces beyond their control," and violent women tend to rationalize their violence, with or without cause, on the grounds that they themselves have been victims of abuse and coercion.

For other related activities, SEE **#30: Crimes and Punishments, #31: Who's the Worst Offender?, #32: How Will We Be Judged?** and **#41: Trying Jekyll for the Crimes of Hyde.**

ACTIVITY #30
Crimes and Punishments (Making Judgments, Defining Consequences)

APPLICATIONS: Criminal justice, ethics, political science

CRITICAL THINKING SKILLS: Examining issues from conflicting viewpoints, evaluating alternative solutions, analyzing the process of making judgments

THE ACTIVITY

Begin by giving students a list of about ten acts that are defined as criminal by state or federal law. Next, ask students to do the following: (1) rank the offenses in order of seriousness according to their own judgments, not the existing legal penalties (2) specify the punishments (if any) they consider appropriate for these offenses, including any recommended alternative means of punishment (e.g. fine or imprisonment) (3) provide a written rationale for both the nature of the punishments and the differences in severity of punishment. Then, students share their responses in class, and the instructor guides a discussion on the purposes of punishment and the appropriateness of different types and degrees of punishment. The class might compare student responses to the actual punishments specified by law, or focus on the differences in the rationales provided by students in their responses. The discussion might also lead to a broader consideration of the principles followed in making legal and ethical judgments, or to an examination of more specific topics such as mandatory sentencing, uniform sentencing, judicial discretion in sentencing, and plea bargaining.

PURPOSES AND BENEFITS

"Does the punishment fit the crime?" is a fundamental question in any system of justice, and this activity is a way for students to take a methodical, analytical look at the purposes of punishment, alternative forms of punishment, and the distinctions made by judicial systems in judging different acts. Students must articulate their reasons for making distinctions and defend their rationales when confronted with other ways of making the same type of distinctions. The exercise may help students to see inconsistencies in their rationales, discrepancies between their views and those of others, and false or narrow assumptions about how judicial systems actually operate. When I use this activity in my Criminals in Literature course, I provide a brief history of both the types of punishment used in different cultures and conflicting ideas about the legitimate purposes of criminal punishments. Some students assume that punishment means imprisonment, and they are surprised to discover that the penitentiary—prison as we know it—is a relatively modern invention, less than 200 years old.

USES, ADAPTATIONS, AND RESOURCES

In *Critical Thinking*, Richard Paul presents a similar exercise, with emphasis on student examination of concepts of fairness. The activity could also be modified to focus less on criminal penalties and more on comparative ethical judgments of different acts, including acts that are morally questionable but not defined as criminal.

For an analysis of the relation of punishment to crime, a good starting point is Cesare Beccaria's *On Crimes and Punishments*, written in 1764, one of the earliest attempts to take a systematic look at the purpose of punishment and to establish a rationale for the proportionality of different punishments. Beccaria tries to answer the following questions: "Is the death penalty really *useful* and *necessary* for the security and good order of society? Are torture and torments *just*, and do they attain the *end* for which laws are instituted? What is the best way to prevent crimes? Are the same punishments equally effective for all times? What influence have they on customary behavior? These problems deserve to be analyzed with that geometric precision which the mist of sophisms, seductive eloquence, and timorous doubt cannot withstand."

Another excellent resource is *Wild Justice: The Evolution of Revenge*, in which author Susan Jacoby uses both historical sources (Voltaire, Machiavelli, Hannah Arendt) and literary sources (*Medea, Hamlet, The Godfather*) to examine the evolution of legal punishments and the concept of "proportional retribution," a punishment that fits the crime. Jacoby takes her title from Francis Bacon, who wrote in his essay "Of Revenge": "Revenge is a kind of wild justice, which the more man's nature runs to it, the more ought law to weed it out." She considers both the general question of the legitimacy of punishments and the more specific question of how public, state-ordained "justice" attempts to satisfy the private desire for vengeance. "Dismissing the legitimate aspects of the human need for retribution," she writes in her conclusion, "only makes us more vulnerable to the illegitimate, murderous, wild impulses that always lie beneath the surface of civilization—beneath, but never so deep that they can be safely ignored."

For related activities, SEE **#31: Who's the Worst Offender?** and **#32: How Will We Be Judged?**

ACTIVITY #31
Who's the Worst Offender? (Making Ethical Judgments)

APPLICATIONS: Ethics, psychology, health care professions, other disciplines

CRITICAL THINKING SKILLS: Examining issues from opposing viewpoints, evaluating alternative solutions, analyzing the process of making judgments

THE ACTIVITY

Begin by having students read this story, taken from Paul Zindel's novel *The Pigman*:

> There's a river with a bridge over it, and a WIFE and her HUSBAND live in a house on one side. The WIFE has a LOVER who lives on the other side of the river, and the only way to get from one side of the river to the other is to walk across the bridge or ask the BOAT-MAN to take you.
>
> One day the HUSBAND tells his WIFE that he has to be gone all night to handle some business in a faraway town. The WIFE pleads with him to take her with him because she knows if he doesn't she will be unfaithful to him. The HUSBAND absolutely refuses to take her because she will only be in the way of his important business.
>
> So the HUSBAND goes alone. When he is gone the WIFE goes over the bridge and stays with her LOVER. The night passes, and dawn is almost up when the WIFE leaves because she must get back to her own house before her husband gets home. She starts to cross the bridge but sees an ASSASSIN waiting for her on the other side, and she knows if she tries to cross, he will murder her. In terror, she runs up the side of the river and asks the BOATMAN to take her across the river,

but he wants 50 cents. She has no money, so he refuses to take her.

The WIFE runs back to the LOVER'S house and explains to him what her predicament is and asks him for 50 cents to pay the BOATMAN. The LOVER refuses, telling her it's her own fault for getting into the situation. As dawn comes up, the WIFE is nearly out of her mind and decides to dash across the bridge. When she comes face to face with the ASSASSIN, he takes out a large knife and stabs her until she is dead.

Next, ask students to write down the names of the five characters—wife, husband, lover, boatman, assassin—in order of their moral responsibility for the wife's death. Then, students share their responses and the rationales for their rankings, and the instructor guides a discussion of students' analysis of the ethical choices in this story, as well as the underlying values or ethical principles students have applied in making judgments about characters in the story.

PURPOSES AND BENEFITS

"The pragmatic dimension of critical thinking," John McPeck says in *Critical Thinking and Education*, "cannot be satisfied until one comes to grips with the value system involved in the judgment." This activity, like the previous one, applies critical thinking to the process of making ethical judgments. It's an exercise in values clarification; students must articulate, defend, and examine their ideas about moral responsibility for behavior. It's also a good example of what psychologists call the use of "discrepant events" to challenge students' assumptions, reasoning, or ethical beliefs. An instructor might use a series of such exercises as a way of determining patterns in making judgments and calling attention to underlying—and perhaps unexamined—standards that students apply in making judgments in different contexts.

USES, ADAPTATIONS, AND RESOURCES

This exercise was passed along to me by Anita Splendore, an English teacher at Driscoll School in Brookline, Massachusetts, who reports that her seventh-grade students tend to be surprisingly hard on both the boatman and wife and surprisingly forgiving of the assassin. Though the situation it presents is simplistic, the exercise can work well as a lesson in values clarification for college students, and it would be interesting to conduct an experiment to determine how students' rankings of responsibility might change as the students grow older. Similar exercises in making relative judgments—such as "triage" decisions— can be tailored to apply to ethical quandaries in specific disciplines such as business or the health professions. Peter Horn's *Clinical Ethics Casebook* and Ralph Baergen's *Ethics at the End of Life* both examine a range of ethical dilemmas in making treatment decisions in medicine.

Many bibliographical sources provide values clarification exercises asking students to make judgments about the behavior of characters in real or hypothetical situations. Several sources, for instance, raise the question: "Would it be ethical to kill a bully who is terrorizing a whole town?" Vincent Ruggiero, in *The Art of Thinking*, discusses common principles used as the basis for moral judgments, and he provides exercises on judging the morality of behavior in various situations—a boy who turns his mother into the authorities for drug use, parents who seek a court order to gain the right to sterilize their retarded daughter. In *Thinking Critically*, John Chaffee presents a framework for establishing the moral basis of actions and decisions, and he quotes an interesting commentary from James R. Kelly on Garrett Hardin's "lifeboat" ethic of survival (SEE **Activity #21**). "If we as a nation," Kelly writes, "allow people to starve while we could, through some sacrifice, make more food available to them, what hope can any person have for the future of international relations? If we cannot agree on this most basic of values—feed the hungry—what hopes for the future can we entertain?"

Diane Halpern, in *Critical Thinking Across the Curriculum*, discusses ethical concepts such as permission schema—if something is true, then you have permission to do something else—and obligation schema—if something is true, then you have an obligation to do something else. *Teaching Critical Thinking in the Arts and Humanities* includes an article by Angel Villarini on "Teaching Critical Thinking Through Moral Deliberation," while in *Teaching Critical Thinking in Psychology*, Hartley and Kasschau provide a collaborative exercise in which students in a group are given a story and required to achieve unanimous consensus in judging the morality of its characters. *de Bono's Thinking Course* contains a number of exercises aimed at examining the ethics of behavior in different situations—a woman accusing her employees of sex discrimination, a government official who wants to retract a piece of confidential information given to a reporter—from all possible points of view.

In a more thorough analysis of the process of forming moral principles, Lawrence Kohlberg's *The Philosophy of Moral Development: Moral Stages and the Idea of Justice* defines six stages that characterize the development of moral judgment from childhood to adulthood. In response to Kohlberg's theory—and to the fact that women "seem to exemplify the third stage of his six-stage sequence"—Carol Gilligan, in her *In a Different Voice: Psychological Theory and Women's Development*, discusses gender differences in the process of moral development and in the means of making decisions and ethical judgments. "Yet herein lies a paradox," Gilligan writes, "for the very traits that have traditionally defined the 'goodness' of women, their care for and sensitivity to the needs of others, are those that mark them as deficient in moral development" according to Kohlberg's theory. She distinguishes between a "morality of rights," based on an individual's belief in universal human rights, and a "morality of responsibility," based on obligations that arise from particular personal relationships.

For a related activity, SEE #32: **How Will We Be Judged?**

ACTIVITY #32
How Will We Be Judged? (Making Historical Judgments)

APPLICATIONS: History, ethics, literature, other disciplines

CRITICAL THINKING SKILLS: Examining issues from different perspectives, detecting false assumptions, making ethical judgments

THE ACTIVITY

Begin by asking students to imagine themselves as Americans living 100 years into the future, in 2104. Then ask them to look back and reflect on American society in the year 2004 and choose some aspect of that society—a widespread belief, a common practice, a law—that most Americans in their own society (in 2104) now view as clearly evil, abhorrent, immoral. Students share their responses in class and provide rationales for their choices. From there, the instructor guides a discussion of specific student choices and more general principles used as grounds for making ethical judgments, especially within a historical context. Students may present their responses orally or in writing.

PURPOSES AND BENEFITS

This activity is intended to get students to shift their perspectives on history, to reflect on the values of their society, and to engage their classmates in a critical discussion of the rationale for ethical judgments. The idea arose from many discussions in literature classes of past practices and beliefs, in America and elsewhere—slavery, witchcraft trials, the Holocaust—that Americans now view as clearly unjustifiable and evil. Students often find it hard to comprehend how these evil practices or beliefs could have been condoned or tolerated by so many people, and they like to think that, if they had lived back then, they would have been among the righteous exceptions. Some students also assume, explicitly or implicitly, that the moral progress of civilization is both natural and inevitable and that certain evils of the past could never be revisited. This activity is a way of challenging that assumption—not to persuade students that humans are inherently wicked or incorrigible, but to suggest that it is easy for any of us to be glib or self-righteous in passing judgment on historical evils that we have no opportunity to rectify. In some classes we have debated the idea of a society making amends for evils perpetrated in the past, such as reparations for the descendants of American slaves.

USES, ADAPTATIONS, AND RESOURCES

This activity could be used in any course in which students are discussing judgments of historical practices or events. I've used the assignment spontaneously, when class discussions of literature have led us to questions about the context of historical judgments—how to view, for instance, the anti-Semitism of a 16th century writer whose whole culture is anti-Semitic. In identifying current practices that future Americans will view as evil, students provide a wide range of responses—legal abortion, animal experimentation, the sexualization of childhood, failure to heed warnings about the disastrous effects of global warming—and the topics they choose may lead to heated debates when some students condemn practices or beliefs that others view as ethical and defensible. Some students exhibit a critical perspective by challenging the assumptions of the exercise, claiming that America in any recognizable form will not exist in 2104 or that, if it does, there's no reason to believe that Americans then will be more enlightened than we are now. We sometimes compare student choices to the past evils depicted in literature in trying to determine to what extent they are analogous.

In *Critical Thinking*, Richard Paul suggests asking students a similar question: What ideas of ours will future generations view as egocentric or irrational? He proposes assignments on the study of national bias, in which students critique articles about the responsibilities of nations for various events (e.g. genocide in Rwanda), determine which nations are blamed for which events on which grounds, and then consider how the judgments might change if the articles had been written from other points of view.

Facing History and Ourselves, a national educational initiative "aimed at stimulating young people and adults to think deeply about what constitutes civic participation in a democracy," offers one way "to promote critical thinking and moral behavior" through a curriculum model that links history to ethics. It sponsors interdisciplinary courses for high school and college students, providing study guides and guest speakers as classroom resources, connections with community groups, professional development through its Summer Institute, and an online campus. The philosophy of the initiative is based on "the belief that education in a democracy must be what Alexis de Tocqueville called 'an apprenticeship in liberty.' Facing History helps students find meaning in the past and recognize the need for participation and responsible decision making." The initiative's pedagogic approach is "shaped by cognitive and moral development theory and practice, which promotes understanding of different perspectives, competing truths, and the need to comprehend one's own motives and those of others." The basic assumption is that "students must be trusted to examine history in all its complexities, including its legacies of prejudice and discrimination, resilience and courage." Students explore topics such as the Holocaust, the Armenian genocide, and the American civil rights movement. Courses are designed to help students make connections "between history and the moral choices individuals confront in their own lives" and "reflect on their thinking in order to be aware of their own development." The initiative's web site (http://www.facinghistory.org) includes its statement of philosophy, a description of its classroom model, methods for evaluation, and resources for teachers.

In a related activity, one that focuses more on historical perspective and less on ethical judgments, I've used a journal assignment inspired by Virginia Woolf's novel *Orlando* about a character who lives for several centuries (switching genders halfway through his/her life span) and witnesses sweeping changes in his/her society. In keeping their journals, students imagine themselves as Orlando-like characters who remain living throughout the entire time period covered by a course— in World Literature II, from about 1700 to the present—while moving continuously from the culture and era of one assigned literary work to the culture and era of the next work. Students react to the assigned literature and comment on how it reflects changes in a given culture over time, changes from one culture to another, changes in literary tastes and subjects, or changes that focus on a certain theme—the rights of women, attitudes against people from other cultures. The assignment develops analytical skills while giving students a sense of cohesion in courses that cover many writers from different cultures and eras.

In the abstract "Creative Writing in the History Classroom," Dixon K. Durham, a history professor at Midlands Technical College in South Carolina, describes a history assignment that requires "each student to create a fictional family and then develop the memorabilia from which an American saga might be written about that family." The idea, Durham says, is for "each student to introduce a newcomer—European or African—into the American colonies and build a family story around that person's descendants through history to the present time." Students are introduced to research in original sources and must include several genuine historical documents in their projects. In addition, the abstract describes a "letterbook" (one-subject notebook) assignment in which students adopt historical personas and write letters to show how individuals (e.g. Pierre, who stormed the Bastille, writing to his pregnant wife) are affected by historical issues and events.

Durham also suggests ways in which letterbooks could be adapted for both mathematics and sociology courses.

ACTIVITY #33
In This Writer's Opinion (Presenting Opinions Persuasively)

APPLICATIONS: Composition, journalism, political science, other disciplines

CRITICAL THINKING SKILLS: Getting relevant information, distinguishing fact from opinion, detecting slanting and bias, using evidence, examining issues from conflicting viewpoints, evaluating alternative solutions, analyzing the process of forming opinions

THE ACTIVITY

In this activity students write editorials or letters to the editor, to be submitted to college or community newspapers or to be displayed on public bulletin boards. Students choose their own controversial issues, conduct research to get relevant facts and a range of opinions and perspectives, and discuss the issues with classmates and their instructor. They then write and revise their editorials or letters, using persuasive reasoning and effective evidence while anticipating criticisms of their opinions. Students may work individually or collaborate in small groups, and they may focus on issues in their colleges, their communities, or the world at large.

PURPOSES AND BENEFITS

In *Critical Thinking and* Education, John McPeck writes: "One must have a justification for one's belief in order to distinguish knowledge from mere opinion." This assignment brings together a number of critical thinking skills that students must demonstrate: getting relevant and reliable information, detecting slanting in the information, examining issues from multiple viewpoints, evaluating alternative solutions to problems, and using reasoning and evidence to make a

---

persuasive case for a point of view. Dialogue with classmates and the instructor helps students to examine the processes they use in forming opinions, and, if their editorials or letters are in fact published, they get the satisfaction of seeing their work in print, while becoming part of a college or community dialogue on the issue at hand.

USES, ADAPTATIONS, AND RESOURCES

Randy Accetta, a writing instructor at Pima Community College in Arizona, describes one version of this assignment in his abstract "The 'We Think' Project." Accetta prepares his students by asking them to freewrite in response to brief editorials and to "address things that anger them—the school, the town, or the world." Students then write three editorials and choose one for a meticulous revision; this one is printed anonymously, attached to poster board, and hung in a public space for two weeks. A guest-lecturing journalism instructor gives his students an overview of the basic purposes and format of editorials, and students work in small groups as they revise their editorials and respond to one another's work. Each student also "creates a press release and fact sheet to submit to the local media," and local newspapers, television, and radio all report on the project.

This activity can be tailored to issues in particular fields: health care, business, gerontology, human services, criminal justice, and so on. I've used similar assignments in both composition and literature courses, sometimes framing them as "muckraking" or "whistleblowing" assignments to connect them to assigned readings such as Henrik Ibsen's depiction of an environmental whistleblower in the play *An Enemy of the People*. In some cases, students research current controversial issues, or pending legislation, and then write letters to legislators or other public officials. I often suggest that students structure their thinking by approaching issues through a problem-solution format (SEE **Activity #35**). We also discuss the necessity of anticipating and addressing potential objections to their opinions. I use examples to illustrate counterarguing strategies such as refuting opposing arguments (both how and when to do so), accommodating objections by establishing common ground with opponents, and conceding points without undermining one's thesis. One technique I demonstrate is explained in John Bean's *Engaging Ideas*—how to qualify a thesis by adding an "although" clause to incorporate a legitimate objection or limitation to the main idea. Bean also discusses how to use thesis-support assignments in different disciplines. He suggests this assignment for a physics course on electricity and magnetism: "An electric dipole is placed above an infinitely conducting plane. The dipole does/does not feel a net force or a torque. Explain." And for a nursing or medical ethics course, he suggests this topic: "People suffering from schizophrenia or manic-depressive disorder should/should not be forced to take their medication."

In *Arguing in Communities*, Gary Hatch presents a framework for viewing editorials or other opinion essays as part of an ongoing "conversation" within a community, academic or otherwise. He examines the organization of communities (including "electronic communities"), the principles of discourse within different communities, and the "sites" at which conversations may take place. He also uses readings to illustrate distinctions between types of appeals (logos, ethos, pathos), types of claims, and types of evidence. Hatch includes a collection of letters to the "Readers' Forum" of Utah's *Deseret News* in response to the governor's proposal to significantly expand the amount of land in Utah to be designated as wilderness.

Dorothy Seyler's *Read, Reason, and Write* presents a method for shaping arguments developed by British philosopher Stephen Toulmin. An argument, Seyler says, "consists of evidence or reasons presented in support of an assertion or claim that is either stated or implied." The Toulmin method, modeled on the types of claims people make in lawsuits, breaks down arguments into (1) claims (2) supporting evidence, and (3) "warrants," defined as "the principles or assumptions that allow us to assert that our evidence or reasons—what Toulmin calls the *grounds*—do indeed support our assertion." Annette Rottenberg's *Elements of Argument*, another text designed for a course on argumentation, is also based on the Toulmin method, starting with Toulmin's three key questions for writers: "(1) What are you trying to prove? (2) What have you got to go on? (3) How did you get from evidence to claims?" This method, she says, "assists students in defending their claims as directly and efficiently as possible" and "reflects the way people actually go about organizing and developing claims outside the classroom." Rottenberg describes this approach as "audience-centered" because actual arguments are intended "to win the adherence of their audience." She provides examples from speeches, editorial opinions, and letters to the editor—some chosen to illustrate effective argumentation, some selected because they are "obviously flawed." In contrast to some texts on argumentation, Rottenberg also treats "motivational appeals"—directed to "the needs and values of an audience, designed to evoke emotional response"— as a legitimate argumentative strategy.

Writer's Guide: Political Science provides guidelines, with examples, on writing letters to editors and public officials and on briefing court decisions. Kathleen Bell's *Developing Arguments*, like Hatch's book, distinguishes between both types of appeals and types of argumentative structures. She also discusses how to "control" the use of language to establish clarity, promote a sense of fairness, and motivate readers to take action. In *Thinking for Yourself*, Marlys Mayfield focuses on the importance of detecting hidden assumptions in evaluating and expressing opinions. She includes writing assignments on "articulating hidden assumptions behind arguments" and "solving a problem by uncovering assumptions." Another assignment, which includes a structured peer review, involves writing a "letter of complaint."

For related activities, SEE **#34: The Devil's Advocate, #35: It's Debatable, #36: What Are the Alternatives?** and **#39: If I Had My Way.**

ACTIVITY #34
The Devil's Advocate (Analyzing Arguments, Responding to Criticism)

APPLICATIONS: Composition, speech, mathematics, education, other disciplines

CRITICAL THINKING SKILLS: Examining issues from opposing viewpoints, evaluating alternative solutions or theories, using evidence to support a thesis

THE ACTIVITY

The term "devil's advocate" originally referred to an official in the Roman Catholic Church who was appointed to present arguments against a proposed canonization or beatification. It now refers to anyone who takes the position of opposing a thesis or proposal in order to test its validity. In this collaborative activity, students who are writing argumentative essays work in groups of four or five. One student (the presenter) begins by briefly summing up the controversial aspects of his/her subject and explaining his/her position on the subject. Then, one by one, the other students in the group each put forth, as persuasively as possible, at least one argument against that position, and the presenter briefly responds to these arguments. Once the first presenter is finished, another student takes on the role of presenter, while the other students continue to play their roles as devil's advocates. Students are required to stay within their roles. Regardless of their personal opinions, they can't agree with the presenters. I allot ten or fifteen minutes for each student in each group to be the presenter.

PURPOSES AND BENEFITS

Critical thinking involves an ongoing dialectic, a running debate between our opinions and conflicting viewpoints, or, in some cases, an internal debate that helps to resolve our own ambivalence on a particular issue. The ability to respond persuasively to opposing viewpoints is especially important in arguing a position or defending a course of action in a problematic situation. This activity has two primary purposes: (1) to make each presenter aware of arguments against the presenter's position (2) to give each presenter a trial run in articulating responses to these arguments. The activity also makes students more aware of the need to view any controversial subject from conflicting viewpoints and to consider alternative solutions to problems. Ultimately, and perhaps most importantly, exercises like this can help students to become their own devil's advocates. In *Time Travels and Papa Joe's Pipe*, Alan Lightman paraphrases a commencement address by Nobel Prize winning physicist Richard Feynman: "When we do scientific research, when we publish our results, we should try to think of every possible way we could be wrong."

USES, ADAPTATIONS, AND RESOURCES

Howard Gardner, in *The Unschooled Mind*, describes exercises like this as a form of "reciprocal education" in which students collaborate while focusing on a text or issue and play such roles as summarizer, clarifier, arguer, and skeptic. As an example he cites Japanese students who learn math through a structured group "conversation." I use this exercise in Composition I shortly after students have chosen their topics and tentative thesis statements for a major research-argument essay. I conjoin the exercise with a written paraphrasing exercise: to provide a thoughtful response to an opinion, one must be able to paraphrase the opinion accurately. This and similar "yes, but" activities can be used in any course with an assignment that requires students to argue positions, present

---

solutions, or propose strategies to arrive at decisions. Possible subjects range from a campaign strategy in a marketing class to a care plan in an allied health class to a proposed solution of an air pollution problem in an environmental science class. Students playing devil's advocate may have trouble carrying out their roles effectively. They may struggle to think of opposing arguments, dislike arguing positions they don't believe in and insist on agreeing with presenters, or abandon the structure of the exercise and fall into freewheeling debates about the subjects at hand or even unrelated subjects. To keep the class focused, I assign one student in each group the role of monitor; it's the monitor's job to make sure that other students stay within their roles and within the allotted time for each presenter. When it's time for the monitor to present, another student takes on the role of monitor.

In another collaborative activity, mathematics professor Theodore Panitz in *Learning Together* describes a "write and swap" exercise to engage paired students in a critical thinking exchange: "One mechanism involves having students choose a sentence or phrase written in a text passage or presented by the teacher, writing their interpretation or opinion of the material and then asking their partner to comment, also in writing. After each person has completed both the written and comment sections of the worksheet, a discussion follows to clarify each other's ideas and reactions to the comments." In *Engaging Ideas*, John Bean suggests questions teachers can use to structure similar "paired interview" exercises, and he outlines classroom procedures for both "response-centered reviews" and "advice-centered reviews" in which students react to drafts of one another's argumentative essays in order to pinpoint ideas in need of clarification, raise potential counterarguments, and focus on problems in the use of reasoning or evidence to support argumentative points

Many instructors also use collaborative "think aloud" activities in class to reveal why students are confused or stuck in their attempts to grasp concepts or solve problems. In the abstract "Talk-Alouds: Windows on the Mind," educational psychologists Laura Hume and Claire Weinstein from the University of Texas describe one variety of this exercise: "For example, during a class discussion in algebra, the instructor could ask a student to solve a problem and instruct a student to say aloud everything she thinks as she attempts to solve the problem. This gives the instructor, as well as the students, a good idea of the processes that the student is going through to arrive at the product. It is an effective and efficient way of catching misconceptions which may be common to the class and correcting those mistakes immediately instead of waiting until after the test." Hume and Weinstein acknowledge that this approach does have limitations; it "may not work with students who have poor verbal skills," and in some cases "it may be difficult, if not impossible, to articulate the thought processes that are being used." However, they believe that talk-alouds can be helpful both in diagnosing student problems and in giving instructors opportunities to model their own means of thinking through problems and arriving at solutions. They suggest the following guidelines for carrying out this activity:

- Keep the students talking.
- Encourage students to say *what* they are thinking and not to stop and analyze *why* they are thinking it.
- Expect false starts and blind alleys.
- Try to diagnose strengths and weaknesses.

Lochhead and Whimbey's "Teaching Analytical Reasoning Through Thinking Aloud," reprinted in Stice's *Developing Critical Thinking and Problem Solving Abilities*, also describes "think aloud" exercises designed to detect inaccuracies in reading, weaknesses in problem solving, and lack of perseverance. Among other sources, Annette Rottenberg's *Elements of Argument*, Kathleen Bell's *Developing Arguments* and Marlys Mayfield's *Thinking for*

Yourself provide more formal and structured approaches for evaluating written arguments.

Richard Murphy, a former coordinator of the Writing Across the Curriculum initiative at Bradford College, offers another approach to collaboration through a handout on "Kinds of Listening and Response," developed by Peter Elbow, Robert Whitney, and the faculty of the Bard College Institute for Writing and Thinking, to be used as guidelines for writers' groups. Categories include:

- *Active Listening or "Sayback"*: The listener says in own words what he or she hears the writer saying The response is usually stated as a kind of question: "I hear your paper saying . . ." or "So, are you saying that . . ." The purpose of sayback is to try to get the writer to say more about the piece; it's an invitation for the writer to explore. The object is not for the listener to "get it right," but to help the writer *discover* his or her ideas.
- *Lurkings*. What do listeners *almost* hear? What's circling around the edges? Where does the piece want to go? What do listeners want to hear more about? These are probative, exploratory kinds of questions. They help the writer push the piece of writing, uncover possibilities. Again, listeners are *inviting* new thinking and discovery.
- *Skeleton-finding*. Listeners identify other ideas they hear, implicit or explicit supporting points. Skeleton-finding is useful with both an early draft and a more finished piece. With a rough draft, listeners can help the writer find a possible outline; with a more finished piece, listeners can make a descriptive outline, writing a sentence for each paragraph, thus helping the writer see (and re-see) the existing structure.
- *Movies of the Reader's Mind*. What did you feel, think, or experience as you read or listened to the piece of writing, and at what points in the text did you feel them? This response reflects the listener's *experience* of the piece, his or her subjective reactions. It lets the writer know the effect of his or her

words on a listener, moment by moment, as the listener experienced them.

Collaborative activities like these can help writers to refine their thinking, flesh out undeveloped ideas, identify points in need of clarification, or detect problems with tone or organization. Another approach Murphy uses—devil's advocacy stood on its head—requires the listener to apply the "principle of charity": "Suspend any disbelief in the argument and become its avid supporter. Allow all the assumptions made, even if repellent to you, and charitably assist the author in developing the best possible argument that can be made. Add data, examples, reasons that might support this argument, entering wholly and enthusiastically into its spirit."

SEE the following page for the paraphrasing exercise I use; all selections have been taken from Penguin's *Fifty Great Essays*. For related activities, SEE **#35: It's Debatable** and **#36: What Are the Alternatives?**

COURSE: Composition I

INSTRUCTOR: John Nelson

SUBJECT: Exercise on Paraphrasing

DIRECTIONS: To "paraphrase" means to express somebody else's idea in your own words. On a separate sheet, write an accurate paraphrase of each of the following five quotations. Each paraphrase should be as concise as possible, without omitting essential details. Write in complete sentences.

"Prudence, indeed, will dictate that Governments long established should not be changed for light and transient causes; and accordingly all experience hath shewn that mankind are more disposed to suffer, while evils are sufferable, than to right themselves by abolishing the forms to which they are accustomed. But when a long train of abuses and usurpations, pursuing invariably the same Object evinces a design to reduce them under absolute Despotism, it is their right, it is their duty, to throw off such Government, and to provide new Guards for their future security." (Thomas Jefferson and others, "The Declaration of Independence")

"What, then, is the basic distinction? The masculine principle is better understood as a driving ethos of superiority designed to inspire straightforward, confident success, while the feminine principle is composed of vulnerability, the need for protection, the formalities of compliance and the avoidance of conflict—in short, an appeal of dependence and good will that gives the masculine principle its romantic validity and its admiring applause." (Susan Brownmiller, "Femininity")

"I don't think I can learn from a wild animal how to live in particular—shall I suck warm blood, hold my tail high, walk with my footprints precisely over the prints of my hands?—but I might learn something of mindlessness, something of the purity of living in the physical senses and the dignity of living without bias or motive. The weasel lives in necessity, and we live in choice, hating necessity and dying at the last ignobly in its talons. I would like to live as I should, as the weasel lives as he should." (Annie Dillard, "Living Like Weasels")

"I believe in aristocracy, though—if that is the right word, and if a democrat may use it. Not an aristocracy of power, based upon rank and influence, but an aristocracy of the sensitive, the considerate, and the plucky. Its members are to be found in all nations and classes, and all through the ages, and there is a secret understanding between them when they meet. They represent the true human condition, the one permanent victory of our queer race over cruelty and chaos." (E. M. Forster, "What I Believe")

"As a boy, I saw countless tough guys locked away; I have buried several, too. They were babies, really—a teenage cousin, a brother of twenty-two, a childhood friend in his mid-twenties—all gone down in episodes of bravado played out in the streets. I came to doubt the virtues of intimidation early on. I chose, perhaps unconsciously, to remain a shadow—timid, but a survivor." (Brent Staples, "Just Walk on By: Black Men and Public Space.")

ACTIVITY #35
It's Debatable (Debating Issues, Refuting Arguments)

APPLICATIONS: Speech, reading and writing courses, business, other disciplines

CRITICAL THINKING SKILLS: Getting relevant information, detecting slanting and false assumptions, using evidence, examining issues from opposing viewpoints, evaluating alternative solutions, analyzing the process of forming opinions

THE ACTIVITY

Students in this activity prepare for and then carry out a class debate on some controversial topic. Students generally choose a topic from a list of possibilities provided by the instructor. They work in teams, dividing up responsibilities and taking on specific roles within the team. One student, for instance, may make the opening statement in the debate, while another is primarily responsible for refuting several opposing arguments. They conduct research on the topic, practice presenting arguments and anticipating their responses to opposing arguments, and then carry out the debate in a format structured by the instructor and/or the debating teams.

PURPOSES AND BENEFITS

This activity, like the two previous ones, brings together a number of critical thinking skills: getting relevant and reliable information, detecting false assumptions and the slanting of information, examining issues from conflicting viewpoints, evaluating alternative solutions to problems, and marshalling evidence to support a point of view persuasively. Students gain experience in collaborating effectively in groups—through, for example, devil's advocate exercises (SEE #34)—and, as with role-playing activities (SEE **#41** and **#42**), the debate format challenges them by testing their abilities to think on their feet. The activity encourages foresight by requiring students to anticipate objections to their positions, and, as they go through the stages of preparation, they gain experience in analyzing the process of forming opinions.

USES, ADAPTATIONS, AND RESOURCES

Ralph Tufo and Sherry Rogers, my colleagues in the Linked Learning program at North Shore Community College, use one form of this activity in their developmental reading and writing classes, in which the debate is integrated with reading and writing assignments. Students vote on topics from a list provided to them. To structure their preparation, they're given worksheets for listing premises and supporting evidence, anticipating and rebutting opposing arguments, and summing up their arguments in "clinchers" or closing statements. The instructors tutor and advise students as they conduct research and prepare for "the great debate," and they've devised a scoring sheet with criteria used by classmates in evaluating the performance of the debate teams. While debates can work well in many contexts, especially speech courses, the approach used by Tufo and Rogers has been particularly effective in building the self-confidence of students in developmental classes.

The evaluation of any collaborative activity, including a debate, presents some special difficulties, especially if the activity is a long-term project that culminates in an oral presentation. Some students may be industrious in preparation and helpful in assisting teammates to prepare, but then freeze up during the debate itself. Others may perform well during the debate but attend irregularly and contribute little to group preparation. And some students may exhibit strong debating skills on a team that is lax in preparation and performs poorly as a whole. When my students engage in debates or other major collaborative projects, I use a scoring sheet with criteria, similar to that designed by professors Tufo and Rogers, but I

---

also use a class participation grade (which generally counts for 15% to 25% of the overall course grade) to allow for evaluation of effort in preparation and for individual demonstration of skills (e.g. the ability to rebut an opposing argument) during both the preparation process and the presentation itself. With any collaborative assignment that involves structured preparation, it's essential, I think, for instructors to meet regularly with teams, as professors Tufo and Rogers do, not only to advise but also to assess contributions to the preparation process.

A discipline-specific version of a debate is described in "Issues for Debate: Increasing Student Participation" by Felipe H. Chia, Coordinator of the Business Management Program at Harrisburg Area Community College in Pennsylvania. Chia uses debates in business management and marketing classes, with topics including the following: "(1) Does a retail store have the right to install TV cameras and special mirrors in dressing rooms in order to control shoplifting? (2) Is it O.K. for an American sales manager working abroad to offer a bribe to a foreign purchasing agent in order to obtain an order, when working in a country where bribes are customarily given? (3) Should an employer have the right to intervene in 'office romances'?" Students carry out research and conduct interviews, prepare for the debate by developing strategies and practicing their presentation of arguments, and incorporate "concepts and principles of the class lectures into the discussion of the issues."

In *Engaging Ideas*, John Bean gives examples of argumentative topics used by finance professor Dean Drenk: "(1) The market is/is not efficient in strong-form, random-walk terms. (2) Bonds are/are not more risky investments than stocks. (3) Random diversification is/is not more reliable than selective diversification." Though Professor Drenk uses these topics for essay assignments in which students learn to practice "the methods of inquiry, research, and argumentation of finance," the topics could be used to frame student debates.

Bean also outlines a step-by-step method of structuring debates, for use in any discipline.

Many speech and composition textbooks, as well as books devoted to the study of argument and persuasion, contain sections on the fundamentals of argumentation with readings on controversial issues. Vincent Ruggiero's *The Art of Thinking* suggests strategies for evaluating arguments and building a persuasive case, with a brief appendix on class presentations and group discussions. Kathleen Bell's *Developing Arguments* offers a section on debates—with such topics as affirmative action, drug testing in college sports, and women in the military—along with argumentative essays on AIDS, discrimination, law and ethics, and the Vietnam War. Dorothy Seyler's *Read, Reason, Write* includes a series of debates—relating to laws, rights, and responsibilities—on topics ranging from immigration to global warming. Gary Hatch's *Arguing in Communities,* Stuart Hirschberg's *Strategies of Argument,* Sally DeWitt Spurgin's *The Power to Persuade,* and Daniel McDonald's *The Language of Argument* all discuss strategies of argumentation and provide a variety of argumentative essays to be used for analysis or to generate debate topics.

SEE #36: **What Are the Alternatives** for a related activity.

ACTIVITY #36
What Are the Alternatives? (Solving Problems, Comparing Solutions)

APPLICATIONS: Composition, government, psychology, environmental science, human services (drug and alcohol rehabilitation), college success seminars, other disciplines

CRITICAL THINKING SKILLS: Getting relevant and reliable information, detecting slanting and false assumptions, testing hypotheses, using evidence, evaluating alternative solutions, foreseeing the consequences of decisions

THE ACTIVITY

In this problem-solving activity students go through the following steps: (1) define a problem (2) examine its causes and effects (3) compare and evaluate alternative solutions to the problem (4) recommend and make a case for one or more proposed solutions (5) suggest ways to implement the solution(s), and (6) if possible, evaluate the effectiveness of implementing the solution(s). This activity comes in many varieties. The instructor may assign problems, or students may choose and define problems of their own. Students may work alone or collaborate in groups. They may present their results in essays, in formal research papers, or in class presentations. The activity can be used as a major assignment in itself or incorporated into broader assignments (SEE **#33**, **#35**, and **#40**). Problems may range from students' personal problems (how to balance school, work, and family responsibilities) to problems within their colleges (how to increase student participation in college governance) to community problems (how to develop a budget that satisfies conflicting interests) to social issues (how to treat or prevent alcoholism) to national or global issues (how to reduce consumption of natural resources).

PURPOSES AND BENEFITS

"Problem solving," Dave Seymour says in his foreword to *Problem Solving Strategies*, "is not simply about figuring out a solution when things go wrong, although it certainly is useful in those situations. Problem solving is also a means of finding ways to improve systems and to better serve people. In this way problem solving is not only *reactive* but also *proactive*."

The ability to formulate and solve problems goes to the heart of critical thinking, and this activity tests most of the essential critical thinking skills defined in the introduction. In particular, problem-solving assignments help students to understand the importance of how issues are framed or defined, as well as the value of questioning assumptions and looking at problems from various angles—or as, John McPeck says, "seeing where a certain common procedure is fruitless by entertaining alternatives to it." Students must use reasoning and evidence both to justify proposed solutions and to evaluate the implementation of solutions. Evaluation of solutions is especially important, since, as McPeck points out in *Critical Thinking and Education*, the whole idea of problem solving is senseless without the question, "Did the solution work?" And, as Seymour notes, before a solution can even be tried, it must first be persuasively presented: "Your being able to provide a clear explanation of your solution and communicate it effectively to others is often what determines whether or not your solution will be implemented." The assignment also affords students an opportunity to use their creativity in solving problems. One good illustration of creative problem-solving is King Hammurabi's realization that, instead of asking how to bring his people to water, he needed to ask how to bring water to his people—a thought that led to the invention of canals, a major step in the development of civilizations.

USES, ADAPTATIONS, AND RESOURCES

One problem-solving approach is explained in the abstract "PBL in the English Classroom" by Larry Armstrong, an English instructor at Itawamba Community College in Mississippi. Armstrong uses a problem-based learning (PBL) method developed in the natural sciences. Students work in groups, playing designated roles such as reporter, scribe, and challenger. The challenger, for example, "plays the role of spoiler by questioning the majority opinion and exposing fallacies in logic wherever they exist." The problems Armstrong uses are "open-ended, requiring groups to shape their own research strategies. There are no right answers, and I am careful not to lead students by revealing my own biases or answering crucial questions for them." One of his classes proposed solutions in response to this scenario: "The president has asked that each state pose solutions to the problem of school violence, and the governor of Mississippi has asked every community college to offer suggestions. Each PBL group must carefully study the problem and submit solutions to the dean of instruction at Itawamba Community College."

In another assignment, presented in Diane Halpern's *Critical Thinking Across the Curriculum*, students compare and choose between two heroin treatment programs, one run by former heroin addicts and the other run by therapists who have studied the psychology and biology of heroin addiction. In another assignment, on reduction of crime, she illustrates how to match goals with feasible solutions. Halpern provides a generalized outline of basic solution steps, a matrix for solving problems, and a list of "strategies for selecting strategies." She also quotes biologist Linus Pauling on the importance of generating multiple solutions: "The best way to have good ideas is to have a lot of ideas." In "The Fishing Trip" exercise, included in Alverno College's *Teaching Critical Thinking in Psychology*, students are given a scenario about four friends stranded on an island; the students must define the problem and achieve consensus in ranking 14 objects in order of importance for the group's survival. *Writer's Guide: Political Science* includes a chapter on more formal problem solving through policy analysis. Students must identify alternative solutions to a problem, relate the alternatives to policy objectives, and then choose the alternative that comes closest to achieving the objectives.

Other bibliographical sources include steps, guidelines, and suggestions for effective problem solving. *de Bono's Thinking Course*, for instance, discusses how to generate alternatives and how to judge alternatives according to their closeness to an ideal solution. de Bono is perhaps best known for his concept of "lateral thinking," which might be characterized as a temporary suspension of critical thinking, or as a means of generating ideas and potential solutions without concern for judgment or logic. "The essence of lateral thinking," writes McPeck in his critique of de Bono's work, "is to avoid looking at familiar patterns and to connect features of ideas or objects that are not normally associated. As de Bono says, 'We want to move *across* tracks sometimes, not along them'; hence, the term 'lateral thinking.'" In *New Think*, de Bono illustrates lateral thinking through the tale of a girl who must save her father from prison while saving herself from marriage to a nasty moneylender (the tale is also reprinted in Marlys Mayfield's *Thinking for Yourself*). McPeck cites a famous quotation from Louis Pasteur—"Chance favors the prepared mind"—in arguing that lateral thinking may have little value unless one is "thoroughly immersed in the knowledge and data of one's field."

Vincent Ruggiero's *The Art of Thinking* provides frameworks for detecting assumptions that interfere with critical analysis of problems, for asking relevant questions about how to implement solutions, and for anticipating negative reactions to solutions. And Barry Commoner's essay "The Ecological Crisis" (in *The Example of Science)* analyzes why a particular solution—in this case a solution to a sewage disposal problem—failed. Sources that present a more in-depth view of problem solving and conflict resolution include Branford and Stein's *The Ideal Problem Solver,* Flower's *Problem-Solving Strategies for Writing,* Polya's *How to Solve It,* Rubinstein's *Patterns of Problem Solving,* Whimbey and Lochhead's *Problem Solving and Comprehension,* and Wicklegren's *How to Solve Problems.*

For related activities, SEE **#39: If I Had My Way** and **#40: Making the Case.**

Section Four

Projects, Experiments, Adventures

ACTIVITY #37
Does a Dog Know Its Name? (Testing Hypotheses)

APPLICATIONS: Sciences, social sciences, composition, other disciplines

CRITICAL THINKING SKILLS: Getting relevant information to solve a problem, making well-founded inferences, testing hypotheses to answer questions, using evidence to support a thesis, evaluating alternative solutions to problems

THE ACTIVITY

The title of this activity was inspired by a Gary Larson cartoon that presents human speech from a dog's point of view: "Blah, blah, blah, Fido, blah, blah, Fido, blah, blah." (A similar cartoon depicts a cat's point of view: "Blah, blah, blah, blah, blah.") Here, each student formulates a hypothesis to answer a problematic question. The student must then determine, carry out, and evaluate some sort of procedure used to test the validity of the hypothesis. When I use the activity as a writing assignment in Composition I, each student composition—and the process used in testing the hypothesis—must include the following five steps: (1) Ask a question, and explain why this question is worth answering—why the question is significant. (2) State a hypothesis—a possible answer to the question—and explain the reasons why you think this is likely to be the best answer. (3) Determine a procedure to test the hypothesis (e.g. an experiment, a poll, a questionnaire), and explain why you are using this procedure. (4) Carry out the procedure and summarize the results. Explain why the hypothesis has been proven valid or invalid by the test OR why the results of the test are inconclusive. (5) Discuss possible flaws or limitations in the procedure used to test the hypothesis—that is, any factors that might make the results questionable or invalid in proving or disproving the hypothesis.

PURPOSES AND BENEFITS

The essence of science, says Howard Gardner in *Frames of Mind*, is the positing of a hypothesis, the stipulation of conditions under which a hypothesis can be rejected, and a willingness to abandon one hypothesis and consider a new one if the original hypothesis is disconfirmed. The purpose of this activity is to introduce students to some basic principles of scientific reasoning as well as the critical thinking skills and processes used by scientists and social scientists to answer problematic questions—that is, questions with no clear-cut right or wrong answers. The activity appeals to the curiosity of students, engages them in active learning, and encourages them to be both creative and methodical in trying to solve problems. They must consider alternative answers to the questions at hand and think about what would constitute valid and sufficient evidence to support answers to the questions. They learn to evaluate procedures that they themselves have designed and to reflect on the processes by which knowledge is obtained. Often the activity is most beneficial when the tests "fail"—that is, when students come up with surprising results and their hypotheses are proven invalid.

USES, ADAPTATIONS, AND RELATED ACTIVITIES

When I use this activity I provide students with a list of about twenty sample questions to answer, such as: Does a dog know its name? Who interrupts more often in conversation, men or women? How would a friend or family member respond to persistent, unexpected compliments? You hear a rumor that a friend of yours is telling nasty lies about you—how can you tell whether or not this rumor is true? Instructors in other disciplines could choose questions relevant to those disciplines. Students in my course spend one class period collaborating in small groups, with each group taking one question from the list and going through the five-step process (except step #4). In one class, a group considering the interruption question above decided to conduct an impromptu experiment in which, as surreptitiously as possible, they observed another group and recorded the number of interruptions. They discovered, among other things, that it is not so easy to determine what constitutes an interruption; each group member came up with different figures for both the total number of interruptions and the percentage by gender. For the composition assignment, students may take questions from the list I provide or come up with questions of their own. They may collaborate in trying to answer one question, but each must write an individual composition using the five-step process.

This is a challenging assignment for many first-semester freshmen, and students may struggle with various aspects of it: understanding the basic notion of a hypothesis, wording their questions precisely, detecting their own biases in formulating answers to the questions, coming up with legitimate procedures to test hypotheses, and seeing the flaws or limitations in the procedures they use. A common limitation of procedures is that few students are in a position to get data from a large, statistically valid sample. Nonetheless, most students rise to the challenge and take a personal stake in the assignment. They're anxious to discover the results of searches for information that they themselves have devised. One student, for instance, hypothesized about the reactions she would get if she told friends and family members that she was planning to join the military. The reactions she got (family members were supportive; friends, discouraging) surprised her and changed her perceptions of those close to her. Several students developed questionnaires to answer the following question, posed in a Milan Kundera story: "A group of men are given a choice of two possibilities: (a) you can spend a night making love to a beautiful, famous model of your choice, on the condition that nobody must know about it (b) you can walk past all your friends with your arm wrapped intimately around the model's waist, on the condition that you never make love to her. Which option would most men choose?" One student found that most of her male respondents chose "(c) neither"—a result that led her to question the candor of her respondents and to consider whether the gender of the questioner (her) might have influenced responses. Another student wrote two questionnaires, one for males and one for females, and distributed them to respondents, to be answered anonymously, in the club where she worked as a bartender. Yet another student developed a questionnaire posing this question: "Which option would you prefer: (a) to have your parents walk in on you while you were engaged in a sexual act with your partner (b) to walk in on your parents while they were engaged in a sexual act?" The responses she got (e.g. "gross") suggest that certain young people are disturbed, if not downright horrified, by the notion that middle-aged persons—even virile ones such as myself—continue to seek erotic pleasure despite having one foot in the grave.

This activity could be modified for use in almost any discipline, and many sources include guidelines for testing hypotheses or evaluating tests of hypotheses. Physicist Alan Lightman, in *Time Travels and Papa Joe's Pipe*, examines the methods used by the ancient Greeks to answer the question, "Is the earth round or flat?" Diane Halpern's *Critical Thinking Across the Curriculum* provides a chart of "hypothesis-testing skills" and an explanation of such common errors as the bias to seek confirmatory evidence. In *Thinking Critically*, John Chaffee presents exercises that require students to evaluate the use of experimental results to support a proposed theory or hypothesis. John McPeck's *Critical Thinking in Education* and Thomas Gilovich's *How We Know What*

Isn't So both discuss the scientific distinction between "the context of discovery" (generating ideas) and "the context of justification" (testing ideas by determining the acceptability of proof). Gilovich also quotes Robert Pirsig in considering the role of the social sciences in challenging dubious beliefs: "The real purpose of the scientific method is to make sure Nature hasn't misled you into thinking you know something you actually don't know." Both *Writer's Guide: Life Sciences* and *Writer's Guide: Political Science* contain chapters on conducting experiments in order to write more formal, in-depth research reports, and many textbooks include examples of testing hypotheses to illustrate the methods of science. For example, in *Biology*, an introductory college text, Sylvia Mader explains the use of mitochondrial DNA analysis to test the hypothesis that "the first Americans came from Siberia in more than one wave of migration." And, as its title suggests, Royston Roberts' *Serendipity: Accidental Discoveries in Science* illustrates how the testing of hypothesis may lead to unexpected and enlightening results.

To return to the title of this module, I would say that my golden retriever, Emmylou, bright as she is, responds only to the commanding tones of her master, not to any specific terms of address. The renowned animal expert Konrad Lorenz would disagree. In *Man Meets Dog*, he writes, "It sometimes seems to me that the word recognition of a clever dog which is firmly attached to its master extends even to whole sentences." As an example he cites his pet schnauzer, Affi: "She knew the names of at least nine people, and would run across the room to them if their names were spoken. She never made a mistake." Lorenz also discusses the difficulties involved in getting dogs to achieve "high feats of word recognition" in a laboratory setting. I'm not fully persuaded by his arguments, but it's because of disagreements like this that scientists try to test hypotheses. Dorothy Seyler's *Read, Reason, Write* includes an essay that poses another canine question: "What paw does your dog shake hands with?" "And why that paw?"

ACTIVITY #38
Anthropology Comes Home (Interpreting Cultural Rituals)

APPLICATIONS: Anthropology, gerontology, marketing, psychology, other social sciences

CRITICAL THINKING SKILLS: Getting relevant information, distinguishing fact from opinion, analyzing the use of symbols and metaphorical language, making inferences, testing hypotheses, evaluating alternative theories to explain phenomenon

THE ACTIVITY

The idea for this activity came from a televised documentary, aired some time ago, about a child whose tribe, from a remote and sparsely settled region of New Guinea, was studied by a series of Western anthropologists. Villagers in the tribe, including this child, were observed at length and interviewed in depth on matters ranging from initiation rites to sexual practices to kinship systems, and the tribe became well known in anthropological circles. Intrigued and inspired by these anthropologists, the child grew to adulthood, immigrated to the United States, and eventually became a graduate student in anthropology at an American university. As he struggled to understand the customs of his new land, he was perplexed and disturbed by much of what he witnessed. Among other things, he was astonished to discover that elders in this society were often segregated—in dwellings called nursing homes—cut off from family members and cared for by strangers. Such a thing was unimaginable in his tribe back home. He wrote his dissertation on American kinship systems

In this activity the student is asked to observe a specific cultural ritual or event in America—wedding, funeral, baby shower, prom, church service, athletic event, dance—and then describe and interpret the ritual from the perspective of a foreign anthropologist (the more foreign the better) who has never before witnessed this ritual in America. The goal is to suspend prior knowledge and assumptions and view the ritual as objectively as possible. The student must: (1) describe the ritual in detail, including the behavior of individuals, the apparent relationships among individuals, the use of objects with apparent symbolic significance, and so on (2) make inferences about the function of the ritual, the protocol of the ritual, and the reasons why it is carried out in a certain manner, and (3) interpret the behavior of individuals and the significance of any symbols used in the ritual. The student may interview participants in the ritual, or attend another similar ritual to get a point of comparison, and the student may offer several potential explanations in interpreting the meaning of details in the ritual.

PURPOSES AND BENEFITS

Like other exercises in this section, this activity encourages critical thinking through active learning that requires a shift in perspective. The main purpose is to help students learn, through direct experience, how anthropologists operate: how they get data, how they analyze and interpret the data, how they evaluate and choose between alternative explanations of data. The activity would probably work best after students have been introduced to basic principles of anthropology, such as the purpose of anthropological studies, common methods of gathering data, and common problems in interpreting data and evaluating sources of information. The activity has other potential benefits for students, including training in being vigilant observers of human behavior, a better appreciation of how cultural rituals in America might be viewed by immigrants to our country, and an enhanced understanding of the specific rituals they're observing. Genuine knowledge, John Dewey wrote, always comes with the discovery of something not understood in what had been taken for granted as obvious.

USES, ADAPTATIONS, AND RESOURCES

This activity could be carried out as a composition assignment, an oral report in class, a collaborative activity, and/or a research project with required use of sources. The activity is designed for an anthropology course but could be modified to focus on principles of psychology or sociology, or used in a course or program designed to make students more aware of differences in cultural perspectives. In *The Silent Language,* anthropologist Edward T. Hall illustrates how people from different cultures have different conceptions of time and space, as well as different interpretations of non-verbal signals and behavior—the "silent language" of his title. For instance, behavior considered "masculine" in one culture may be viewed as "feminine" in another, and even definitions of death may vary from culture to culture. Harry Wade, in his article "Making the Given Problematic: A Cross-Cultural Approach to Critical Thinking" (included in Alverno College's *Teaching Critical Thinking in the Arts and Humanities*), also discusses ways to help students become more aware of their "hidden cultural grammar." Alverno's *Teaching Critical Thinking in Psychology* includes a "Culture Puzzles" exercise in which students explain an apparently bizarre custom from another culture, while John Bean's *Engaging Ideas* suggests an assignment in which students analyze the "local subcultures" of groups such as kindergartners, cheerleaders, and owners of recreational vehicles.

One key concept in anthropology is ethnocentrism, the belief that the customs of one's own society or ethnic group are superior or at least normative. In *Thinking for Yourself,* Marlys Mayfield examines ethnocentrism as a barrier to critical thinking, while Hall, in *The Silent Language,* illustrates how it leads to conflicts in cross-cultural communication. He also stresses the importance of becoming more aware of our ethnocentric tendencies—one potential benefit of the activity explained above. One essay I use in literature courses,

"On Cannibals" by the 16th century French essayist Montaigne—my personal favorite as a model of critical thinking—discusses the ethnocentrism of 16th century Europeans in their attitudes toward a South American tribe. "I can see nothing barbarous or uncivilized about it," Montaigne says in regards to the tribe's practice of cannibalism, "except that we all call barbarism that which does not fit in with our usages. And indeed we have no other level of truth and reason but the examples and model of the opinions and usages of the country we live in. There we always see the perfect religion, the perfect government, the perfect and accomplished manner of doing all things."

In *Local Knowledge*, Clifford Geertz critically examines both the objectives and the methods of anthropology. Anthropology, he says, is "mostly engaged in trying to determine what this people or that take to be the point of what they are doing." He illustrates the relativism of anthropology in his discussion of common sense—common to whom?—as a "cultural system." And, in his introduction, he articulates his view of the value of anthropology:

> To see ourselves as others see us can be eye-opening. To see others as sharing a nature with ourselves is the merest decency. But it is from the far more difficult achievement of seeing ourselves among others, as a local example of the forms human life has locally taken, a case among cases, a world among worlds, that the largeness of mind, without which objectivity is self-congratulation and tolerance a sham, comes. If interpretive anthropology has any general office in the world, it is to keep reteaching this fugitive truth.

The methods of anthropology can be applied in a wide variety of contexts. Mark Feeney's *Boston Globe* article "She Knows What You Want" profiles social anthropologist Ilsa Schumacher, whose firm, Cultural Dynamics, "has been practicing anthropology not on some primitive tribe or distant ethnic group but on the American buying public." Schumacher interviews people, observes their everyday behavior, and sits down to meals with them, all in the course of conducting market research in order to sell products. "If you're not an anthropologist," she says, "and you're a business person, you think of it as marketing. We think of it as interpreting how things fit into our lives." Students investigating this topic might focus on the validity of such market research or the ethics of using anthropology for commercial purposes.

Finally, another way to prompt students to shift perspectives—in this case, from species to species instead of from culture to culture—is suggested in Robin Dunbar's *Grooming, Gossip, and the Evolution of Language*. Dunbar's thesis is that human "gossip"—defined as conversation about social behavior—serves the same basic functions as the constant mutual grooming carried out by our fellow primates. "We are social beings," he says, "and our world—no less than that of the monkeys and apes—is cocooned in the interests and minutiae of everyday social life. They fascinate us beyond measure." Furthermore, he claims, the main reason we use language—and perhaps the main reason why language evolved—is to gain social information and build cohesion in social relationships. In other words, we're all gossips:

> Next time you are in a café or a bar, just listen for a moment to your neighbours. You will discover, as we have in our research, that around two-thirds of their conversation is taken up with matters of social import. Who is doing what with whom, and whether it's a good or a bad thing; who is in and who is out, and why; how to deal with a difficult social situation involving a lover, child or colleague. You may happen on a particularly intense exchange about a technical problem at work or a book just read. But listen on, and I'll wager that, within five minutes at the most, the conversation has drifted away again, back to the natural rhythms of social life.

Students exploring this subject might start with some research of their own—say, a collaborative eavesdropping exercise in which they keep track of the topics discussed, the time devoted to each topic, and the apparent motives of speakers in a series of everyday conservations.

ACTIVITY #39
If I Had My Way (Creating a Model)

APPLICATIONS: Human services, criminal justice, future studies, social sciences, other disciplines

CRITICAL THINKING SKILLS: Examining issues from conflicting viewpoints, evaluating solutions to problems, foreseeing the consequences of decisions, making judgments

THE ACTIVITY

"We learn most," wrote Jean Piaget, "when we have to invent." In this activity students, working individually or collaborating in teams, create and describe a model institution: a high school, business, nursing home, mental health care facility, rehabilitation clinic, prison, probation department, registry of motor vehicles, and so on. The more detailed the model, the better. Students explain, with a rationale, the purpose of the model institution, its organizational structure, its everyday methods of operation, its criteria for hiring employees, its funding, and other aspects of the institution. Students also discuss how the model would address significant problems faced by existing institutions of this type and explain why the model might be able to solve or minimize these problems. The model could be presented as an in-class report, a written essay, or a full-scale research project.

PURPOSES AND BENEFITS

It's relatively easy to play the role of critic or devil's advocate and find fault with existing institutions. It's far more challenging—and a greater test of critical thinking skills—to design an institution that might work effectively and then provide a rationale for the details of the design. This activity requires students to look at the big picture as they analyze the goals, values, structure, and operations of some type of institution. They must consider a

---

variety of potentially conflicting perspectives (clients, employees, managers, the general public), compare and evaluate different possible designs, and make judgments about alternative solutions to problems. As with other problem-posing assignments, they must also try to project and foresee the likely consequences of the decisions they make in determining the details of their models. The activity tests students' ability to use reasoning effectively, to use language precisely and persuasively, and to anticipate objections to their models. Finally, it provides an excellent opportunity for a critical exchange of ideas within the context of group collaboration.

USES, ADAPTATIONS, AND RESOURCES

This activity could be used in various courses, especially those in which students examine institutional organization or the effectiveness of specific institutions, and it would work best after students have already spent significant time studying the operations and problems in existing institutions. It's an ambitious assignment, one that could be *the* major project in a course, and the instructor should set up the assignment in stages to give students sufficient time for brainstorming, research, incubation, exploratory writing, revision, and feedback from both classmates and the instructor. With full-scale projects like this, it's especially important for students to resist what John Bean calls the tendency "to reach closure too quickly." Too often, Bean says in *Engaging Ideas*, students "do not suspend judgment, question assumptions, imagine alternative answers, play with data, enter into the spirit of opposing views, and just plain linger over questions. As a result, they often write truncated and underdeveloped papers. To deepen students' thinking, teachers need to build into their courses time, space, tools, and motivation for exploratory thinking." Before beginning the project, students should read and discuss some analyses of existing institutions. As they develop their models, they might review and critique the designs of their classmates or compare several groups' designs for the same type of institution.

To initiate the project, the instructor might assign a work like Thomas More's *Utopia* or B.F. Skinner's *Walden Two* that describes a model society or a model version of some social institution. The anthology *The Good Life*, edited by Jerry Richard, presents an interesting history of experiments in building Utopian communities in the United States, including both some excerpts from Skinner's book and a critique of *Walden Two* by Joseph Wood Krutch. For criminal justice students, Michel Foucault's *Discipline and Punish* offers a provocative view of the history of penal institutions, attempts to design model prisons, and an analysis of why these attempts have failed and why efforts to rehabilitate inmates may actually stimulate or refine criminal behavior. And, in *Asylums*, sociologist Erving Goffman examines what he calls the "total institution"—"a place of residence and work where a large number of like-situated individuals, cut off from the wider society for an appreciable period of time, together lead an enclosed, formally administered round of life"—and finds striking similarities in the structure and operations of total institutions designed for widely different purposes, including prisons, mental institutions, army training camps, boarding schools, nunneries, and nursing homes. Goffman examines mental institutions in some depth, but more generally he finds that in total institutions, regardless of the institution's purported function, staff members invariably spend much of their time establishing and enforcing the rules of the institution, while inmates tend to devote themselves to negotiating and, in many cases, subverting these rules.

For a related activity, SEE **#40: Making the Case**.

ACTIVITY #40
Making the Case (Students as Consultants: The Case Method)

APPLICATIONS: Business, economics, statistics, history, law, composition, other disciplines

CRITICAL THINKING SKILLS: Getting relevant information to solve a problem, using evidence to support a claim, evaluating alternative solutions to problems, foreseeing the consequences of decisions, evaluating effectiveness of decision-making strategies

THE ACTIVITY

Ann Marie Radaskiewicz, English professor at Western Piedmont Community College in North Carolina, describes this activity in her abstract "Writing for the Real World." Early in the semester, students in her composition class select a project involving some proposed improvement to their college. The class then forms a mock company, a fictional consulting firm. Radaskiewicz explains: "We pretend the college has hired our firm to research and prepare a formal report on the topic. This report will discuss the problem or issue in detail and include our recommendations for improvement." The ultimate objective is to write a formal research report for the college's president. In carrying out this activity, students write business letters and short reports, conduct interviews, deliver oral presentations of reports, and develop research skills by using the Internet and library resources. Students collaborate within "departments" to write sections of the final formal report.

PURPOSES AND BENEFITS

This activity is an effective way to teach the critical thinking skills essential for practical problem-solving—skills such as getting relevant and reliable information, using evidence to support a proposal, generating potential solutions, evaluating alternative solutions, and foreseeing the consequences of decisions. Radaskiewicz reports that the assignment is engaging and meaningful to students because it serves a definite purpose for a real audience. She adds that students become more proficient not only in problem-solving but also in their writing skills, computer skills, and their ability to collaborate effectively. In her conclusion she states that students "experience a sense of accomplishment when the pieces of the final report finally fit into place and the document is presented to a real audience."

USES, ADAPTATIONS, AND RESOURCES

This project could easily be modified for use in business courses or other courses with problem-solving components. In *Engaging Ideas*, John Bean outlines a similar assignment in which the student acts as a research assistant to a business consultant for a beer company. In another related activity, an instructional team from the University of Texas at Austin—Norvell Northcutt, Sue Darby, and Leann Ellis—describe a research project in their abstract "Teaching the Big Picture." In this collaborative research project the instructor acts as both instructor and client, and the class is "hired" as a "team of researchers to conduct a large-scale qualitative study examining his organization's office of institutional effectiveness." Students study the literature of qualitative research, conduct interviews, gather and analyze data, and produce a final written report. In its scope, its use of statistical data, and the sophistication of its research methodology, this project is far more complex and demanding than the previous one. However, it develops many of the same critical thinking skills using research, collaboration, and applied problem solving. The authors of the abstract state: "Although the class described here is a graduate-level, qualitative research course, the pedagogical design and theoretical principles are applicable to any course that includes a research project component (e.g. English composition or statistical methods)."

Another form of the student-as-consultant model, discussed by Richard Neustadt and Ernest May in *Thinking in Time: The Uses of History*, has been used in a course for graduate students in business administration at the University of North Carolina. The course uses a case study approach to focus on the uses of history in making business decisions. In one case the student consultants must decide on whether or not to advise an electronics company to bid on a component for a new government tank. UNC Professor Lester Garner says about the project: "We discuss factors such as the political web of relationships that direct weapon procurement decisions, American attitudes toward the military and big business, and the problems of manufacturing when dealing with new technologies, all of which should influence the firm's decision on the bid. We look at these factors throughout their relevant pasts, and by the end of the module many students perceive that the financial data may be the least influential factor to consider in such a decision." Another case simulates Mexican-U.S. negotiations of compensation for Mexico's nationalization of oil companies in the 1930s. This case study project, like the one used at Texas, is aimed at graduate students but could be modified and simplified for use in undergraduate courses. It's also an excellent illustration of how a course can integrate the concerns and methods of two different disciplines, in this case business and history.

In his article "Making the Case," David Garvin, professor of business administration at Harvard Business School, provides a useful overview of the case method of teaching, from which the student-as-consultant model derives. The case method—a methodology aimed at cultivating critical thinking and now widely used in law, business, medicine, and other disciplines—was pioneered in the 1870s by Harvard law professor Christopher Langdell, who abandoned the then popular Dwight Method (a combination of lecture, recitation, and drill) for an approach in which students: (1) read and analyze original sources—actual cases (2) are questioned by the instructor about the facts of the case, the issues to be decided, the underlying judicial principles, and comparisons to other cases, and (3) then form their own conclusions about how to decide or resolve issues. Ideally, Garvin states, the case method combines "tough, relentless questioning by instructors" and a careful critique of "boundary problems," defined by Yale Law School dean Anthony Kronman as problems that "involve a clash of principles in which as much, or nearly as much, may be said on one side or the other." Instructors often assign multiple cases, chosen because they involve apparently contradictory principles, and raise hypothetical questions that sharpen the tension between conflicting principles by slighting changing the facts or issues in a case. "Learning to think like a lawyer means understanding and accepting the importance of small differences," Garvin says. "Decisions often turn on matters of seemingly insignificant detail. Precedents may or may not apply in this particular set of circumstances Doctrines and rules are seldom unequivocal or easy to apply." His viewpoint is reinforced by law professor Elizabeth Warren, who asserts that the mark of a good lawyer (and, I would add, a good critical thinker) is "the ability to make fine discriminations, to think of two things that are closely interconnected but keep them separate from one another."

Garvin also discusses how the case method has been adopted, and in some cases modified, in business, medicine, and other disciplines. For business students, he says, case discussions have three primary benefits:

- They help students develop and refine diagnostic skills "in a world where markets and technologies are constantly changing."
- They help develop persuasive skills. "Management is a social art: it requires working with and through others.

The ability to tell a compelling story, to marshal evidence, and to craft persuasive arguments is essential to success."

- They cultivate the habit of making critical decisions in problematic situations in which knowledge may be limited but a course of action must be determined—what business administration professor Thomas Piper calls "the courage to act under uncertainty."

Business cases typically involve real, not hypothetical, problems that require students to cope with limited information, to distinguish between relevant and irrelevant information, and to choose a solution from a number of possible options. The primary challenge, Garvin explains, is "making and implementing decisions, often in the face of considerable uncertainty." Garvin also addresses criticisms regarding the limitations or drawbacks of the case method approach. One problem, he claims, is that preoccupation with decisiveness and persuasiveness may lead students to become "trigger-happy" in making decisions, inflexible, or unwilling to admit errors in public. Another problem is that the current trend of presenting case studies on valuation and forecasting may lead to less emphasis on "diagnosis, decision-making, and implementation—the action skills the case method was originally designed for."

SEE **Activity #45: Thinking Online and Off** for ideas on using information-technology and multimedia approaches to enhance the teaching of case studies.

ACTIVITY #41
Trying Jekyll for the Crimes of Hyde
(Conducting Mock Trials)

APPLICATIONS: Literature, history, criminal justice, business law, political science, speech, other disciplines

CRITICAL THINKING SKILLS: Determining the reliability or relevance of information, distinguishing fact from opinion, making inferences, using evidence, examining issues from opposing viewpoints, analyzing the process of making judgments

THE ACTIVITY

Students in this activity play roles in conducting mock trials of characters from literature or history. I've used this approach in world and American literature courses as well as in my "Criminals in Literature" course. We've tried Medea for the murder of her children, the king of Corinth, and the king's daughter. We've tried Dr. Jekyll for the crimes of Mr. Hyde, raising issues of intent and criminal responsibility. We've put Ben Franklin's heroine, Polly Baker, on the stand and heard her plea that she should be memorialized, not punished, for bearing five illegitimate children. In a variation on this approach, we've conducted a child custody hearing based on Henrik Ibsen's play *A Doll's House*.

Students list (in order) the three roles they would most prefer to play, and then, using these lists, I determine which students will be defendants, prosecutors, defense attorneys, witnesses, and jury members. I give extra credit to students willing to play especially difficult roles such as Medea. When our trials are based on works from ancient Greece, several class members are transformed into gods or goddesses—picture a wisecracking, gumsmacking Venus in bluejeans who chastises those who would dare to blame *her* for the murders committed by Medea. Students spend two periods working in small groups, based on their roles.

They prepare trial strategy, decide how to play their roles most effectively, and anticipate questions that might be raised during the trial. The trial itself takes two or three 50-minute class periods. I distribute a handout that includes a list of participants and their roles, ground rules for the trial, and the sequence of events for the trial. As the instructor, I act as a moderator, not a judge; student jury members determine all verdicts and punishments. I maintain order, and I may question witnesses and defendants to insure that important issues are fully explored and that each student plays a significant role in the trial. All jury members must participate in questioning defendants and witnesses. Verdicts are determined by a majority vote of the jury, and I ask jury members to provide a brief rationale for their votes.

PURPOSES AND BENEFITS

In this activity students develop critical thinking skills by inhabiting roles. Students enjoy the trials as a departure from the usual lecture or discussion format, and for the most part they take their roles quite seriously. In addition to fostering collaboration among students, the format encourages them to study the assigned text carefully so they can perform their roles with some self-assurance. The trial also helps students to clarify and articulate their responses to the literature; once they have testified and deliberated with their classmates, they are better able to express their interpretations in writing. Role-playing activities bring out the resourcefulness and creativity in students, and every trial we've conducted has had its revelations and unexpected developments. The most bashful, self-doubting student may blossom into a relentless prosecutor, an ingeniously self-justifying Dr. Jekyll—"I was addicted to being Mr. Hyde!"—or an indignant, impassioned Polly Baker.

USES, ADAPTATIONS, AND RESOURCES

This activity is well suited to a speech course, and it could be carried out in any course or field—history, criminal justice, business law—that focuses on criminal behavior or legal issues. In his abstract "Court Is Now in Session," Daniel H. Holt, business instructor at Southeastern Illinois College, describes a mock trial exercise he uses in Business Law. Holt gives his students a written narrative about a legal dispute between two parties. Some students are assigned to be attorneys for the plaintiffs and defendants; other serve as jury members. The attorneys present their cases in a mock trial, while the jury members rate the attorneys' presentations in terms of "effectiveness, organization, clarity, and persuasiveness of their arguments." The instructor does his own rating as well. The project, Holt says, "promotes skills in critical thinking, research, communication, planning, and evaluation of self and others."

Tom Bateman, political science instructor at Mount Royal College in Calgary, Alberta, describes a similar exercise in his abstract "Moot Court Exercise." Students in his "Law, Politics, and the Judicial Process" course create a fictional Supreme Supreme Court of Canada that hears an appeal of an actual decision rendered by the real Supreme Court of Canada. Students play the roles of court members, attorneys, journalists, and academic commentators on the judicial process. Bateman also enlists the support and direct involvement of local members of the legal community. The moot court exercise, he says, includes "serious argument, attentive listening, questioning, and solemn deliberation." At the end of his abstract, Bateman provides a useful list of suggestions for faculty planning similar projects.

In *Thinking Critically*, John Chaffee includes an interesting article by Daniel Goleman, "Jurors Hear Evidence and Turn It into Stories," about the way jurors think and reason during the process of reaching a verdict. Jurors, Goleman says, must form narratives to give coherence to testimony, and they must use inferences and assumptions to justify or "sell" their verdicts to their fellow jurors. Often, he claims, they tend to focus on whether the victims could have avoided becoming victims, perhaps because it

---

reassures them that they need not become victims themselves. This view is supported by anecdotes from trial lawyers—and research done by consultants who advise attorneys on jury selection—which indicates that jury members often fail to grant significant damages to claimants demographically similar to themselves, because the jury members like to think that, in these situations, *they* would have avoided being injured or victimized. On a similar note, Alverno College's *Teaching Critical Thinking in Psychology* presents a "You, the Jury" exercise in which students in a hypothetical trial represent the defendant by questioning prospective jurors in the process of jury selection.

In literature courses, I've found it helpful to present students with an analogy between jurors evaluating evidence in a trial and readers interpreting and making inferences about the "evidence" in literary works. Both must determine whether evidence is important and reliable; both must weigh conflicting interpretations of the same information; both need to be attuned to their own biases and subjective slants; and for both, in the end, the final decision (or interpretation) is theirs and theirs alone.

For related activities, SEE **#42: Suddenly You're Old** and **#43: Playing with Literature.**

ACTIVITY #42
Suddenly You're Old (Students as Actors: Playing Roles)

APPLICATIONS: Nursing and other health care professions, gerontology, human services, criminal justice, engineering, philosophy, literature, speech and drama, other disciplines

CRITICAL THINKING SKILLS: Examining issues from different viewpoints, evaluating solutions, foreseeing consequences of decisions, evaluating effectiveness of strategies

THE ACTIVITY

In this activity, like the previous one, students learn by playing roles in simulated, structured, or more open-ended situations. One variety is explained by Lynn M. Young, Director of Nursing Education at Mohave Community College in Arizona, in "Teaching Empathy and Understanding with a Game." In this role-playing game nursing students take on the roles of elderly patients: "They started at the 'identity table' where they were asked to select an age (older than 65), an occupation from which they have retired, a retirement lifestyle, three personal possessions that they would like to take with them to a nursing home." As they proceed through the game, students are given "simulated deficits associated with aging" (infirmities, financial losses), placed in one of three "functional levels of elder living" (independent, assisted, and totally dependent), draw cards with positive or (in most cases) negative consequences, and contend with role-playing "operators" who have been "coached to display biases and discriminatory practices typical of those seen in society." After the game students verbalize their feelings and observations in a discussion, and critique the game as a learning experience.

PURPOSES AND BENEFITS

This particular role-playing game was designed for students to "think critically about their own attitudes and increase their understanding and empathy for the problems of the elderly." Young reports that the game achieves these goals by enabling students to "explore their feelings and examine biases from a perspective designed to promote insights and understanding." More generally, role-playing activities help students learn by shifting their perspectives, requiring them to improvise and think on their feet in structured contexts, and by setting up situations that enable students to test problem-solving strategies and evaluate the effectiveness of these strategies. Role-playing games can also build student self-confidence and in some cases help students evaluate their career choices.

USES, ADAPTATIONS, AND RESOURCES

For students entering the health professions, Nancy Mairs' essay on multiple sclerosis, "On Being a Cripple," and Frank DeFord's "Cystic Fibrosis" both provide insight into the perspectives of patients with serious illnesses and the problems faced by family members of those patents.

Role-playing activities can be used effectively in virtually any discipline. For instance, Alverno College's *Teaching Critical Thinking in Psychology* includes "The Client" exercise used in Abnormal Psychology: the instructor or guest actor roleplays a client during the initial clinical contact, while class members play the roles of counselors. More elaborate exercises are presented in "Law and Security Simulations: Integrating Theory and Practice" by Colleen Clarke, Professor of Law and Security Administration at the Confederation College of Applied Arts & Technology in Thunder Bay, Ontario. Clarke describes role-playing simulations for Law & Security students that "set up teaching conditions that are as close to real life as possible—e.g. roadways on college property are blocked off for accident scenes; the campus pub, college plant, conference dining room, storage rooms, and any other useful areas are borrowed for crime settings." Exercises involve members from the law enforcement community, actors from high school drama clubs, and college professors who analyze student responses. After the exercises, students present their evidence in simulated courtrooms. The simulations, Clarke says, "test student skills and allow them to apply their working knowledge and instinctive reactions to seemingly real situations." The simulations build student self-confidence and "afford students a realistic look at their career choices."

In "The Supercop Scenario," Joe Klein describes the use of similar role-playing scenarios in the training for the Police Corps, an elite federal program for recent college graduates. Klein quotes Colonel Hy Rothstein, one of the trainers, on the purpose of the program: "We teach a skills set. But what we are really interested in is teaching people how to think. We want to see how you behave in uncertain situations you haven't been prepared for—and that's what comes out when we run them through scenarios." The Police Corps scenarios, like the simulations used in Clarke's program, exemplify what might be called high-speed critical thinking. We tend to consider critical thinking a leisurely process of analysis and reflection, but in some professions, such as law enforcement or air traffic control, critical evaluations of situations—and actions based on those evaluations—must be carried out quickly and decisively, under pressure, with little or no time for reflection. Simulation exercises are especially well suited for such professions.

In his abstract "Dramatizations: Philosophers (and Students) Come Alive," Don Foran, who teaches English and philosophy at Centralia College in Washington, describes an activity in which student explore philosophical issues by taking on the roles of philosophers or contemporary figures and presenting dramatizations for their classmates. As examples he cites jail-cell conversations, "Dating Game" dilemmas, and a "poker party hosted by

Machiavelli for his friends Karl Marx, Simone Weil, and Lao-Tzu."

In *Engaging Ideas*, John Bean recommends the use of role-playing exercises, simulations, and "what if" situations to "encourage what Piaget calls decentering—getting students outside of the assumptions of their own worldviews." One simulation, which Bean links to a writing assignment, focuses on a patient suffering from kidney failure who has been missing his dialysis treatments and failing to follow a prescribed diet. Students play the roles of the patient, the patient's wife, a patient on the waiting list for use of the dialysis machine, members of the hospital staff, and medical ethicists with conflicting viewpoints. Bean also recommends the use of dialogues and argumentative scripts to help students define issues and understand the differences between conflicting viewpoints. "The freedom from traditional thesis-governed form," he writes, "as well as the necessity to role-play each of the opposing views in the conversation, often stimulates more complex thinking than traditional argumentative papers, in which students often try to reach closure too quickly." Bean cites the following example of a dialogue in a mechanical engineering course:

> For the design application we have been studying, your design team has proposed four alternative solutions: conventional steel roller bearings, ceramic bearings, air bearings, and magnetic bearings. As a team, write a dialogue in which each team member argues the case for one of the alternative solutions and shows weaknesses in the other solutions.

In another abstract, "Using Role-Playing to Teach Thinking," Richard Jewell, education specialist at the University of Minnesota, describes role-playing exercises he has used in teaching Composition I, Problem Solving, and World Religions. His students have become business managers creating a TV ad campaign, founders of a new religion, and mental health professionals evaluating family problems. Jewell suggest the following guidelines for developing role-playing activities to develop critical thinking: (1) Isolate the thinking pattern or skill you want to teach. (2) If the thinking skill appears complex to students, break it down further into steps, parts, or separate functions. (3) Decide if the skill can be practiced best by small groups, in class or out. (4) Imagine enjoyable, challenging, dramatic roles for students to try. (5) Collect brief written or oral evaluations within the same day or week.

In addition to the mock trials described in **Activity #41**, I've conducted a mock classroom exercise when I've taught George Orwell's *1984*. The purpose of this activity is to give students a taste of life in a totalitarian society and an experience with some of the conflicts faced by characters in the novel. I play the Thought Trainer, indoctrinating students with the principles of Big Brother, and students play the roles of students within the context of the totalitarian society that Orwell depicts. In their roles, students are punished—by verbal reprimands, threats, sarcasm, or isolation from the group—for any behavior I choose to consider an infraction, including dangerous questions, inappropriate smiles or body language, the slightest rebelliousness, or any other sign of unacceptable thinking. Students must decide whether to act as obedient disciples of Big Brother or risk punishment for showing signs of independent thinking. I've used a similar exercise when I've taught Margaret Atwood's futuristic novel *A Handmaid's Tale*, which focuses on indoctrination according to gender roles. A note of warning: this type of exercise is intended to build an atmosphere of tension and mistrust, where any freedom of thought is prohibited, and the exercise can be draining for the instructor and disturbing for students, especially students with emotional problems or those who don't respond well to displays of authority in their faces. The instructor must be quite clear in explaining the purpose and format of the exercise, and it's also essential to adhere rigidly to the Thought Trainer role, so that students will stay within their roles. I allow students to opt out of the exercise entirely or at any point in the exercise.

ACTIVITY #43
Playing with Literature (Students as Collaborators: Playing with Texts)

APPLICATIONS: Literature, composition

CRITICAL THINKING SKILLS: Testing hypotheses, examining issues from opposing viewpoints, evaluating alternative solutions and alternative interpretations

THE ACTIVITY

This activity—playing with literature—comes in many varieties. One is illustrated by these directions for a writing assignment on Albert Camus' *The Stranger*: "Narrate the events on the day of the murder from the point of view of the Arab who is killed by Meursault. This topic is an experiment in point of view; you should focus on developing the Arab's character and providing motives for his behavior. Before beginning your narrative, reread the relevant section of the novel." Another variation is illustrated by these directions for a writing assignment on Jonathan Swift's *Gulliver's Travels*: "Assume that you are one of Swift's Yahoos and that you are capable of human speech. Narrate several scenes that reveal your image of yourself and your attitude toward the Houyhnhnms. Give careful thought to the questions of what words a Yahoo would use (or would not be able to use) and what thoughts and feelings a Yahoo would be capable of expressing."

PURPOSES AND BENEFITS

In this activity students show their understanding of literature by becoming authors themselves. Instead of directly analyzing a literary work, they write narratives that collaborate with it, comment on it, revise it, respond to it, extrapolate from it, or play with its point of view. The activity appeals to the creativity of students, and it provides them with an alternative means to demonstrate their insights into the behavior of characters, their grasp of issues that authors have raised and in some cases left unresolved, or their critiques of the ways in which authors have presented characters or themes. The activity also focuses attention on the importance of point of view in literature. To carry out the activity well, students must read the literary work carefully and reflect on it thoughtfully, and they must confront the challenge of writing narratives that are consistent—in tone, language, or theme—with the original.

USES, ADAPTATIONS, AND RESOURCES

I've used different forms of this activity with a wide range of literary works. An assignment might require students to do one or more of the following: (1) to write a scene from the point of view of a specific (often secondary) character, such as the Arab in *The Stranger* or the African woman at Kurtz's station in Joseph Conrad's *Heart of Darkness* (2) to write or summarize an alternative ending for a literary work, such as Mark Twain's *Huckleberry Finn* or Richard Wright's *Native Son,* and provide a rationale for any changes from the original (3) to write an unwritten scene or extrapolate and write a scene that takes place after the conclusion of events in the original work—a final conversation between Fielding and Adela from E. M. Forster's *A Passage to India*, a narration of Orlando's trance from Virginia Woolf's *Orlando* (4) to write a scene based on a premise or assumption—that Swift's Yahoos can speak, that Jake in Ernest Hemingway's *The Sun Also Rises* has regained his sexual potency, that the student must use the language of Newspeak from George Orwell's *1984* to write a report for the Ministry of Love on Winston's political "cure" (5) to place a character from literature in a new, usually contemporary context—Huck Finn on the river in 2004, or Lewis Carroll's Alice engaged in a dialogue with a modern hookah smoker imagined by the student. To provide examples of authors who have played with the creations of other authors, the instructor might refer students to such works as Jean

Rhys' *Wide Sargasso Sea*—the backstory of Charlotte Bronte's *Jane Eyre*—or Tom Stoppard's *Rosencrantz and Guildenstern Are Dead*, in which Hamlet recedes to a minor role and secondary characters take center stage.

A related activity—Therapy for Fictional Characters—was inspired in part by the televised drama *The Sopranos*. Here, students are asked to provide psychological advice or a therapeutic plan for a literary character in the throes of a dilemma, such as Dostoyevsky's "underground man" in *Notes from the Underground* or Emma Bovary from Flaubert's *Madame Bovary*. This idea may make both psychologists and English professors wince, and the activity does have its drawbacks. A little knowledge, they say, is a dangerous thing, and students may be glib with their advice or simplistic in their application of therapeutic concepts or in their grasp of the dilemmas faced by characters. They may come up with ideas that are silly or far-fetched or that seem to sully the integrity of the original work. Nonetheless, this approach can be a creative way for students to demonstrate both psychological insight and their comprehension of the conflicts faced by literary characters. I've used one such assignment when I've taught Shakespeare's *Othello*: "Assume that you are an old, close friend of Othello's who shows up in Cyprus at the end of Act Four. Othello tells you why he believes that Desdemona has been unfaithful to him, and he tells you that he intends to kill her. What questions would you ask him, what advice would you give him, and why would you give him this advice? Remember, all you know so far about the situation in the play is what Othello himself has told you."

ACTIVITY #44
Drawing on the Right Side of the Brain
(Students as Artists)

APPLICATIONS: Art, education, psychology, biology, physics, mathematics, computer science, graphic design, other disciplines

CRITICAL THINKING SKILLS: Examining phenomena from conflicting viewpoints, evaluating alternative solutions to problems, using metacognition to develop creativity

THE ACTIVITY

This activity—or rather, this progression of integrated activities—is explained by Dr. Betty Edwards, professor of art at California State University in Long Beach, in her book *Drawing on the Right Side of the Brain*, which applies recent discoveries in brain research to the teaching of drawing. Edwards' book is based largely on psychobiologist Roger Sperry's studies of "the dual nature of human thinking—verbal, analytic thinking mainly located in the left hemisphere, and visual, perceptual thinking mainly located in the right hemisphere." Her key principle in teaching drawing is that it is "a global (or 'whole') skill requiring only a limited set of basic components." These components, she explains, are not drawing skills but perceptual skills: the perception of edges, the perception of spaces, the perception of relationships, the perception of light and shadows, and the perception of the whole, or *gestalt*. The strategy of her book is "to explain in basic terms the relationship of drawing to visual, perceptual brain processes and to provide methods of accessing and controlling these processes." To help students access and control these processes, she offers a number of specific activities such as upside-down drawing, contour drawing, negative-space drawing, sighting techniques, and exercises on the perception of shadows. In her postscript Edwards makes recommendations to teachers of drawing, parents of drawing students, and art students, both beginners and more advanced.

PURPOSES AND BENEFITS

Edwards' book, which is widely used by art teachers, is an excellent illustration of how to apply metacognitive critical thinking—the brain examining its own functions and processes—to teaching in a way that is both practical and creative. Students gain "access to powerful brain functions often obscured by language" while developing their ability to draw. "In the process of learning to draw," she explains, "one also learns to control how one's own brain handles information." Students develop more confidence in their skills and find both aesthetic pleasure and "deeper artistic perceptions" through explorations of their own creativity.

USES, ADAPTATIONS, AND RESOURCES

Edwards' book was among the first to present some practical educational applications of dual brain research. In her postscript she points out, in general terms, the potential for other applications, "whether writing or painting, developing a new theory in physics, or dealing with environmental problems." She suggests three primary methods for tapping this potential: (1) training both hemispheres of the brain (2) training students to use "the cognitive style *suited to the task at hand*" and (3) training students to integrate the functions of both hemispheres or learning styles. "Without abandoning training in traditional verbal and computational skills," she writes, "concerned teachers are looking for teaching techniques that will enhance children's intuitive and creative powers, thus preparing students to meet new challenges with flexibility, inventiveness, and imagination and with the ability to grasp complex arrays of interconnected ideas and facts, to perceive underlying patterns of events, and to see old problems in new ways."

In *Time Travels & Papa Joe's Pipe: Essays on the Human Side of Science*, astrophysicist Alan Lightman discusses the potential of Edwards' teaching methods in his examination of "two different ways of approaching problems—the intuitive and the analytic." What Edwards demonstrates, he says, is that "we can all learn to draw better by consciously holding at bay our left hemisphere with its preconceptions about what things *should* look like." He's especially fond of her exercise in which "you take a Picasso line drawing of a man sitting in a chair, turn it upside down, and copy what you see." Lightman suggests that fellow scientists could "profit by trying some of these exercises, perhaps in a different version" in order to cultivate intuitive thinking, and he cites his own experience with the study of the acceleration of objects under the influence of gravity.

Another fascinating slant on artistic creation and metacognition is presented in *Metamagical Themas* by mathematician Douglas Hofstadter, who describes himself as a "relentless quester after the chief patterns of the universe—certain organizing principles, clear and powerful ways to categorize what is 'out there.'" In his search for the basic patterns of our minds, Hofstadter explores how musical and visual patterns can stir our emotions. "All my research," he writes, "is aimed at finding patterns that will help us to understand the mysteries of musical and visual beauty." In one chapter he looks at "parquet deformations," which he describes as "a highly geometric form of art that, though mathematical or 'computerish' in appearance, relies on many human judgments for its charm." He relates this art form to the woodcuts of M. C. Escher, as well as musical compositions by Bach and Steve Reich, while considering both the general question of how computers might be used to understand creativity and the specific challenge of programming a computer to "invent' parquet deformations. Students in graphic design might be given an assignment to create parquet deformations of their own. Hofstadter's discussion also leads him to the theoretical question, "Is there an architecture to creativity? Is there a plan, a scheme, a set of principles that, if elucidated clearly, could account for all the creativity embodied in the collection of all parquet deformations, past, present, and future?"

Patricia Thomas' article "Brainy Women: At the Frontiers of Neuroscience" also makes connections between art, the biology of perception, and the use of computers. Thomas profiles Carla Shatz, chair of the neurobiology department at Harvard, who was inspired to become a neurobiologist by Harvard professor George Wald's course on the chemistry of vision, by Rudolf Arnheim's course on visual perception in art and science, and by the influence of her mother, an artist: "Her painting got me interested in vision from the artistic side, and in some subliminal way guided my decision to work on the visual system." Shatz and other neurobiologists are conducting research aimed at refuting "the notion that the human brain [can] not comprehend its own complexity." They have studied nerve cells to "construct a map showing how input from the eyes journeys to the back of the brain, where the visual cortex transforms these signals into what we see. They also discovered that these pathways are established during a critical period early in life, and that blocking signals during that time will result in permanent visual impairment." With recombinant DNA and other new technologies, neurobiologists can now study thousands of cells, genes, or proteins. Professor Shatz says, "Even the simplest action involves more than one nerve cell at a time, so the goal is to study the functioning of many, many cells simultaneously— and we can't do that without computers."

For related activities, SEE **#45: Thinking Online and Off** and **#46: My Aquatic Uncle.**

ACTIVITY #45
Thinking Online and Off (Using Technology to Teach Critical Thinking)

APPLICATIONS: Computer science, environmental science, biology, business, health care, law, developmental reading, education, other disciplines

CRITICAL THINKING SKILLS: Getting relevant and reliable information, testing hypotheses, evaluating evidence, evaluating alternative solutions and theories

THE ACTIVITY

One means of using technology to develop critical thinking is presented in the abstract "Use of Select-and-Fill-In Concept Maps" by Charles Kaminski, Director of Instructional Services at Middlesex Community College in Massachusetts. A concept map, Kaminski explains, is a "graphical representation of the meaningful relationships between concepts within a domain of knowledge." Concept maps are usually hierarchical and drawn in a tree-like structure, with the concepts indicated by geometrical shapes labeled with words to identify them. In his online environmental studies course, Kaminski uses computer software such as *Inspiration* to create Select-and-Fill-In (SAFI) concept maps that must be filled in by students: "SAFI maps begin with a teacher-created master map. Then, while maintaining the structural integrity of the map, some or all of the concepts or link labels from the map are eliminated. Students are asked to fill in the missing concepts or links by choosing them from a provided list of terms." Kaminski uses SAFI maps to organize information and concepts, "giving students a bare, skeletal structure onto which further knowledge will be constructed." As an example he cites a concept map on ecological succession. After students complete the SAFI task, they must "apply the succession knowledge contained in the SAFI map" by taking a quiz with the following instructions: "Describe, in a few short sentences, the succession of plants which occurs after a volcanic blast like that at Mt. Saint Helens in 1980. Is this a primary or secondary succession?" The abstract includes an illustration of a concept map on ecological succession.

PURPOSES AND BENEFITS

This activity requires active, dynamic learning by students, and it's an effective way of using computer software—and visualization of ideas—in teaching students to analyze concepts and apply these concepts to specific situations. As Kaminski explains, "By providing students with an advance organizer—a SAFI map—instructors may elicit a more accurate understanding of concepts within a domain, resulting in higher student achievement." He reports that many students enjoy carrying out SAFI exercises and find them helpful in clarifying how concepts are interrelated. His assignments on ecological principles are particularly valuable given that so many animals and plants in the world are currently jeopardized by habitat destruction. Kaminski also says, "Many students have observed that the SAFI maps help them think about their own learning, indicating that the SAFI maps may play a metacognitive, as well as the intended cognitive, role."

USES, ADAPTATIONS, AND RESOURCES

Kaminski uses e-mail to provide feedback to students as they fill in the concept maps, and he's added an online tutorial on the construction and components of concept maps. Though he has used SAFI maps in online courses, he says that "there is no reason that they could not be used, formatively or summatively, in the traditional classroom. They are simple to construct, are easy to administer, and can be graded quickly."

In *The Unschooled Mind*, Howard Gardner advocates the use of computer software such as *Envisioning Machine* and *Thinker Tool* to illustrate discrepancies between student intuition and formal physics laws. He also suggests means of using software to make accurate predictions or to collect data about issues of concern—acid rain, waste disposal—and then create methods to analyze the data. Jenine L. Tanabe, a Life Sciences instructor at Yuba College in California, discusses one such use of computers to gather and analyze data in her abstract "Science Laboratory—Teaching Concepts and Content." Her goal, she says, is "to emphasize scientific thinking and hands-on experimentation." To achieve this goal she uses the Biopac Student Lab System, a networked computer system that includes "a 4-channel A-D data converter, assorted transducers and sensors, user-friendly software, and versatile student lessons to capture and manipulate real physiologic data." This system enables her "to offer a powerful lab exploring the effects of drugs on frog heart rate and contraction strength," and it enables students "to record and manipulate high quality data, such as EEG, EMG and pulmonary function" and to gain "an appreciation for subject variability, measurement errors, and procedural precision." Tanabe concludes her abstract by saying: "This curriculum model used computers to enhance, not replace, experimentation. It emphasized both concepts and content. It produced extraordinary learning and could serve as a model for improved science laboratory instruction."

Harvard Magazine's article "Casing the Future" examines ways in which information-technology has been used to enhance the case method approach to teaching (SEE **Activity #40: Making the Case**) "in ways that produce greater realism, engagement, and interaction." For instance, faculty at the Harvard Business School have developed a number of wide ranging multimedia cases on such topics as the marketing of a new Microsoft software product and the development of an advertising campaign for Mountain Dew. One case, Pacific Dunlap, studies the operation of a textile factory in China through video interviews, an interactive spreadsheet, and a video tour of the manufacturing floor. In another multimedia approach, Harvard Medical School has developed ICON (Interactive Case-based Online Network), a network that gives students easy Web access to case studies and relevant research material. The network includes a "Virtual Contact" module that permits students to interact with "participants" in the case, whose roles are played by medical school faculty: "Students pose questions, and the faculty members respond—true to form and wholly in character. A renowned specialist might curtly dismiss a naïve question, while a family member might provide intimate details about a patient's condition. Students in one tutorial were paged in the middle of class and told that their patient had been admitted unexpectedly to the emergency room at two the previous morning. How did they plan to respond?" Harvard Law School, in turn, has used multimedia and simulation technologies to facilitate dialogue on case studies, including a tool called H2O, a polling and messaging system that allow students and faculty to swap messages: "A professor might ask members of her class to take a position on a hypothetical law; for example, are they for or against it, and for what reasons? Arguments must be written up and submitted to the system. Then, at a preset time, H2O randomly trades students' comments: every student in favor of the law is sent an argument from a student who is opposed, and vice versa. Students must then frame rebuttals to the arguments they have received."

In another activity designed to enhance student thinking through technology, Kathleen Yanchus, a colleague in our Linked Learning learning community at North Shore Community College, uses a "Webquest" project to teach developmental reading. Students use online sources and other readings to study the fishing community of Gloucester, Massachusetts and relate their study to such topics as local history, meteorology, the mythology of the sea, and two narratives about the challenges and hazards of fishing, Sebastian Junger's *The Perfect Storm* and Linda Greenlaw's *The Hungry Ocean*. This project helps students develop both online research and reading comprehension skills while stimulating their creativity. The activity encourages them to become more independent learners and challenges them to synthesize knowledge from different disciplines, in different modes. Using diagrams, music, scenarios, scientific charts, and other resources, students share the results of their research in classroom presentations.

For students interested in the use of computers to study artificial intelligence, Douglas Hofstadter's *Metamagical Themas* is a good starting point. Hofstadter covers topics such as "the seeming paradox of mechanizing creativity," the use of analogies in human and machine thinking, and the relation between computation and cognition. He also discusses the Turing Test, or the "Imitation Game" as its inventor, mathematician Alan Turing, called it: "You want to know if that machine can think? Put it behind a curtain and see if it can fool people into thinking it is human on the basis of what it types to them." Richard Powers' novel *Galatea 2.2* (the title refers to Pygmalion's creation in the ancient Greek myth) presents a fictional version of an attempt by a cognitive neurologist to model the human brain and invent a machine that will pass one form of the Turing Test.

SEE the **Appendix** for a list of online sources on teaching critical teaching. Some sources include online tutorials.

ACTIVITY #46
My Aquatic Uncle (Bringing the Disciplines Together)

APPLICATIONS: Sciences, humanities, social sciences, computer science, other disciplines

CRITICAL THINKING SKILLS: Examining issues from multiple viewpoints, using metaphorical language, evaluating alternative theories and interpretations, integrating knowledge

THE ACTIVITY

One interdisciplinary approach to teaching critical thinking is exemplified in the abstract "An Interdisciplinary Technology Model That Works" by Lillian Cook, Chair of the Letters Division at Panola College in Texas. Cook and a physics colleague use assignments that connect physics and literature. For example, after reading and analyzing Robert Frost's poem "Mending Wall," students "write an analysis which includes an examination of metaphorical language and theme, and a short analysis of the physics principle of entropy—a scientific term for randomness in nature or a move toward disorganization of objects." In another assignment, students read and analyze Edgar Allen Poe's "The Pit and the Pendulum" and then "describe the maximum energy of the pendulum, the potential and kinetic energies, and the velocity of the honed edge at its most threatening position." Students also use computer software in this interdisciplinary technology program and review each other's papers electronically.

PURPOSES AND BENEFITS

Activities like these help students to examine issues or concepts from multiple viewpoints, to integrate their knowledge, to find connections between seemingly unconnected disciplines, and to transfer their understanding of concepts from one context to another. Cook states: "One of the most important results is that students expand their scientific knowledge and learn that relationships and connections exist among disciplines and between school work and real-life activities. Moreover, they develop problem-solving and group-work skills that will transfer to the workplace." She also cites interdisciplinary approaches used by colleagues in art, developmental math, history, and political science courses.

USES, ADAPTATIONS, AND RESOURCES

Interdisciplinary approaches afford unlimited opportunities for innovations in teaching critical thinking skills. For instance, the Learning Communities program at Holyoke Community College in Massachusetts has developed an integrated curriculum dedicated to "reuniting the arts and the sciences" and offers courses like the following: "You Are Here: Nature, Ecology, and Home" (combining topics in science and English), "Our Changing Universe: Understanding the Nature of Nature" (team taught by a natural scientist and a physical scientist), and "The (R)evolution of Becoming Human" (taught by instructors from biology, business, English, library research, and psychology). One value of a team-teaching approach is that it can help students understand both the distinctiveness of different disciplines—how each has its own assumptions, its own mode of inquiry, its own core questions—and the connections between these disciplines. Here are the kinds of questions psychologists ask. This is what biologists want to know. This is what intrigues linguists. And here's where their different modes of inquiry come together.

In his abstract "Promoting the Humanities in Technical Curricula," Philip Bailey of Edgecombe Community College in North Carolina suggests some "creatively tailored assignments" to "teach cultural literacy in traditionally technical courses, combining the goals of business/technical and liberal arts education." Examples he cites include the analysis of *Death of a Salesman* in a sales management course and, for a nursing course, an examination of cultural communication differences among patients who have emigrated from different countries. In their abstract "Team-Teaching in an Interdisciplinary Environment," Deborah Vess and David Hutto of DeKalb College in Georgia discuss their efforts to integrate World Civilization to 1300 and Western Humanities to 1550. Their students, they report, "learned that great literature cannot be understood without a knowledge of the era in which it was written, that great art reflects the philosophical and political events of its day, and that political events do not occur in isolation, but rather grow out of deeply held philosophical and ethical beliefs."

Another interdisciplinary approach is explained in the abstract "Multi-course Projects as Bridges Between Disciplines" by chemistry professor Laura Precedo-Choudhury and physics professor Carey Witkov of Broward Community College in Florida. The authors are part of a team—all from the Science, Mathematics, Engineering, and Technology faculty—that "designed interdisciplinary projects that served as bridges between existing courses." One module, the "Wetlands Project," requires students "to collect and analyze environmentally sensitive parameters from a wetland habitat" and to reach conclusions about the overall health of the habitat. And in the "To Ship or Not to Ship Project," students are given a scenario about shipping oil along the west coast of Florida and "then divided into groups (citizens, EPA, oil company, environmental group) that must research and eventually debate the fate of whether or not to ship the oil." In arguing the benefits of such interdisciplinary approaches, the authors write that the "tendency to compartmentalize knowledge effectively negates the inherent interconnections of 'real-world' problems and discourages students" from seeking out those connections. "In today's information age," they add, "we need to teach our students to exploit the vast amount of information available by providing a global overview that stresses the importance of the interconnected parts." Their abstract lists questions to be asked in developing and assessing such projects, and they have included a student assessment instrument on their website (http://fs.broward..cc.fl.us/north/math/nsf/).

My own experience with interdisciplinary approaches includes a literature-and-science module in a world literature course. The project was designed to achieve the following goals: (1) to increase understanding of scientific principles and the scientific process of developing knowledge (2) to explore how science and literature interrelate and influence each other (3) to focus on ethical issues involving the role of science and technology in modern society. Students examined the scientific and political aspects of water pollution in Henrik Ibsen's play *An Enemy of the People*, the suspension or violation of rules of logic and physical science in Lewis Carroll's *Alice's Adventures in Wonderland*, and fictional (and wildly imaginative) versions of the origins of different life forms and evolutionary processes in Italo Calvino's *Cosmicomics*. Calvino depicts the evolution of the universe by making characters out of mathematical formulae and simple cellular structures. Each of his stories begins with a brief scientific fact or concept that becomes the focus of a personal dilemma for—well, not a character in the usual sense, but a life form. My favorite story, "The Aquatic Uncle," is about an anthropomorphic love triangle involving a charming and classy amphibian (almost reptilian in her sophistication), the insecure first-generation amphibian that pursues her, and the suitor's reactionary uncle, a fish. One value of this approach is that scientific ideas are made more accessible, more alive, to liberal arts students because they are presented in the form of narratives. Students grasp and apply biological principles (e.g. the risks and benefits of migrating to a new habitat) while gaining a fuller understanding of the possibilities of the narrative form. This kind of project is a way to help students realize that knowledge need not be fragmented, that science and literature (or the humanities generally) need not be segregated in mutually exclusive disciplines, and that a well-educated person should be fluent in a range of disciplines.

A number of excellent books could be used in different courses to make enlightening and sometimes unexpected connections between disciplines. Examples include Jared Diamond's *Guns, Germs, and Steel* (a study of world civilizations, integrating history, anthropology, biology, and linguistics), Robert Wright's *The Moral Animal* (human motivation and ethics viewed from the perspective of evolutionary psychology), Susan Griffin's *A Chorus of Stones* (a collage of memoir, history, technology, and philosophy, on the effects of war on private lives), C. P. Snow's *The Two Cultures and the Scientific Revolution* (on how to bridge the divide between the sciences and the humanities), Susan Sontag's *Illness as Metaphor* (on social attitudes toward illness and the language used to label the ill), Primo Levi's *The Periodic Table* (personal and historical reflections, from an Italian chemist and Holocaust survivor, organized by elements from the periodic table), and Samuel Florman's *The Existential Pleasures of Engineering* (on the satisfactions of engineering and the social responsibility of engineers, as well as a rebuttal to anti-technological arguments). My latest project is to design an interdisciplinary assignment on the Tower of Babel, which would combine, for starters, the cultural and symbolic significance of this and other towers, artistic and literary representations of the tower, and the engineering of structures in both the ancient and modern world.

Cultivating Judgment

Section Five

Student as Teacher, Teacher as Student

ACTIVITY #47
Seminaring (Students as Collaborative Teachers)

APPLICATIONS: Any discipline

CRITICAL THINKING SKILLS: Determining the importance of information, making inferences, using evidence, examining issues from conflicting viewpoints, analyzing the process of forming opinions, self-regulation of learning

THE ACTIVITY

This activity is described in detail in the booklet *Learning About Learning Communities: What is Our Common(wealth) Interest?*, sponsored by the Massachusetts Board of Higher Education and Holyoke Community College in Massachusetts. A seminar is defined as "a focused group discussion of a book or a work of art." Seminars are commonly used in coordinated studies programs, and the students generally select the book or work of art to be discussed. "Students in the program meet once or twice a week for an extended discussion of the text for that week. Generally, faculty members take a back seat in seminar, and ask that students develop responsibility and skills in working with their peers to understand the texts and their relationship to the program's themes." Jim Harnish, a history professor at North Seattle Community College, describes the basic process in a seminar: "A seminar brings together an interested group of learners who have done some preparation, including having read, thought about and written about a particularly good book. This solitary preparation should include marking the text for interesting passages, reviewing those sections, organizing one's thoughts on paper and producing significant questions that need to be explored." Harnish suggests that students structure their discussions of each book by focusing on three questions: "(1) What is the author saying? (2) What does the author mean? (3) Why is this point important?"

PURPOSES AND BENEFITS

This activity stimulates students' intellectual curiosity and encourages self-reliance, student responsibility for their own learning, and critical thinking through reflection on readings and a structured exchange of ideas. Harnish states: "In the seminar the group is responsible for exploring the text and probing the ideas people have brought from their individual reading of the text. It is a time to 'mine' the text, to work it over as a group, to think aloud about it, and to test some ideas against the group." Gilbert G. Salcedo, a faculty member at Evergreen State College in Washington, adds that seminars have three main purposes: "(a) to develop skills of verbal expression in the forceful and persuasive articulation of ideas (b) to develop skills in the logical analysis of ideas by listening carefully to oneself and others (c) to pool or exchange information through cooperative discussion geared toward improved factual understanding of a topic." Seminars also help to develop intellectual self-confidence and a sense of common purpose among students and faculty.

USES, ADAPTATIONS, AND RESOURCES

This activity is most commonly carried out within learning communities but could be adapted for use in individual courses in various disciplines. The *Learning About Learning Communities* booklet includes "Hints for Seminaring" by Professor Harnish, "An Etiquette for Seminar" by Professor Salcedo, an account of a seminar experience by Evergreen State College student Mary Young, a "Seminar Group Assessment" prepared by Professor Jerry Zimmeran of Lower Columbia College, and a "Seminar Process Assessment" by

Professor K. Ann McCartney of Shoreline Community College. All these materials provide helpful guidance to faculty in setting up seminars and assessing their value.

Faculty at other colleges have developed worthwhile activities in which students take on active roles as leaders or collaborators in designing, implementing, and assessing assignments. In "On the Lookout: Evaluation Forms," Barbara Gorzycki, an instructor of Speech and English at Lee College in Texas, explains an assignment in which students "create and design an evaluation form" that she uses in her classes to evaluate student speeches. *Teaching Critical Thinking in Psychology* from Alverno College includes a "Create an Exam" assignment in which students construct a one-hour exam and then describe the processes used in constructing it. In another exercise, "Test Pilot," students in work groups design simple measures of intellectual functioning, then merge as a class to combine their results into a battery of tests and design a procedure for administering the tests. And in *Learning Together*, mathematics professor Theodore Panitz includes a "write your own textbook chapter" exercise in which students explain "the process/procedure for solving word problems."

Other related activities involve students not as teachers but as collaborators in making decisions or in evaluating the effectiveness of activities and programs. During the orientation for our Linked Learning program at North Shore Community College, we break into work groups—consisting of students, teachers, and staff members—to share ideas and brainstorm answers to questions like the following: (1) What skills should we be trying to teach students? Why? (2) What are the characteristics of an effective thinker? How can we best cultivate these characteristics? (3) Of the following list of classroom activities [e.g. lecture, small group discussion, writing, student presentations], which are most likely to be productive and worthwhile? Which are not? At the end of each year we invite a panel of students to an informal luncheon for a candid and open-ended evaluation of all the activities in the program. Also, on several occasions when our college was establishing an interview procedure for hiring a new program director, I assigned students to write down at least three questions that they would like to ask a potential director. Some of their responses were ultimately used as formal interview questions.

ACTIVITY #48
Back to the Classroom (Teachers as Students)

APPLICATIONS: Any discipline

CRITICAL THINKING SKILLS: Examining issues from different perspectives, evaluating alternative solutions to problems, self-regulation of learning

THE ACTIVITY

Here, the teacher becomes—or continues to be—the student. There are many ways to go about this. Teachers may write essays, conduct experiments, or take on other projects they've assigned to their students. If they're collaborating with fellow teachers within learning communities, they may sit in on colleagues' classes and join students in participating in class discussions They may gain new insights into the teaching/learning process by teaching different populations of students or by using different modes of instruction. They may use feedback from student evaluations, discussions with colleagues, or review of videotaped classes to examine and modify their teaching methods. Or they may literally become students again and take workshops, credit courses, or whole programs of courses—or carry out less formal independent research on subjects that capture their imaginations— as part of their professional development.

PURPOSES AND BENEFITS

There are various reasons for teachers to carry out activities like these: (1) to provide students with models of how to approach particular assignments (2) to test the value of their assignments or the clarity of their directions (3) to identify with the challenges and perhaps the frustrations their students face when carrying out assignments (4) to build cohesion and a sense of common purpose within a learning community (5) to learn new teaching methods by observing their colleagues in action (6) to develop new skills, such as the ability to use online resources in teaching (7) to deepen their knowledge in their fields of expertise (8) to keep themselves intellectually stimulated, and (9) to reflect critically on their teaching methods. Personally, I've found that some of my best insights about teaching have arisen in situations in which I've had to change perspective, from teacher to student, beginning with my first semester of graduate school when, in back-to-back classes within the same classroom, I had to shift abruptly from being a student in the course Theories of Criticism to being the teacher in Composition I. While tutoring my writing students now, I also recall my own experience as a student in a writing seminar, when I sat back and watched as the instructor ruthlessly (or so it felt) crossed out every adverb in my short story and then tactfully (and quite persuasively) explained why all these adverbs were unnecessary. I've also learned new skills and teaching techniques—and had the pleasure of observing some fine teachers at work—by taking computer workshops at my college and joining students in my colleagues' classes within our Linked Learning program.

USES, ADAPTATIONS, AND RESOURCES

I regularly carry out one form of this activity in composition and literature courses, when I assign students to write in-class essays and then write along with them. A similar approach is explained in the abstract "Practicing What You Teach" by Stephen A. Calatrello, an English instructor at Calhoun Community College in Georgia. The abstract opens with an anecdote about a professor speaking to a class of would-be teachers in an introductory graduate level education course: "Never," the professor said, "under any circumstances, ask your students to do an assignment that you either can't do or won't do yourself." Calatrello, who was then teaching part-time while working full-time for an aerospace trade magazine ("paid to make the inaccessible prose of aerospace engineers accessible to the populace"), was led by this remark to share one of his recently completed articles with his composition students. "I wanted my students to see," he says, "how one of my projects evolved from invention and research to planning and drafting, and how it ultimately appeared in a final, approved draft ready for release." Later, as a full-time instructor, he decided to write along with his composition students as they worked on their narrative essays: "We did everything together—brainstorming, planning, drafting, revising, editing, and proofreading." While Calatrello notes that it's clearly unrealistic for teachers to do this with every assignment, he says that the experience was "remarkable" in helping him to understand the pressures students face and in enabling students to see him as both an exemplar and "just another writer in the class."

I've also seen the value of teaching in new contexts—and felt reinvigorated as a teacher—through such personal experiences as team-teaching in classes for high school students, tutoring inmates who were preparing to take GED exams, and teaching in the "Changing Lives Through Literature" program, administered through the Massachusetts judicial system. In this program, judges, probation officers, and a group of men on probation come together as students with a common purpose: to help the probationers become more reflective about their lives, and more aware of belonging to a community, through discussions of the conflicts, challenges, and choices faced by characters in literature. We've studied such works as James Dickey's novel *Deliverance,* Russell Banks' novel *Continental Drift*, Lorraine Hansberry's play *A Raisin in the Sun,* and Tim O'Brien's novel about the Vietnam War, *The Things They Carried.* I've been especially inspired by the judges and probation officers who have volunteered their time (I'm paid) and taken the risk of stepping outside their customary roles, all because of their belief in the value of public reflection and dialogue. Several of the student probationers in my classes have gone on to become full-time college students.

Just as students need to take regular inventory of their strategies as learners (SEE activity **#49**), it's also essential for faculty to continue to be "students" of their own strategies as teachers. In *Engaging Ideas,* for instance, John Bean outlines a procedure for having a colleague critique an assignment handout in order to predict how students might react to it. Neil Browne's article "Student Evaluation of Teaching as if Critical Thinking Really Mattered," published in *The Journal of General Education*, suggests that while most faculty would call themselves teachers of critical thinking, many fail to evaluate their own teaching methods—or the assumptions they make when teaching—according to the principles they purport to teach. Early in my career, I reevaluated my approach to teaching—specifically, my means of conveying expectations to students—after reviewing research on teachers' expectations of students. In *The Art of Thinking*, Vincent Ruggiero describes one experiment in which researchers administered an intelligence test to all students at an elementary school. Researchers told teachers that the test would identify certain students about to go through a "learning spurt," though in fact the researchers had merely selected these students at random. At the end of the year, when students were tested again, those who had been identified as "learning spurt" students gained twice as many IQ points as the other students. In another experiment I came across, college composition teachers were asked to compare and evaluate two student essays. One essay used more advanced vocabulary and more complex sentence constructions but was repetitive and verbose; the other essay was simpler in style but clearer and more concise. The teachers in the experiment consistently preferred the long-winded essay.

Finally, the most important element of professional development is an ongoing dialogue with colleagues, both within and outside of our own disciplines. Too often as teachers, and as students of teaching, we neglect to consult our most valuable resource—the judgment and experience of our peers. It's this idea of sharing our experiences—what works and what doesn't, what's important to teach and what isn't, which ideas are most stimulating to colleagues in other fields—that's at the very heart of this sourcebook.

ACTIVITY #49
Time to Take Inventory (Conducting Self-evaluations)

APPLICATIONS: Any discipline

CRITICAL THINKING SKILLS: Evaluating problem-solving strategies, analyzing the process of forming opinions and making decisions, self-regulation of learning

THE ACTIVITY

In this activity the instructor asks a series of self-inventory questions to prompt students to reflect on how they study and learn and what they could do to learn more effectively. Instructors might ask questions like the following: (1) Are you an active learner? Do you take notes in class? Do you come to class prepared to think about the assigned material and to engage your classmates in discussion? Do you ask questions in class? (2) What, typically, is your first reaction when you are given a new assignment? Will this reaction help you to succeed on the assignment? (3) What one thing causes you the most difficulty in this course? What can you do to ease this difficulty? If you are currently struggling in this or any other course, have you talked to the instructor one-on-one? Have you sought tutorial help? (4) Are you using your time efficiently? If not, what could you do to use it more efficiently? (5) If you are feeling stressed out by your courses, what are you doing to help yourself? Students answer the questions in writing, and the instructor responds to their answers. In some cases the instructor may suggest a meeting with a student to discuss problem-solving strategies in more depth.

PURPOSES AND BENEFITS

Periodic reflection on how one thinks and learns is an essential element of the critical thinking process. This exercise can help students think about their approach to learning, identify sources of frustration and difficulties in comprehension, and focus on problem-solving strategies to learn more effectively. It also initiates or continues a dialogue between students and instructor so that they can work together to help the students achieve to their full potential.

USES, ADAPTATIONS, AND RESOURCES

I use exercises like this about four weeks into each semester, when students are starting to show signs of wear and tear, and again about midway through the semester. The activity can be used in any course or discipline, and instructors can modify it to focus on specific learning methods appropriate to their courses. I also use more focused self-assessment prompts, in writing and in tutorials, for students working on particular assignments. When Composition I students are working on their argumentative research papers, I give them questions like the following: Why is this topic important to you? What element of this topic is most confusing to you? Is your thesis precisely defined? Have you found specific, reliable, and sufficient evidence to support any claims you are making? Have you anticipated and addressed arguments that might be raised against your thesis? John Bean's *Engaging Ideas* includes a helpful chapter illustrating how instructors can guide critical self-evaluation through the kinds of comments they write when tutoring students' rough drafts or grading papers

Ralph Tufo, a colleague in our Linked Learning learning community at North Shore Community College, uses a portfolio project as a self-inventory tool in his developmental reading course. The portfolio's purpose is "to help students establish learning goals in the area of college reading and to reflect upon their progress in attaining these goals throughout the semester." In creating their portfolios, students respond to questions like the following: Does the portfolio accurately and honestly demonstrate the student's progress in college reading skills? What self-assessments were made about the student's strengths and weaknesses? What self-knowledge or new insights were gained, and how could these insights be applied to future academic endeavors?

George Medelinskas, a former Linked Learning colleague and now a professor at Northern Essex Community College in Massachusetts, teaches a Problem Solving course in which he regularly asks students to provide written responses to questions like the following: What makes somebody a good problem solver, or a poor problem solver? What are five things you can do to help yourself solve a problem that you are stuck on? Identify the person in your life who most irritates you—what keeps the two of you from more effective communication? What one thing could you do on a regular basis that would make a tremendous difference in your personal life?

In *Learning Together*, mathematics professor Theodore Panitz provides guidelines for a number of regular self-inventory activities, including a post-exam questionnaire, a mid-semester course review and student self-evaluation (with a "push" plan to "survive the demands of instructors"), and an end-of-semester self-evaluation. Kathleen McWhorter's *Study and Critical Thinking Skills in College* presents a more thorough program for integrating study skills and critical thinking skills to help students achieve success in college. In her chapter "Critical Analysis of Course Content," she offers guidelines and exercises for synthesizing material from different sources, for raising critical questions about assigned reading, and for recognizing and evaluating subjective content in readings. She suggests to students: "To overcome the natural tendency to pay more attention to points of view with which you agree and treat opposing viewpoints superficially, deliberately spend more time reading, thinking about, and examining ideas that differ from your own." She includes a detailed self-assessment questionnaire at the end of her book.

ACTIVITY #50
What's Missing from This Course?
(Evaluating Courses)

APPLICATIONS: Any discipline

CRITICAL THINKING SKILLS: Determining the importance of information, detecting slanting, examining issues from conflicting viewpoints, evaluating alternatives

THE ACTIVITY

The idea here is simple. Near the end of the semester, ask your students to write a composition—a paragraph, a page—in which they answer the question: What's missing from this course? That is, what material, issues, points of view, or activities merited inclusion in the course but were neglected or omitted?

PURPOSES AND BENEFITS

This activity stimulates critical thinking by both students and faculty while providing faculty with feedback as they consider possible modifications of their courses. The activity may be inappropriate in courses that allow little latitude in covering material, but it can be a useful element of evaluation in any survey course where instructors must cover some material or issues at the expense of other material. The question requires each student to reflect on curricular goals and to think about a course as a whole. What were we trying to achieve in this course? What did I expect to learn? What guided the selection of material we've covered? In what ways has the course been slanted by the professor's own preferences or interests? The question also prompts students to consider a course from a professor's point of view. If I were teaching this course, how would I do it differently?

I've posed the question to students in my literature classes and received a variety of responses, ranging from "more women writers" to "Stephen King" to "stories that aren't so depressing." The only answer I won't allow is "nothing." Naturally, some responses are more helpful than others, but the responses have led to changes in both content and delivery, ranging from inclusion of the Arabic "1001 Nights" in my World Literature I course to a greater reliance on small group work to maximize class participation.

The value of this question is demonstrated in Meredith Rode's essay "The Hunt for Democracy: The Lion's Perspective." Professor Rode begins her essay with an African proverb: "Until the lions have their own historians, tales of the hunt will always glorify the hunter." She goes on to discuss her inclusion of a "Blacks in Antiquity" unit in an art history course. For many students, the idea that there were black people in antiquity came as a revelation. As one student put it, "I had never considered the presence of Africans in Greece and Rome, and had never been exposed to the idea." In some courses I've seen, such as a study of the Vietnam War that contained no Vietnamese sources, the question "what's missing here?" was begging to be asked by someone. The question can also be asked of an entire department or an entire curriculum in a college. When I started teaching at North Shore Community College, the English Department offered American, British, and Western literature as sophomore literature options. If one wanted to teach Lady Murasaki's *Tale of Genji* or Chinua Achebe's *Things Fall Apart*, the curriculum offered no home for such works. After questioning our own curriculum, we now teach the literature of the world, as well as Native American literature.

USES, ADAPTATIONS, AND RESOURCES

The question can be posed by itself or as part of general, informal course evaluation, or be discussed in class as a means

---

of determining what students have learned—or haven't learned—in a course. I've also asked my students the questions: What questions remain in your mind? What did we cover in this course that you wish had been omitted? SEE the following page for a student feedback survey that I've used in my literature classes.

WORLD LITERTURE I
Student Feedback Survey

READING

1. Did this course improve your understanding and/or appreciation of literature? If so, how?
2. Was the amount of required reading fair?
3. Were there assigned readings that you found particularly worthwhile?
4. Are there any readings that should be deleted from the course? Why?
5. What can be done to insure that students keep up with the required reading?

WRITING

1. Did this course help you to improve as a writer? If so, how? If not, why not?
2. Was the amount of required writing reasonable?
3. Were the topics stimulating? Are there other types of topics that you would recommend?
4. Was the grading fair? Was the basis for grading clear?
5. Did the instructor clearly explain the strengths and weaknesses of compositions?

CLASS MEETINGS

1. Was class time spent in interesting, worthwhile ways?
2. Should there be more/less lecture? Whole-class discussion? Small-group discussion?
3. What can be done to get more students involved in class discussions?

OVERALL

1. Did the course achieve the objectives specified in the syllabus?
2. What's missing from this course? That is, what readings, issues, points of view, or activities should have been included but were neglected or omitted?
3. What did we cover in this course that you wish had been omitted?
4. What questions remain in your mind from our studies of literature? `

Appendix
&
Bibliography

APPENDIX
Selected Critical Thinking Websites

Of the many websites devoted to the teaching of critical thinking, I have found these to be particularly useful. All include links to other sites and resources.

Critical Thinking Across the Curriculum Project
    http://www.kemetro.cc.mo.us/longview/ctac/ctac.htm
Developed at Longview Community College in Lee's Summit, Missouri, this site includes sections on core critical thinking concepts, the structure and analysis of arguments, detection of fallacies, Power Point presentations (one is on the nursing process and critical thinking), resources for integrating critical thinking into college classes in specific disciplines, links to online tutorials and software for teaching critical thinking, a bibliography of critical thinking textbooks and other bibliographical materials.

Critical Thinking Consortium
    http://www.criticalthinking.org/
This site, from the Foundation for Critical Thinking, directed by Richard Paul of Sonoma State University in California, offers start-up materials—sample syllabi, lesson plans, assessment tools, and online resources—for faculty who want to infuse critical thinking skills into courses across the curriculum. The site includes a "thinker's guide" series, available for purchase, and an overview of the International Critical Thinking Essay Test.

Critical Thinking and Information Literacy Across the Curriculum
    http://www.bcc.ctc.edu/lmc/ilac/default.htm
Funded by the National Science Foundation at Bellevue Community College in Bellevue, Washington, this project incorporates scientific concepts and information technology to infuse critical thinking and scientific literacy across the curriculum.

It includes assignments and assessment tools for a wide variety of disciplines, a section on critical thinking and cultural diversity, and links to online critical thinking sites.

Critical Thinking Across the Curriculum
http://planet.tvi,cc.nm.us/ctac/Default.htm
This site, developed at Albuquerque TVI Community College in Albuquerque, New Mexico, offers a forum for discussion of critical thinking, an archive of teaching assignments and ideas (e.g. Role Playing in Computer Science, Polya Math Strategy, Chemistry Unknowns, and History in Context), an annotated bibliography, and links to online resources.

Critical Thinking on the Web
http://www.austhink.org.critical/
Dedicated to cultivating "advanced reasoning and analysis," and developed by Tim van Gelder at Trinity College in Melbourne, Australia, this side offers online tutorials and sections on argument mapping, cognitive bias and blind spots, statistical probability, and great critical thinkers (Francis Bacon, George Orwell), as well as links to other resources.

BIBLIOGRAPHY

Accetta, Randy. "The 'We Think' Project." *Innovation Abstracts.* National Institute for Staff and Organizational Development. Vol. 16, No. 11, April 8, 1994.

Ackerman, Diane. *A Natural History of the Senses.* New York: Vintage Books, 1990.

Aristotle. *Politics and Poetics.* New York: The Viking Press, 1967.

Armstrong, Larry. "PBL in the English Classroom." *Innovation Abstracts.* National Institute for Staff and Organizational Development. Vol. 23, No. 10, March 30, 2001.

Bacon, Francis. "Of Studies." Rpt. in *Fifty Great Essays.* Ed. Robert Diyanni. New York: Penguin Academics, 2002: 60-62.

Baergen, Ralph, ed. *Ethics at the End of Life.* Belmont, CA: Wadsworth Publishing, 2001.

Bailey, Philip. "Promoting the Humanities in Technical Curricula." *Innovation Abstracts.* National Institute for Staff and Organizational Development. Vol. 24, No. 4, Feb. 8, 2002.

Bateman, Tom. "Moot Court Exercise." *Innovation Abstracts.* National Institute for Staff and Organizational Development. Vol. 16, No. 2, Jan. 28, 1994.

Bean, John.C. *Engaging Ideas: The Professor's Guide to Interpreting Writing, Critical Thinking and Active Learning in the Classroom.* San Francisco: Jossey Bass Inc., 1996.

Beccaria, Cesare. *On Crimes and Punishments.* New York: The Bobbs-Merrill Company, 1963.

Begley, Sharon. "Memory's Mind Games." *Newsweek* 16 July 2001: 52-56.

Bell, Kathleen. *Developing Arguments: Strategies for Reaching Audiences.* Belmont, CA: Wadsworth Publishing, 1990.

Biddle, Arthur W. and Daniel J. Bean. *Writer's Guide: Life Sciences*. Lexington: D.C. Heath, 1987.

Biddle, Arthur W. and Kenneth M. Holland. *Writer's Guide: Political Science*. Lexington: D.C. Heath, 1987.

Bloom, Benjamin S. et al. *The Taxonomy of Educational Objectives: Affective and Cognitive Domains*. New York: David McKay, 1974.

Bond, Lynne A. and Anthony S. Magistrale. *Writer's Guide: Psychology*. Lexington: D.C. Heath, 1987.

Boorstein, Daniel. "The Historian: 'A Wrestler With an Angel.'" *The New York Times Book Review*: 20 September 1987: 1, 28-29.

Borges, Jorge Luis. *The Book of Imaginary Beings*. New York: Avon Books, 1969.

Branscomb, H. Eric. *Casting Your Net: A Student's Guide to Research on the Internet*. 2nd Edition. Boston: Allyn & Bacon, 2001.

Bransford, John and Barry Stein. *The Ideal Problem Solver*. New York: W.H. Freeman, 1984.

Browne, M. Neil, et al. "Student Evaluation of Teaching as if Critical Thinking Really Mattered." *The Journal of General Education*. Penn State University Press. Vol. 46, No. 3, 1997: 192-206.

Brownmiller, Susan. *Femininity*. New York: Simon & Schuster, 1983.

Calatrello, Stephen A. "Practicing What You Teach." *Innovation Abstracts*. National Institute for Staff and Organizational Development. Vol. 24, No. 9, March 22, 2002.

"Casing the Future." *Harvard Magazine* September-October 2003: 64-65.

Chaffee, John. *Thinking Critically*. Boston: Houghton Mifflin, 1997.

Chaffee, John, Christine McMahon, and Barbara Stout. *Critical Thinking, Thoughtful Writing*. Boston: Houghton Mifflin, 1999.

Chia, Felipe H. "Issues for Debate: Increasing Student Participation." *Innovation Abstracts*. National Institute for Staff and Organizational Development. Vol. 16, No. 29, Dec. 2, 1994.

Clark, Virginia, Paul A. Eschholz, and Alfred E. Rosa. *Language: Introductory Readings*, 4ᵗʰ Edition. New York: St. Martin's, 1985.

Clarke, Colleen M. "Law and Security Simulations: Integrating Theory and Practice." *Innovation Abstracts*. National Institute for Staff and Organizational Development. Vol. 14, No. 21, Sept. 25, 1992.

Commoner, Barry. "The Ecological Crisis." Rpt. in *The Example of Science*. Eds. Robert E. Lynch and Thomas B. Swanzey. Englewood Cliffs, NJ: Prentice-Hall, 1981: 168-177.

Cook, Janet. "Surprise! Something a Little Different Today." *Innovation Abstracts*. National Institute for Staff and Organizational Development. Vol. 23, No. 13, April 20, 2001.

Cook, Lillian. "An Interdisciplinary Technology Model That Works." *Innovation Abstracts*. National Institute for Staff and Organizational Development. Vol. 20, No. 1, Jan. 23, 1998.

Costanza, Michele N. "Tracing the Family Tree: Meeting the Research Aim in Composition." *Innovation Abstracts*. National Institute for Staff and Organizational Development. Vol. 22, No. 24, Oct. 20, 2000.

Cromwell, Lucy, ed. *Teaching Critical Thinking in the Arts and Humanities*. Milwaukee: Alverno Publications, 1986.

Crossman, Richard, ed. *The God That Failed*. New York: Bantam Books, 1965.

de Bono, Edward. *de Bono's Thinking Course.* New York: Facts on File, 1986.

de Bono, Edward. *New Think.* New York: Basic Books, 1971.

Deford, Frank. "Cystic Fibrosis." Rpt. in *Readings for Writers.* 7ᵗʰ Edition. Eds. Jo Ray McCuen and Anthony Winkler. Fort Worth: Harcourt Brace Jovanovich, 1992: 440-445.

Dewey, John. *How We Think.* Boston: D. C. Heath, 1910.

Diamond, Jared. *Guns, Germs, and Steel: The Fates of Human Societies.* New York, W.W. Norton & Company, 1998.

Dixon, Dougal. *After Man: A Zoology of the Future.* New York: St. Martin's, 1981.

Dorff-Pennea, Nancy. "Overcoming Roadblocks to Learning Math." *Innovation Abstracts.* National Institute for Staff and Organizational Development. Vol. 18, No. 3, Feb. 2, 1996.

Dunbar, Robin. *Grooming, Gossip, and the Evolution of Language.* Cambridge, MA: Harvard University Press, 1996.

Durham, Dixon K. "Creative Writing in the History Classroom." *Innovation Abstracts.* National Institute for Staff and Organizational Development. Vol. 16, No. 21, Sept. 30, 1994.

Edwards, Betty. *Drawing on the Right Side of the Brain.* New York: Jeremy Tarcher/Perigree Books, 1989.

"Facing History and Ourselves: Examining History and Human Behavior." *2002.* http//www.facinghistory.org (30 Aug. 2002).

Feeney, Mark. "She Knows What You Want." *The Boston Globe* 19 March 2002: E1.

Fendal, Dan, et al. *Interactive Mathematics Program: Year 2.* Emeryville, CA: Key Curriculum Press, 1998.

Feynman, Richard. *"Surely You Must Be Joking, Mr. Feynman": Adventures of a Curious Character.* New York: W. W. Norton, 1985.

Feynman, Richard. *What Do YOU Care What Other People Think?: Further Adventures of a Curious Character.* Boston: G.K. Hall, 1988.

Florman, Samuel. *The Existential Pleasures of Engineering.* New York: St. Martin's, 1976.

Flower, Linda. *Problem-Solving Strategies for Writing.* New York: Harcourt Brace Jovanovich, 1981.

Foran, Don. "Dramatizations: Philosophers (and Students) Come Alive." *Innovation Abstracts.* National Institute for Staff and Organizational Development. Vol. 21, No. 10, April 2, 1999.

Foran, John. "The Case Method and Interactive Classroom." *Thought and Action.* National Education Association. Summer 2001: 41-50.

Forster, E. M. "What I Believe." Rpt. in *Fifty Great Essays.* Ed. Robert Diyanni. New York: Penguin Academics, 2002: 158-167.

Foucault, Michel. *Discipline and Punish: The Birth of the Prison.* New York: Vintage Books, 1979.

Freire, Paulo. *Pedagogy of the Oppressed.* New York, Herder and Herder, 1970.

Freire, Paulo. *Education for Critical Consciousness.* New York: Continuum, 1987.

Gardiner, Lion F. "Why We Must Change: The Research Evidence." *Thought and Action.* National Education Association. Fall 2000: 121-138.

Gardner, Howard. *Frames of Mind.* New York: Basic Books, 1983.

Gardner, Howard. *The Unschooled Mind: How Children Think and How Schools Should Teach.* New York: Basic Books, 1991.

Garvin, David A. "Making the Case." *Harvard Magazine* September-October 2003: 56-65, 107.

Gawande, Atul. *Complications: A Surgeon's Notes on an Imperfect Science.* New York: Metropolitan Books, 2002.

Gawande, Atul. "Under Suspicion." *The New Yorker* 8 January 2001: 50-53

Geertz, Clifford. *Local Knowledge: Further Essays in Interpretive Anthropology.* New York: Basic Books, 1983.

Gibson, Joanna. *Perspectives: Case Studies for Readers and Writers.* New York: Addison Wesley Longman, 2002.

Gilligan, Carol. *In a Different Voice: Psychological Theory and Women's Development.* Cambridge, MA: Harvard University Press, 1982.

Gilovich, Thomas. *How We Know What Isn't So: The Fallibility of Human Reason in Everyday Life.* New York: Macmillan, 1991.

Gladwell, Malcom. "The Naked Face." *The New Yorker* 5 August 2002: 38-49.

Goffman, Erving. *Ayslums: Essays on the Social Situation of Mental Patients and Other Inmates.* New York: Anchor Books, 1961.

Goleman, Daniel. *Emotional Intelligence.* New York: Bantam, 1995.

Gorzycki, Barbara. "On the Lookout: Evaluation Forms." *Innovation Abstracts.* National Institute for Staff and Organizational Development. Vol. 23, No. 19, Sept. 21, 2001.

Goshgarian, Gary, ed. *Exploring Language.* 8th Edition. New York: Addison-Wesley Longman, 1998.

Griffin, Susan. *A Chorus of Stones: The Private Life of War.* New York: Anchor Books, 1992.

Hall, Donald. *Writing Well.* Boston: Little, Brown and Company, 1973.

Hall, Edward T. *The Silent Language*. New York: Anchor Books, 1973.

Halpern, Diane F. *Critical Thinking Across the Curriculum*. Mahwah, NJ: Lawrence Erlbaum Associates, 1997.

Halonen, Jane S., ed. *Teaching Critical Thinking in Psychology*. Milwaukee: Alverno Publications, 1986.

Hammons, Jim and Ken Turner. "Using a Cost-Benefit Proposal to Help Improve Teaching." *Innovation Abstracts*. National Institute for Staff and Organizational Development. Vol. 20, No. 11, April 10, 1998.

Hardin, Garrett. "The Tragedy of the Commons." Rpt. in *Writing About Science*. Eds. Mary E. Bishop and Joseph A. Mazzeo. New York: Oxford University Press, 1979: 331-348.

Hardwick, Elizabeth. *Seduction and Betrayal: Women and Literature*. New York: Vintage Books, 1975.

Hatch, Gary Layne. *Arguing in Communities*. Mountain View, CA: Mayfield Publishing Company, 1996.

Hayakawa, S. I. *Language in Thought and Action*. New York: Harcourt Brace, 1964.

Hirschberg, Stuart. *Strategies of Argument*. Boston: Allyn & Bacon, 1996.

Hofstadter, Douglas R. *Metamagical Themas: Questing for the Essence of Mind and Pattern*. New York: Basic Books, 1985.

Holt, Daniel H. "Court Is Now in Session." *Innovation Abstracts*. National Institute for Staff and Organizational Development. Vol. 15, No. 6, Feb. 26, 1993.

Holton, Gerald. *Thematic Origins of Scientific Thought: Kepler to Einstein*. Cambridge, MA: Harvard University Press, 1973.

Holyoke Community College. *Learning About Learning Communities: What is Our Common(wealth) Interest?* March 31, 2000.

Horn, Peter. *Clinical Ethics Casebook.* 2nd Edition. Belmont, CA: Wadsworth Publishing, 2002.

Hult, Christine A. *Researching and Writing Across the Curriculum.* 2nd Edition. New York: Longman, 2002.

Hume, Laura M. and Claire E. Weinstein. "Talk-Alouds: Windows on the Mind." *Innovation Abstracts.* National Institute for Staff and Organizational Development. Vol. 16, No. 16, August 26, 1994.

Jacoby, Susan. *Wild Justice: The Evolution of Revenge.* New York: Harper Torchbooks, 1983.

Jacobs, Harold R. *Mathematics: A Human Endeavor.* 2nd Edition. New York: W. H. Freeman & Company, 1982.

Jefferson, Thomas. "The Declaration of Independence." Rpt. in *Fifty Great Essays.* Ed. Robert Diyanni. New York: Penguin Academics, 2002: 197-205.

"Jesus Seminar Forum." Rutgers University Department of Religion. 2002. http://religion.rutgers.edu/jseminar/index.html (30 Aug. 2002).

Jewell, Richard. "Using Role-Playing to Teach Thinking." *Innovation Abstracts.* National Institute for Staff and Organizational Development. Vol. 20, No. 9, March 20, 1998.

Johnson, Ken and Ted Herr. *Problem Solving Strategies: Crossing the River with Dogs and Other Mathematical Adventures.* 2nd Edition. Emeryville, CA: Key Curriculum Press, 2001.

Kafka, Franz. "Letter to His Father." Rpt. in *The Basic Kafka.* Ed. Erich Heller. New York: Pocket Books, 1971: 185-235.

Kagan, Jerome and Julius Segal. *Psychology: An Introduction.* 8th Edition. Fort Worth: The Harcourt Press, 1995.

Kaminski, Charles. "Use of Select-and-Fill-In Concept Maps." *Innovation Abstracts.* National Institute for Staff and Organizational Development. Vol. 23, No. 18, Sept. 14, 2001.

Katz, Jack. *Seductions of Crime: Moral and Sensual Attractions in Doing Evil.* New York: Basic Books, 1988.

Klein, Joe. "The Supercop Scenario." *The New Yorker* 18 March 2002: 72-78.

Kohlberg, Lawrence. *The Philosophy of Moral Development: Moral Stages and the Idea of Justice.* New York: Harper and Row, 1981.

Kuhn, Thomas. *The Structure of Scientific Revolutions.* Chicago: The University of Chicago Press, 1962.

Kurfiss, Joanne. *Critical Thinking: Theory, Research, Practice and Possibilities.* Washington: Association for the Study of Higher Education, 1988.

Lambert, Craig. "Stealthy Attitudes." *Harvard Magazine* July-August 2002: 18-19.

LeDoux, Joseph. *The Emotional Brain.* New York, Simon & Schuster, 1998.

Levi, Primo. *The Periodic Table.* New York: Schocken Books, 1984.

Lightman, Alan. *Time Travels and Papa Joe's Pipe: Essays on the Human Side of Science.* New York: Penguin Books, 1986.

Lindeman, Peter V. "Want to Cut Up Something Different in Biology? Try a Journal Article Dissection." *Innovation Abstracts.* National Institute for Staff and Organizational Development. Vol. 16, No. 24, Oct. 21, 1994.

Lorenz, Konrad. *Man Meets Dog.* New York: Penguin Books, 1964.

Mader, Sylvia S. *Biology.* 5th Edition. Dubuque, IA: William C. Brown, 1996.

Mairs, Nancy. "On Being a Cripple." Rpt. in *Fifty Great Essays.* Ed. Robert Diyanni. New York: Penguin Academics, 2002: 251-264.

Mayfield, Marlys. *Thinking for Yourself: Developing Critical Thinking Skills Through Reading and Writing.* 3rd Edition. Belmont, CA: Wadsworth Publishing, 1994.

McDonald, Daniel. *The Language of Argument.* 2nd Edition. New York: Thomas Y. Crowell Company, 1975.

McLaughlin, Terence. "Dirt." Rpt. in *The Example of Science.* Eds. Robert E. Lynch and Thomas B. Swanzey. Englewood Cliffs, NJ: Prentice Hall, 1981: 30-37.

McPeck, John. *Critical Thinking and Education.* New York: St. Martin's Press, 1981.

McWhorter, Kathleen T. *Study and Critical Thinking Skills in College.* 3rd Edition. New York: Harper Collins, 1996.

Miller, Jonathan. *The Body in Question.* New York: Vintage Books, 1982.

Montaigne, Michel de. *The Complete Essays of Montaigne.* Ed. Donald M. Frame. Stanford, CA: Stanford University Press, 1958.

More, Thomas. *Utopia.* New York: Appleton-Century-Crofts, 1949.

Murray, Barbara and Jennifer Walsh. "Collaborative Writing: English and Math." *Innovation Abstracts.* National Institute for Staff and Organizational Development. Vol. 14, No. 21, Sept. 25, 1992.

Murray, Bridget. "Teaching Today's Pupils to Think More Critically." *Monitor: Journal of the American Psychological Association.* March 1997: 51.

Nelson, John. "Criminals in Literature." *Innovation Abstracts.* National Institute for Staff and Organizational Development. Vol. 16, No. 13, April 22, 1994.

Neustadt, Richard E. and Ernest R. May. *Thinking in Time: The Uses of History for Decision Makers.* New York: The Free Press, 1986.

Northcutt, Norvel, Sue Darby, and Leann Ellis. "Teaching the Big Picture." *Innovation Abstracts*. National Institute for Staff and Organizational Development. Vol. 17, No. 23, Oct. 13, 1995.

Orwell, George. "Politics and the English Language" and "Shooting an Elephant." *A Collection of Essays by George Orwell*. Garden City, NY: Doubleday Anchor Books, 1954.

Panitz, Theordore. *Learning Together: Keeping Teachers and Students Actively Involved in Learning by Writing Across the Curriculum*. Stillwater, OK: New Forums Press Inc., 2001.

Paul, Richard. *Critical Thinking: How to Prepare Students for a Rapidly Changing World*. Foundation for Critical Thinking, 1995.

Paul, Richard and Linda Elder. *Critical Thinking Development: A Stage Theory*. Foundation for Critical Thinking. 2000.

Pearson, Patricia. *When She Was Bad: How and Why Women Get Away with Murder*. New York: Viking Penguin, 1998.

Piaget, Jean. *The Essential Piaget*. H. E. Gruber and J. J. Voneche, eds. New York: Basic Books, 1977.

Pinker, Steven. *The Language Instinct*. New York: Harper Collins, 1995.

Polya, George. *How to Solve It*. Princeton, NJ: Princeton University Press, 1957.

Postman, Neil and Charles Weingartner. *Teaching as a Subversive Activity*. New York: Delacorte, 1969.

Powers, Richard. *Galatea 2.2*. New York: Harper Perennial, 1996.

Precedo-Choudhury, Laura and Carey Witkov. "Multi-Course Projects as Bridges Between Disciplines." *Innovation Abstracts*. National Institute for Staff and Organizational Development. Vol. 24, No. 11, April 5, 2002.

Radaskiewicz, Ann Marie. "Writing for the Real World." *Innovation Abstracts*. National Institute for Staff and Organizational Development. Vol. 19, No. 27, Nov. 14, 1997.

Rasool, Joan, Caroline Banks, and Mary-Jane McCarthy. *Critical Thinking: Reading and Writing in a Diverse World*. New York: Wadsworth, 1996.

Richard, Jerry, ed. *The Good Life*. New York: New American Library, 1973.

Rivkin, Mary S. "Discovery: Taking Critical Thinking Outdoors." *Scholastic Early Childhood Today* May 2002: 37-44.

Rivers, William L. *Finding Facts: Interviewing, Observing, Using Reference Sources*. Englewood Cliffs, NJ: Prentice Hall, 1975.

Roberts. Royston M. *Serendipity: Accidental Discoveries in Science*. New York: John Wiley, 1989.

Robertson, Julie Fisher and Donna Rane-Szostak. "Using Dialogues to Develop Critical Thinking Skills: A Practical Approach." *Journal of Adolescent and Adult Literacy*. April 1996: 39-45.

Rode, Meredith. "The Hunt for Democracy: The Lion's Perspective." *Thought and Action*. National Education Association. Summer 2000: 21-32 .

Rosenhan, David. "On Being Sane in Insane Places." *Science* #179 (1973): 250-258.

Rottenberg, Annette. *Elements of Argument: A Text and Reader*. New York: St. Martin's, 1985.

Rubinstein, Moshe. *Patterns of Problem Solving*. Englewood Cliffs, NJ: Prentice-Hall, 1975.

Ruggiero, Vincent. *The Art of Thinking: A Guide to Critical and Creative Thought*. New York: Longman, 1998.

Sacks, Oliver. *The Man Who Mistook His Wife for a Hat and Other Clinical Tales*. New York: Harper Perennial, 1987.

Seyler, Dorothy U. *Read, Reason, Write*. 5th Edition. Boston: McGraw-Hill, 1999.

Schelling, Thomas C. *Choice and Consequence: Perspectives of an Errant Economist*. Cambridge: Harvard University Press, 1984.

Schmidt, Gary D. and William J. VandeKopple. *Communities of Discourse: The Rhetoric of Disciplines*. Englewood Cliffs: Prentice Hall, 1993.

Schoenfeld, Allen. *Mathematical Problem Solving*. New York: Academic Press, 1985.

Schumacher, E. F. *Small Is Beautiful: Economics as if People Mattered*. New York: Harper & Row Perennial, 1975.

"Seven: A Thousand Years of Deadly Sin." *The Boston Globe Magazine* 3 October 1999.

Shea, Christopher. "Mad for Risk at Harvard." *The Boston Globe.* 4 January 2004: C5.

Skinner, B. F. *Walden Two*. New York: The MacMillan Company, 1962.

Snow, C. P. *The Two Cultures and the Scientific Revolution*. London: Cambridge University Press, 1965.

Sontag, Susan. *Illness as Metaphor*. New York: Vintage Books, 1979.

Spurgin, Sally DeWitt. *The Power to Persuade: A Rhetoric and Reader for Argumentative Writing*. 2nd Edition. Englewood Cliffs, NJ: Prentice Hall, 1989.

Stanton, Elizabeth Cady. "Declaration of Sentiments and Resolutions." Rpt. in *Fifty Great Essays*. Ed. Robert Diyanni. New York: Penguin Academics, 2002: 313-316.

Steffens, Henry J. and Mary Jane Dickerson. *Writer's Guide: History.* Lexington: D.C. Heath, 1987.

Stice, James, ed. *Developing Critical Thinking and Problem-Solving Abilities.* San Francisco: Jossey Bass, 1987.

Tanabe, Jenine L. "Science Laboratory—Teaching Concepts and Content." *Innovation Abstracts.* National Institute for Staff and Organizational Development. Vol. 21, No. 23, Oct. 15, 1999.

Tannen, Deborah. *You Just Don't Understand: Women and Men in Conversation.* New York: Ballantine, 1990.

Thomas, Glen and Gaye Smoot. "Critical Thinking: A Vital Work Skill." *Thrust for Educational Leadership.* February/March 1994: 34-38.

Thomas, Patricia. "Brainy Women: At the Frontiers of Neuroscience." *Harvard Magazine* May-June 2002: 37-43, 85-86.

Thompson, Clive. "He and She: What's the Real Difference?" *The Boston Globe* 6 July 2003: H1.

Toulmin, Stephen. *The Uses of Argument.* Cambridge, England: Cambridge University Press, 1958.

Tudge, Colin. *Last Animals at the Zoo.* Washington, D.C.: Island Press, 1992.

Vincent, Jean-Didier. *The Biology of Emotions.* Cambridge, MA: Basil Blackwell, 1990.

Viola, Herman J. and Carolyn Margolis, eds. *Seeds of Change.* Washington: Smithsonian Institution Press, 1991.

Vess, Deborah, and David Hutto. "Team-Teaching in an Interdisciplinary Environment." *Innovation Abstracts.* National Institute for Staff and Organizational Development. Vol. 18, No. 19, Sept. 20, 1996.

Watson, G. and E.M. Glaser. *The Watson-Glaser Critical Thinking Appraisal*. San Antonio: The Psychological Association, 1994.

Whimbey, Arthur and Jack Lochhead. *Problem Solving and Comprehension*. Philadelphia: Franklin Institute Press, 1982.

Wicklegren, W. A. How to Solve Problems. San Francisco: W.H. Freeman, 1974.

Wilson, Edward O. *The Diversity of Life*. New York: W. W. Norton and Company, 1993.

Wilson, Edward O. *Sociobiology*. Cambridge, Mass. Harvard University Press, 1980.

Winterowd, W. Ross and Geoffrey Winterowd. *The Critical Reader, Thinker and Writer*. Mountain View, CA.: Mayfield Publishing, 1997.

Wollstonecraft, Mary. "A Vindication of the Rights of Women." Rpt. in *Fifty Great Essays*. Ed. Robert Diyanni. New York: Penguin Academics, 2002: 390-393.

Woolf, Virginia. *Orlando*. New York: Harcourt Brace Jovanovich, 1956.

Wright, Carolyn L. "The 12 Ball Problem, or How I Stopped Hating the Assignment and Learned to Love Thinking." *Innovation Abstracts*. National Institute for Staff and Organizational Development. Vol. 16, No. 23, Oct. 14, 1994.

Wright, Robert. *The Moral Animal: Why We Are the Way We Are: The New Science of Evolutionary Psychology*. New York: Vintage Books, 1994.

Young, Lynn M. "Teaching Empathy and Understanding With a Game." *Innovation Abstracts*. National Institute for Staff and Organizational Development. Vol. 16, No. 30, Dec. 9, 1994.

Zimbardo, Philip. "The Pathology of Imprisonment." *Society* April 1972: 4-8.

Zindel, Paul. *The Pigman*. New York, Bantam Books, 1983.

ABOUT THE AUTHOR

John Nelson's education background includes a B.A. with honors from Harvard University, graduate work at Oxford University, and an M.A. in English from the University of Illinois. He has taught speech, basic communications, composition, literature, creative writing, and English in higher education for over 30 years. He received the National Institute for Staff & Organizational Development Teaching Excellence Award in 1999, and Commonwealth of Massachusetts Outstanding Service Awards in 1985 and 1995, among others.

Throughout his career at North Shore Community College, he was deeply involved in curriculum development, including two decades of leadership on the college curriculum committee. As curriculum coordinator for a TRIO program serving 400 students, he teamed with colleagues to develop and implement an integrated curriculum centered on critical thinking. He has conducted seminars on how to teach critical thinking, and has received numerous grants and published articles on curricular innovations.